# Rust Standard Library Cookbook

Over 75 recipes to leverage the power of Rust

**Jan Hohenheim**
**Daniel Durante**

**BIRMINGHAM - MUMBAI**

# Rust Standard Library Cookbook

**Commissioning Editor:** Merint Mathew
**Acquisition Editor:** Aiswarya Narayanan, Alok Dhuri
**Content Development Editor:** Lawrence Veigas
**Technical Editor:** Mehul Singh
**Copy Editor:** Safis Editing
**Project Coordinator:** Prajakta Naik
**Proofreader:** Safis Editing
**Indexer:** Rekha Nair
**Graphics:** Jisha Chirayil
**Production Coordinator:** Deepika Naik

First published: March 2018

Production reference: 2020322

Published by Packt Publishing Ltd.
Livery Place
35 Livery Street
Birmingham
B3 2PB, UK.

ISBN 978-1-78862-392-6

www.packtpub.com

`mapt.io`

Mapt is an online digital library that gives you full access to over 5,000 books and videos, as well as industry leading tools to help you plan your personal development and advance your career. For more information, please visit our website.

# Why subscribe?

- Spend less time learning and more time coding with practical eBooks and Videos from over 4,000 industry professionals

- Improve your learning with Skill Plans built especially for you

- Get a free eBook or video every month

- Mapt is fully searchable

- Copy and paste, print, and bookmark content

# PacktPub.com

Did you know that Packt offers eBook versions of every book published, with PDF and ePub files available? You can upgrade to the eBook version at `www.PacktPub.com` and as a print book customer, you are entitled to a discount on the eBook copy. Get in touch with us at `service@packtpub.com` for more details.

At `www.PacktPub.com`, you can also read a collection of free technical articles, sign up for a range of free newsletters, and receive exclusive discounts and offers on Packt books and eBooks.

# Contributors

## About the authors

**Jan Hohenheim** is a senior software engineer and an active contributor to, and advocator of, the open source community.

Over the years, he has acquired a deep understanding of systems programming through languages such as C++ and Rust by modernizing and refactoring big and complex codebases. His passions include all things AI and Blockchain. In his free time, he researches innovative approaches to bringing biology and technology closer together, which has led him to develop his own Machine Learning framework. You can follow his projects on GitHub. His username is `jnferner`.

**Daniel Durante** is an avid coffee drinker/roaster, motorcyclist, archer, welder, and carpenter whenever he isn't programming. Right from the age of 12, he has been involved with web and embedded programming with PHP, Node.js, Golang, Rust, and C.

He has worked on text-based browser games that have reached over 1,000,000 active players, created bin-packing software for CNC machines, embedded programming with cortex-m and PIC circuits, high-frequency trading applications, and helped contribute to one of the oldest ORMs of Node.js (SequelizeJS).

*I would like to thank my parents, brother, and friends who've all put up with my insanity sitting in front of a computer day in and day out. I would not be here today if it wasn't for their patience, guidance, and love.*

# About the reviewer

**Ruben Schmidmeister** is a senior software engineer. He has a broad knowledge of all things web and Unix. Over the last 2 years, he has been coding in Rust. His latest Rust project is an open source production-oriented server deployment tool called Toby.

He open sources most of his projects on GitHub under the username `bash`, so be sure to check that out.

# Packt is searching for authors like you

If you're interested in becoming an author for Packt, please visit `authors.packtpub.com` and apply today. We have worked with thousands of developers and tech professionals, just like you, to help them share their insight with the global tech community. You can make a general application, apply for a specific hot topic that we are recruiting an author for, or submit your own idea.

# Table of Contents

# Preface

Mozilla's Rust is slowly gaining attention, with amazing features and a powerful library. This book will take you through varied recipes that will teach you how to leverage the standard library to implement efficient solutions.

The book begins with a brief look at the basic modules of the standard library and collections. From there, the recipes will cover crates, which support file/directory handling and (de)serialization for the most common data formats. You will learn about crates related to advanced data structures, error handling, and networking. You will also learn to work with futures and experimental nightly features. The book also covers the most relevant external crates in Rust. You will be able to compose your own algorithms using the standard modules of the library.

By the end of the book, you will be proficient at using the *Rust Standard Library Cookbook*.

## Who this book is for

This book is for developers who would like to explore the power of Rust and learn to use the standard library for various functionalities. Basic Rust programming knowledge and Terminal skills are assumed.

## What this book covers

Chapter 1, *Learning the Basics*, builds a strong foundation of fundamental principles and techniques that are useful in all kinds of situations. It will also show you how to accept user input on the command line so that you can write, all the coming chapters in an interactive way if you wanted to.

Chapter 2, *Working with Collections*, gives you a comprehensive overview of all the major data collections in Rust, which includes illustrations of how data is stored in your RAM so that you're ready to choose the right collection for the right task.

Chapter 3, *Handling Files and the Filesystem*, shows you how to connect your existing tools with the filesystem, allowing you to store, read, and search files on your computer. We will also learn how to compress data in order to send it efficiently over the internet.

Chapter 4, *Serialization*, introduces you to today's most common data formats and how to (de)serialize them in Rust, enabling you to connect your programs to many services by communicating across tools.

Chapter 5, *Advanced Data Structures*, builds a foundation for the chapters to come by providing useful information about general modules and Rust's smart pointers. You will also learn how to generate code for annotated structures at compile time by using custom #[derive()] statements.

Chapter 6, *Handling Errors*, teaches you about Rust's error-handling concept and how to interact seamlessly with it by creating custom errors and loggers for your use case. We will also look at how to design structures in a way that cleans up a user's resources without them noticing.

Chapter 7, *Parallelism and Rayon*, brings you to the world of multithreading and proves to you that Rust really gives you *fearless concurrency*. You will learn how to effortlessly adapt your algorithms in order to use the full power of your CPU.

Chapter 8, *Working with Futures*, introduces you to asynchronous concepts for your program and prepares you for all libraries that work with *futures*, which are Rust's version of tasks that can run in the background of your program.

Chapter 9, *Networking*, helps connect you to the internet by teaching you how to set up low-level servers, respond to requests in different protocols, and communicate with the World Wide Web.

Chapter 10, *Using Experimental Nightly Features*, ensures that you stay ahead in your knowledge of Rust. It will show you tomorrow's way of programming by giving you a tour of the most anticipated features that are still considered unstable.

# To get the most out of this book

This book has been written with and tested for the Rust versions rustc 1.24.1 and rustc 1.26.0-nightly; however, Rust's strong backward compatibility should make it possible for you to use any newer versions for all chapters except the last. Chapter 10, *Using Experimental Nightly Features*, is working with cutting-edge technology that is expected to improve through ground-breaking changes.

To download the newest Rust version, visit `https://rustup.rs/`, where you will be able to download a Rust installer for your operating system. It's okay to leave it at the standard settings. Make sure to call rustup default nightly before starting `Chapter 10`, *Using Experimental Nightly Features*. Don't worry, you'll be reminded again when it's time.

An active internet connection is required for many recipes, as we will work intensively with crates. These are Rust's way of distributing libraries over the internet, and they are hosted at `https://crates.io/`.

You might wonder why a book about Rust's standard library, or std for short, uses so much code from outside the std. That's because Rust, in contrast to most other system languages, was designed with strong dependency management in mind from the beginning. It's so easy to pull crates into your code that a lot of specific functionality has been outsourced to officially recommended crates. This helps the core standard library that is distributed with Rust to stay simple and very stable.

The most official group of crates after the std is the *nursery* (`https://github.com/rust-lang-nursery?language=rust`). These crates are the standard for many operations and are nearly stable or generic enough to be in the std.

If we can't find a crate for a recipe in the nursery, we look at the crates of the Rust core team members (`https://github.com/orgs/rust-lang/people`), who put a lot of effort into providing functionality that is missing from the standard library. These crates are not in the nursery because they are usually specific enough that it is not worth allocating too many resources to actively maintaining them.

All the code in this book has been formatted with the newest rustfmt (rustfmt-nightly v0.4.0), which you can optionally download using rustup component add rustfmt-preview and run with cargo fmt. The code on GitHub (`https://github.com/jnferner/rust-standard-library-cookbook`) is going to be actively maintained and consequently formatted using a newer version of rustfmt, if available. In some cases, this means that the source code line markings can become outdated. It should not be hard to find the code, however, as this shift is usually no greater than two or three lines.

All code has also been checked by Rust's official linter, clippy (`https://github.com/rust-lang-nursery/rust-clippy`), using version 0.0.187. If you want, you can install it with cargo +nightly install clippy and run it with cargo +nightly clippy. The newest version tends to break quite often though, so don't be surprised if it doesn't work outright.

Some clippy and rustc warnings have been left in the code intentionally. Most of these are either dead code, which happens when we assign a value to a variable to illustrate a concept and then don't need to use the variable anymore, or usage of placeholder names such as foo, bar, or baz, which are used when the exact purpose of a variable is irrelevant to the recipe.

# Download the example code files

You can download the example code files for this book from your account at `www.packtpub.com`. If you purchased this book elsewhere, you can visit `www.packtpub.com/support` and register to have the files emailed directly to you.

You can download the code files by following these steps:

1. Log in or register at `www.packtpub.com`.
2. Select the **SUPPORT** tab.
3. Click on **Code Downloads & Errata**.
4. Enter the name of the book in the **Search** box and follow the onscreen instructions.
5. Once the file is downloaded, please make sure that you unzip or extract the folder using the latest version of:

   - WinRAR/7-Zip for Windows
   - Zipeg/iZip/UnRarX for Mac
   - 7-Zip/PeaZip for Linux

The code bundle for the book is also hosted on GitHub at `https://github.com/PacktPublishing/Rust-Standard-Library-Cookbook/`. If there's an update to the code, it will be updated on the existing GitHub repository.

We also have other code bundles from our rich catalog of books and videos available at `https://github.com/PacktPublishing/`. Check them out!

# Conventions used

There are a number of text conventions used throughout this book.

`CodeInText`: Indicates code words in text, database table names, folder names, filenames, file extensions, pathnames, dummy URLs, user input, and Twitter handles. Here is an example: "In the `bin` folder, create a file called `dynamic_json.rs`."

A block of code is set as follows:

```
let s = "Hello".to_string();
println!("s: {}", s);
let s = String::from("Hello");
println!("s: {}", s);
```

When we wish to draw your attention to a particular part of a code block, the relevant lines or items are set in bold:

```
let alphabet: Vec<_> = (b'A' .. b'z' + 1) // Start as u8
.map(|c| c as char)            // Convert all to chars
.filter(|c| c.is_alphabetic()) // Filter only alphabetic chars
.collect(); // Collect as Vec<char>
```

Any command-line input or output is written as follows:

```
name abraham
age 49
fav_colour red
hello world
(press 'Ctrl Z' on Windows or 'Ctrl D' on Unix)
```

**Bold**: Indicates a new term, an important word, or words that you see onscreen. For example, words in menus or dialog boxes appear in the text like this.

Warnings or important notes appear like this.

Tips and tricks appear like this.

# Sections

In this book, you will find several headings that appear frequently (*Getting ready*, *How to do it...*, *How it works...*, *There's more...*, and *See also*).

To give clear instructions on how to complete a recipe, use these sections as follows:

## Getting ready

This section tells you what to expect in the recipe and describes how to set up any software or any preliminary settings required for the recipe.

## How to do it...

This section contains the steps required to follow the recipe.

## How it works...

This section usually consists of a detailed explanation of what happened in the previous section.

## There's more...

This section consists of additional information about the recipe in order to make you more knowledgeable about the recipe.

## See also

This section provides helpful links to other useful information for the recipe.

# Get in touch

Feedback from our readers is always welcome.

**General feedback**: Email `feedback@packtpub.com` and mention the book title in the subject of your message. If you have questions about any aspect of this book, please email us at `questions@packtpub.com`.

**Errata**: Although we have taken every care to ensure the accuracy of our content, mistakes do happen. If you have found a mistake in this book, we would be grateful if you would report this to us. Please visit `www.packtpub.com/submit-errata`, selecting your book, clicking on the Errata Submission Form link, and entering the details.

**Piracy**: If you come across any illegal copies of our works in any form on the internet, we would be grateful if you would provide us with the location address or website name. Please contact us at `copyright@packtpub.com` with a link to the material.

**If you are interested in becoming an author**: If there is a topic that you have expertise in and you are interested in either writing or contributing to a book, please visit `authors.packtpub.com`.

# Reviews

Please leave a review. Once you have read and used this book, why not leave a review on the site that you purchased it from? Potential readers can then see and use your unbiased opinion to make purchase decisions, we at Packt can understand what you think about our products, and our authors can see your feedback on their book. Thank you!

For more information about Packt, please visit `packtpub.com`.

# Disclaimer

Where explicitly stated, this book contains code and excerpts from the The Rust Programming Language (`https://doc.rust-lang.org/stable/book/`), first and second edition, which are both distributed under the MIT license under the following terms:

# Learning the Basics

1

In this chapter, we will cover the following recipes:

- Concatenating strings
- Using the format! macro
- Providing a default implementation
- Using the constructor pattern
- Using the builder pattern
- Parallelism through simple threads
- Generating random numbers
- Querying with regexes
- Accessing the command line
- Interacting with environment variables
- Reading from stdin
- Accepting a variable number of arguments

## Introduction

There are some code snippets and patterns of thought that prove time and again to be the bread and butter of a certain programming language. We will start this book by looking at a handful of such techniques in Rust. They are so quintessential for elegant and flexible code that you will use at least some of them in just about any project you tackle.

The next chapters will then build on this foundation and work hand in hand with Rust's zero costs abstractions, which are as powerful as the ones in higher-level languages. We are also going to look at the intricate inner aspects of the standard library and implement our own similar constructs with the help of fearless concurrency and careful use of `unsafe` blocks, which enable us to work at the same low level that some system languages, such as C, operate at.

# Concatenating strings

String manipulation is typically a bit less straightforward in system programming languages than in scripting languages, and Rust is no exception. There are multiple ways to do it, all managing the involved resources differently.

# Getting ready

We will assume for the rest of the book that you have an editor open, the newest Rust compiler ready, and a command line available. As of the time of writing, the newest version is `1.24.1`. Because of Rust's strong guarantees about backward compatibility, you can rest assured that all of the recipes shown (with the exception of Chapter 10, *Using Experimental Nightly Features*) are always going to work the same way. You can download the newest compiler with its command-line tools at `https://www.rustup.rs`.

# How to do it...

1. Create a Rust project to work on during this chapter with `cargo new chapter-one`
2. Navigate to the newly created `chapter-one` folder. For the rest of this chapter, we will assume that your command line is currently in this directory
3. Inside the `src` folder, create a new folder called `bin`
4. Delete the generated `lib.rs` file, as we are not creating a library
5. In the `src/bin` folder, create a file called `concat.rs`
6. Add the following code and run it with `cargo run --bin concat`:

```
1  fn main() {
2    by_moving();
3    by_cloning();
4    by_mutating();
```

```
5  }
6
7  fn by_moving() {
8    let hello = "hello ".to_string();
9    let world = "world!";
10
11   // Moving hello into a new variable
12   let hello_world = hello + world;
13   // Hello CANNOT be used anymore
14   println!("{}", hello_world); // Prints "hello world!"
15  }
16
17  fn by_cloning() {
18    let hello = "hello ".to_string();
19    let world = "world!";
20
21   // Creating a copy of hello and moving it into a new variable
22   let hello_world = hello.clone() + world;
23   // Hello can still be used
24   println!("{}", hello_world); // Prints "hello world!"
25  }
26
27  fn by_mutating() {
28    let mut hello = "hello ".to_string();
29    let world = "world!";
30
31   // hello gets modified in place
32   hello.push_str(world);
33   // hello is both usable and modifiable
34   println!("{}", hello); // Prints "hello world!"
35  }
```

# How it works...

In all functions, we start by allocating memory for a string of variable length.
We do this by creating a string slice (&str) and applying the to_string function on it [8, 18 and 28].
The first way to concatenate strings in Rust, as shown in the by_moving function, is by taking said allocated memory and **moving** it, together with an additional string slice, into a new variable [12]. This has a couple of advantages:

- It's very straightforward and clear to look at, as it follows the common programming convention of concatenating with the + operator

- It uses only immutable data. Remember to always try to write code in a style that creates as little stateful behavior as possible, as it results in more robust and reusable code bases
- It reuses the memory allocated by `hello` [8], which makes it very performant

As such, this way of concatenating should be preferred whenever possible.
So, why would we even list other ways to concatenate strings? Well, I'm glad you asked, dear reader. Although elegant, this approach comes with two downsides:

- `hello` is no longer usable after line [12], as it was moved. This means you can no longer read it in any way
- Sometimes you may actually prefer mutable data in order to use state in small, contained environments

The two remaining functions address one concern each.
`by_cloning`[17] looks nearly identical to the first function, but it clones the allocated string [22] into a temporary object, allocating new memory in the process, which it then moves, leaving the original `hello` untouched and still accessible. Of course, this comes at the price of redundant memory allocations at runtime.

`by_mutating`[27] is the stateful way of solving our problem. It performs the involved memory management in-place, which means that the performance should be the same as in `by_moving`. In the end, it leaves `hello` mutable, ready for further changes. You may notice that this function doesn't look as elegant as the others, as it doesn't use the + operator. This is intentional, as Rust tries to push you through its design towards moving data in order to create new variables without mutating existing ones. As mentioned before, you should only do this if you really need mutable data or want to introduce state in a very small and manageable context.

# Using the format! macro

There is an additional way to combine strings, which can also be used to combine them with other data types, such as numbers.

# How to do it...

1. In the `src/bin` folder, create a file called `format.rs`
2. Add the following code and run it with `cargo run --bin format`

```
1  fn main() {
2    let colour = "red";
3    // The '{}' it the formatted string gets replaced by the
   parameter
4    let favourite = format!("My favourite colour is {}", colour);
5    println!("{}", favourite);
6
7    // You can add multiple parameters, which will be
8    // put in place one after another
9    let hello = "hello ";
10   let world = "world!";
11   let hello_world = format!("{}{}", hello, world);
12   println!("{}", hello_world); // Prints "hello world!"
13
14   // format! can concatenate any data types that
15   // implement the 'Display' trait, such as numbers
16   let favourite_num = format!("My favourite number is {}", 42);
17   println!("{}", favourite_num); // Prints "My favourite number
   is 42"
18
19   // If you want to include certain parameters multiple times
20   // into the string, you can use positional parameters
21   let duck_duck_goose = format!("{0}, {0}, {0}, {1}!", "duck",
   "goose");
22   println!("{}", duck_duck_goose); // Prints "duck, duck, duck,
   goose!"
23
24   // You can even name your parameters!
25   let introduction = format!(
26     "My name is {surname}, {forename} {surname}",
27     surname="Bond",
28     forename="James"
29   );
30   println!("{}", introduction) // Prints "My name is Bond, James
   Bond"
31 }
```

# How it works...

The `format!` macro combines strings by accepting a format string filled with formatting parameters (example, `{}`, `{0}`, or `{foo}`) and a list of arguments, which are then inserted into the *placeholders*.

We are now going to show this on the example in line [16]:

```
format!("My favourite number is {}", 42);
```

Let's break down the preceding line of code:

- `"My favourite number is {}"` is the format string
- `{}` is the formatting parameter
- `42` is the argument

As demonstrated, `format!` works not only with strings, but also with numbers. In fact, it works with all `struct`s that implement the `Display` trait. This means that, by providing such an implementation by yourself, you can easily make your own data structures printable however you want.

By default, `format!` replaces one parameter after another. If you want to override this behavior, you can use positional parameters like `{0}` [21]. With the knowledge that the positions are zero-indexed, the behavior here is pretty straightforward, `{0}` gets replaced by the first argument, `{1}` gets replaced by the second, and so on.

At times, this can become a bit unwieldy when using a lot of parameters. For this purpose, you can use named arguments [26], just like in Python. Keep in mind that all of your unnamed arguments have to be placed before your named ones. For example, the following is invalid:

```
format!("{message} {}", message="Hello there,", "friendo")
```

It should be rewritten as:

```
format!("{message} {}", "friendo", message="Hello there,")
 // Returns "hello there, friendo"
```

# There's more...

You can combine positional parameters with normal ones, but it's probably not a good idea, as it can quite easily become confusing to look at. The behavior, in this case, is as follows—imagine that `format!` internally uses a counter to determine which argument is the next to be placed. This counter is increased whenever `format!` encounters a `{}` *without* a position in it. This rule results in the following:

```
format!("{1} {} {0} {}", "a", "b") // Returns "b a a b"
```

There are also a ton of extra formatting options if you want to display your data in different formats. `{:?}` prints the implementation of the `Debug` trait for the respective argument, often resulting in a more verbose output. `{:.*}` lets you specify the decimal precision of floating point numbers via the argument, like so:

```
format!("{:.*}", 2, 1.234567) // Returns "1.23"
```

For a complete list, visit `https://doc.rust-lang.org/std/fmt/`.

All of the information in this recipe applies to `println!` and `print!` as well, as it is essentially the same macro. The only difference is that `println!` doesn't return its processed string but instead, well, prints it!

# Providing a default implementation

Often, when dealing with structures that represent configurations, you don't care about certain values and just want to silently assign them a standard value.

# How to do it...

1. In the `src/bin` folder, create a file called `default.rs`

2. Add the following code and run it with `cargo run --bin default`:

```
1  fn main() {
2      // There's a default value for nearly every primitive type
3      let foo: i32 = Default::default();
4      println!("foo: {}", foo); // Prints "foo: 0"
5
6
```

```
 7    // A struct that derives from Default can be initialized like
      this
 8    let pizza: PizzaConfig = Default::default();
 9    // Prints "wants_cheese: false
10    println!("wants_cheese: {}", pizza.wants_cheese);
11
12    // Prints "number_of_olives: 0"
13    println!("number_of_olives: {}", pizza.number_of_olives);
14
15    // Prints "special_message: "
16    println!("special message: {}", pizza.special_message);
17
18    let crust_type = match pizza.crust_type {
19      CrustType::Thin => "Nice and thin",
20      CrustType::Thick => "Extra thick and extra filling",
21    };
22    // Prints "crust_type: Nice and thin"
23    println!("crust_type: {}", crust_type);
24
25
26    // You can also configure only certain values
27    let custom_pizza = PizzaConfig {
28      number_of_olives: 12,
29      ..Default::default()
30    };
31
32    // You can define as many values as you want
33    let deluxe_custom_pizza = PizzaConfig {
34      number_of_olives: 12,
35      wants_cheese: true,
36      special_message: "Will you marry me?".to_string(),
37      ..Default::default()
38    };
39
40 }
41
42 #[derive(Default)]
43 struct PizzaConfig {
44    wants_cheese: bool,
45    number_of_olives: i32,
46    special_message: String,
47    crust_type: CrustType,
48 }
49
50 // You can implement default easily for your own types
51 enum CrustType {
52    Thin,
53    Thick,
```

```
54  }
55  impl Default for CrustType {
56    fn default() -> CrustType {
57      CrustType::Thin
58    }
59  }
```

# How it works...

Nearly every type in Rust has a `Default` implementation. When you define your own `struct` that only contains elements that already have a `Default`, you have the option to derive from `Default` as well [42]. In the case of enums or complex structs, you can easily write your own implementation of `Default` instead [55], as there's only one method you have to provide. After this, the `struct` returned by `Default::default()` is implicitly inferrable as yours, if you tell the compiler what your type actually is. This is why in line [3] we have to write `foo: i32`, or else Rust wouldn't know what type the default object actually should become.

If you only want to specify some elements and leave the others at the default, you can use the syntax in line [29]. Keep in mind that you can configure and skip as many values as you want, as shown in lines [33 to 37].

# Using the constructor pattern

You may have asked yourself how to idiomatically initialize complex structs in Rust, considering it doesn't have constructors. The answer is simple, there is a constructor, it's just a convention rather than a rule. Rust's standard library uses this pattern very often, so we need to understand it if we want to use the std effectively.

# Getting ready

In this recipe, we are going to talk about how a **user** interacts with a `struct`. When we say *user* in this context, we don't mean the end user that clicks on the GUI of the app you're writing. We're referring to the programmer that instantiates and manipulates the `struct`.

# How to do it...

1. In the `src/bin` folder, create a file called `constructor.rs`

2. Add the following code and run it with `cargo run --bin constructor`:

```
1  fn main() {
2      // We don't need to care about
3      // the internal structure of NameLength
4      // Instead, we can just call it's constructor
5      let name_length = NameLength::new("John");
6
7      // Prints "The name 'John' is '4' characters long"
8      name_length.print();
9  }
10
11 struct NameLength {
12     name: String,
13     length: usize,
14 }
15
16 impl NameLength {
17     // The user doesn't need to setup length
18     // We do it for him!
19     fn new(name: &str) -> Self {
20         NameLength {
21             length: name.len(),
22             name,
23         }
24     }
25
26     fn print(&self) {
27         println!(
28             "The name '{}' is '{}' characters long",
29             self.name,
30             self.length
31         );
32     }
33 }
```

# How it works...

If a struct provides a method called new that returns Self, the user of the struct will not configure or depend upon the members of the struct, as they are considered to be in an internal *hidden* state.

In other words, if you see a struct that has a new function, always use it to create the structure.
This has the nice effect of enabling you to change as many members of the struct as you want without the user noticing anything, as they are not supposed to look at them anyway.

The other reason to use this pattern is to guide the user to the correct way of instantiating a struct. If one has nothing but a big list of members that have to be filled with values, one might feel a bit lost. If one, however, has a method with only a few self-documenting parameters, it feels way more inviting.

# There's more...

You might have noticed that for our example we really didn't need a length member and could have just calculated a length whenever we print. We use this pattern anyway, to illustrate the point of its usefulness in hiding implementations. Another good use for it is when the members of a struct themselves have their own constructors and one needs to *cascade* the constructor calls. This happens, for example, when we have a Vec as a member, as we will see later in the book, in the, *Using a vector* section in Chapter 2, *Working with Collections*.

Sometimes, your structs might need more than one way to initialize themselves. When this happens, try to still provide a new() method as your default way of construction and name the other options according to how they differ from the default. A good example of this is again vector, which not only provides a Vec::new() constructor but also a Vec::with_capacity(10), which initializes it with enough space for 10 items. More on that again in the Using a vector section in Chapter 2, *Working with Collections*.

When accepting a kind of string (either `&str`, that is, a borrowed string slice, or `String`, that is, an owned string) with plans to store it in your `struct`, like we do in our example, also considering a `Cow`. No, not the big milk animal friends. A `Cow` in Rust is a *Clone On Write* wrapper around a type, which means that it will try to borrow a type for as long as possible and only make an owned clone of the data when absolutely necessary, which happens at the first mutation. The practical effect of this is that, if we rewrote our `NameLength` struct in the following way, it would not care whether the called passed a `&str` or a `String` to it, and would instead try to work in the most efficient way possible:

```rust
use std::borrow::Cow;
struct NameLength<'a> {
    name: Cow<'a, str>,
    length: usize,
}

impl<'a> NameLength<'a> {
    // The user doesn't need to setup length
    // We do it for him!
    fn new<S>(name: S) -> Self
    where
        S: Into<Cow<'a, str>>,
    {
        let name: Cow<'a, str> = name.into();
        NameLength {
            length: name.len(),
            name,
        }
    }

    fn print(&self) {
        println!(
            "The name '{}' is '{}' characters long",
            self.name, self.length
        );
    }
}
```

If you want to read more about `Cow`, check out this easy-to-understand blog post by Joe Wilm: `https://jwilm.io/blog/from-str-to-cow/`.

The `Into` trait used in the `Cow` code is going to be explained in the Converting types into each other section in `Chapter 5`, *Advanced Data Structures*.

# See also

- *Using a vector* recipe in `Chapter 2`, *Working with Collections*
- *Converting types into each other* recipe in `Chapter 5`, *Advanced Data Structures*

# Using the builder pattern

Sometimes you need something between the customization of the constructor and the implicitness of the default implementation. Enter the builder pattern, another technique frequently used by the Rust standard library, as it allows a caller to fluidly chain together configurations that they care about and lets them ignore details that they don't care about.

# How to do it...

1. In the `src/bin` folder, create a file called `builder.rs`

2. Add all of the following code and run it with `cargo run --bin builder`:

```
1    fn main() {
2      // We can easily create different configurations
3      let normal_burger = BurgerBuilder::new().build();
4      let cheese_burger = BurgerBuilder::new()
         .cheese(true)
         .salad(false)
         .build();
5      let veggie_bigmac = BurgerBuilder::new()
         .vegetarian(true)
         .patty_count(2)
         .build();
6
7      if let Ok(normal_burger) = normal_burger {
8        normal_burger.print();
9      }
10     if let Ok(cheese_burger) = cheese_burger {
11       cheese_burger.print();
12     }
13     if let Ok(veggie_bigmac) = veggie_bigmac {
14       veggie_bigmac.print();
15     }
16
17     // Our builder can perform a check for
```

```
18   // invalid configurations
19   let invalid_burger = BurgerBuilder::new()
       .vegetarian(true)
       .bacon(true)
       .build();
20   if let Err(error) = invalid_burger {
21     println!("Failed to print burger: {}", error);
22   }
23
24   // If we omit the last step, we can reuse our builder
25   let cheese_burger_builder = BurgerBuilder::new().cheese(true);
26   for i in 1..10 {
27     let cheese_burger = cheese_burger_builder.build();
28     if let Ok(cheese_burger) = cheese_burger {
29       println!("cheese burger number {} is ready!", i);
30       cheese_burger.print();
31     }
32   }
33 }
```

This is the configurable object:

```
35 struct Burger {
36     patty_count: i32,
37     vegetarian: bool,
38     cheese: bool,
39     bacon: bool,
40     salad: bool,
41 }
42 impl Burger {
43     // This method is just here for illustrative purposes
44     fn print(&self) {
45         let pretty_patties = if self.patty_count == 1 {
46             "patty"
47         } else {
48             "patties"
49         };
50         let pretty_bool = |val| if val { "" } else { "no " };
51         let pretty_vegetarian = if self.vegetarian { "vegetarian
"
              }
            else { "" };
52         println!(
53             "This is a {}burger with {} {}, {}cheese, {}bacon and
                {}salad",
54             pretty_vegetarian,
55             self.patty_count,
56             pretty_patties,
```

```
57              pretty_bool(self.cheese),
58              pretty_bool(self.bacon),
59              pretty_bool(self.salad)
60          )
61      }
62  }
```

And this is the builder itself. It is used to configure and create a `Burger`:

```
64  struct BurgerBuilder {
65    patty_count: i32,
66    vegetarian: bool,
67    cheese: bool,
68    bacon: bool,
69    salad: bool,
70  }
71  impl BurgerBuilder {
72    // in the constructor, we can specify
73    // the standard values
74    fn new() -> Self {
75      BurgerBuilder {
76        patty_count: 1,
77        vegetarian: false,
78        cheese: false,
79        bacon: false,
80        salad: true,
81      }
82    }
83
84    // Now we have to define a method for every
85    // configurable value
86    fn patty_count(mut self, val: i32) -> Self {
87      self.patty_count = val;
88      self
89    }
90
91    fn vegetarian(mut self, val: bool) -> Self {
92      self.vegetarian = val;
93      self
94    }
95    fn cheese(mut self, val: bool) -> Self {
96      self.cheese = val;
97      self
98    }
99    fn bacon(mut self, val: bool) -> Self {
100      self.bacon = val;
101      self
102    }
```

```
103    fn salad(mut self, val: bool) -> Self {
104      self.salad = val;
105      self
106    }
107
108    // The final method actually constructs our object
109    fn build(&self) -> Result<Burger, String> {
110      let burger = Burger {
111        patty_count: self.patty_count,
112        vegetarian: self.vegetarian,
113        cheese: self.cheese,
114        bacon: self.bacon,
115        salad: self.salad,
116    };
117    // Check for invalid configuration
118    if burger.vegetarian && burger.bacon {
119      Err("Sorry, but we don't server vegetarian bacon
             yet".to_string())
120      } else {
121        Ok(burger)
122      }
123    }
124 }
```

# How it works...

Whew, that's a lot of code! Let's start by breaking it up.

In the first part, we illustrate how to use this pattern to effortlessly configure a complex object. We do this by relying on sensible standard values and only specifying what we really care about:

```
let normal_burger = BurgerBuilder::new().build();
let cheese_burger = BurgerBuilder::new()
    .cheese(true)
    .salad(false)
    .build();
let veggie_bigmac = BurgerBuilder::new()
    .vegetarian(true)
    .patty_count(2)
    .build();
```

The code reads pretty nicely, doesn't it?

In our version of the builder pattern, we return the object wrapped in a `Result` in order to tell the world that there are certain invalid configurations and that our builder might not always be able to produce a valid product. Because of this, we have to check the validity of our burger before accessing it[7, 10 and 13].

Our invalid configuration is `vegetarian(true)` and `bacon(true)`. Unfortunately, our restaurant doesn't serve vegetarian bacon yet! When you start the program, you will see that the following line will print an error:

```
if let Err(error) = invalid_burger {
    println!("Failed to print burger: {}", error);
}
```

If we omit the final `build` step, we can reuse the builder in order to build as many objects as we want. [25 to 32]

Let's see how we implemented all of this. The first thing after the `main` function is the definition of our `Burger` struct. No surprises here, it's just plain old data. The `print` method is just here to provide us with some nice output during runtime. You can ignore it if you want.

The real logic is in the `BurgerBuilder`[64]. It should have one member for every value you want to configure. As we want to configure every aspect of our burger, we will have the exact same members as `Burger`. In the constructor [74], we can specify some default values. We then create one method for every configuration. In the end, in `build()` [109], we first perform some error checking. If the configuration is OK, we return a `Burger` made out of all of our members [121]. Otherwise, we return an error [119].

# There's more...

If you want your object to be constructable without a builder, you could also provide `Burger` with a `Default` implementation. `BurgerBuilder::new()` could then just return `Default::default()`.

In `build()`, if your configuration can inherently not be invalid, you can, of course, return the object directly without wrapping it in a `Result`.

# Parallelism through simple threads

Every year, parallelism and concurrency become more important as processors tend to have more and more physical cores. In most languages, writing parallel code is tricky. Very tricky. Not so in Rust, as it has been designed around the principle of *fearless concurrency* since the beginning.

## How to do it...

1. In the `src/bin` folder, create a file called `parallelism.rs`

2. Add the following code and run it with `cargo run --bin parallelism`

```
1    use std::thread;
2
3    fn main() {
4      // Spawning a thread lets it execute a lambda
5      let child = thread::spawn(|| println!("Hello from a new
       thread!"));
6      println!("Hello from the main thread!");
7      // Joining a child thread with the main thread means
8      // that the main thread waits until the child has
9      // finished it's work
10     child.join().expect("Failed to join the child thread");
11
12     let sum = parallel_sum(&[1, 2, 3, 4, 5, 6, 7, 8, 9, 10]);
13     println!("The sum of the numbers 1 to 10 is {}", sum);
14   }
15
16   // We are going to write a function that
17   // sums the numbers in a slice in parallel
18   fn parallel_sum(range: &[i32]) -> i32 {
19     // We are going to use exactly 4 threads to sum the numbers
20     const NUM_THREADS: usize = 4;
21
22     // If we have less numbers than threads,
23     // there's no point in multithreading them
24     if range.len() < NUM_THREADS {
25       sum_bucket(range)
26     } else {
27       // We define "bucket" as the amount of numbers
28       // we sum in a single thread
29       let bucket_size = range.len() / NUM_THREADS;
30       let mut count = 0;
```

```
31        // This vector will keep track of our threads
32        let mut threads = Vec::new();
33        // We try to sum as much as possible in other threads
34        while count + bucket_size < range.len() {
35            let bucket = range[count..count +
                                 bucket_size].to_vec();
36          let thread = thread::Builder::new()
37            .name("calculation".to_string())
38            .spawn(move || sum_bucket(&bucket))
39            .expect("Failed to create the thread");
40          threads.push(thread);
41
42          count += bucket_size
43      }
44      // We are going to sum the rest in the main thread
45      let mut sum = sum_bucket(&range[count..]);
46
47      // Time to add the results up
48      for thread in threads {
49        sum += thread.join().expect("Failed to join thread");
50      }
51      sum
52    }
53  }
54
55  // This is the function that will be executed in the threads
56  fn sum_bucket(range: &[i32]) -> i32 {
57    let mut sum = 0;
58    for num in range {
59      sum += *num;
60    }
61      sum
62  }
```

# How it works...

You can create a new thread by calling thread::spawn, which will then begin executing the provided lambda. This will return a JoinHandle, which you can use to, well, join the thread. Joining a thread means waiting for the thread to finish its work. If you don't join a thread, you have no guarantee of it actually ever finishing. This might be valid though when setting up threads to do tasks that never complete, such as listening for incoming connections.

Keep in mind that you cannot predetermine the order in which your threads will complete any work. In our example, it is impossible to foretell whether *Hello from a new thread!* or *Hello from the main thread!* is going to be printed first, although most of the time it will probably be the main thread, as the operating system needs to put some effort into spawning a new thread. This is the reason why small algorithms can be faster when not executed in parallel. Sometimes, the overhead of letting the OS spawn and manage new threads is just not worth it.

As demonstrated by line [49], joining a thread will return a `Result` that contains the value your lambda returned.

Threads can also be given names. Depending on your OS, in case of a crash, the name of the responsible thread will be displayed. In line [37], we call our new summation threads *calculation*. If one of them were to crash, we would be able to quickly identify the issue. Try it out for yourself, insert a call to `panic!()`; at the beginning of `sum_bucket` in order to intentionally crash the program and run it. If your OS supports named threads, you will now be told that your thread *calculation* panicked with an *explicit panic*.

`parallel_sum` is a function that takes a slice of integers and adds them together in parallel on four threads. If you have limited experience in working with parallel algorithms, this function will be hard to grasp at first. I invite you to copy it by hand into your text editor and play around with it in order to get a grasp on it. If you still feel a bit lost, don't worry, we will revisit parallelism again later.

Adapting algorithms to run in parallel normally comes at the risk of data races. A data race is defined as the behavior in a system where the output is dependent on the random timing of external events. In our case, having a data race would mean that multiple threads try to access and modify a resource at the same time. Normally, programmers have to analyze their usage of resources and use external tools in order to catch all of the data races. In contrast, Rust's compiler is smart enough to catch data races at compile time and stops if it finds one. This is the reason why we had to call `.to_vec()` in line [35]:

```
let bucket = range[count..count + bucket_size].to_vec();
```

We will cover vectors in a later recipe (the *Using a vector* section in Chapter 2, *Working with Collections*), so if you're curious about what is happening here, feel free to jump to Chapter 2, *Working with Collections* and come back again. The essence of it is that we're copying the data into `bucket`. If we instead passed a reference into `sum_bucket` in our new thread, we would have a problem, the memory referenced by `range` is only guaranteed to live inside of `parallel_sum`, but the threads we spawn are allowed to outlive their parent threads. This would mean that in theory, if we didn't `join` the threads at the right time, `sum_bucket` might get unlucky and get called late enough for `range` to be invalid.

This would then be a data race, as the outcome of our function would depend on the uncontrollable sequence in which our operating system decides to launch the threads.

But don't just take my word for it, try it yourself. Simply replace the aforementioned line with `let bucket = &range[count..count + bucket_size];` and try to compile it.

## There's more...

If you're experienced with parallelism, you might have noticed how suboptimal our algorithm here is. This is intentional, as the elegant and efficient way of writing `parallel_sum` would require using techniques we have not discussed yet. We will revisit this algorithm in `Chapter 7`, *Parallelism and Rayon*, and rewrite it in a professional manner. In that chapter, we will also learn how to concurrently modify resources using locks.

## See also

- *Access resources in parallel with RwLocks*, recipe in `Chapter 7`, *Parallelism and Rayon*

# Generating random numbers

As described in the preface, the Rust core team left some functionality intentionally out of the standard and put it into its own external crate. Generating pseudo-random numbers is one such functionality.

## How to do it...

1. Open the `Cargo.toml` file that was generated earlier for you
2. Under `[dependencies]`, add the following line:

   ```
   rand = "0.3"
   ```

3. If you want, you can go to rand's crates.io page (`https://crates.io/crates/ rand`) to check for the newest version and use that one instead

4. In the `bin` folder, create a file called `rand.rs`

5. Add the following code and run it with `cargo run --bin rand`:

```
1   extern crate rand;
2
3   fn main() {
4     // random_num1 will be any integer between
5     // std::i32::MIN and std::i32::MAX
6     let random_num1 = rand::random::<i32>();
7     println!("random_num1: {}", random_num1);
8     let random_num2: i32 = rand::random();
9     println!("random_num2: {}", random_num2);
10    // The initialization of random_num1 and random_num2
11    // is equivalent.
12
13    // Every primitive data type can be randomized
14    let random_char = rand::random::<char>();
15    // Altough random_char will probably not be
16    // representable on most operating systems
17    println!("random_char: {}", random_char);
18
19
20    use rand::Rng;
21    // We can use a reusable generator
22    let mut rng = rand::thread_rng();
23    // This is equivalent to rand::random()
24    if rng.gen() {
25      println!("This message has a 50-50 chance of being
                   printed");
26    }
27    // A generator enables us to use ranges
28    // random_num3 will be between 0 and 9
29    let random_num3 = rng.gen_range(0, 10);
30    println!("random_num3: {}", random_num3);
31
32    // random_float will be between 0.0 and 0.999999999999...
33    let random_float = rng.gen_range(0.0, 1.0);
34    println!("random_float: {}", random_float);
35
36    // Per default, the generator uses a uniform distribution,
37    // which should be good enough for nearly all of your
38    // use cases. If you require a particular distribution,
39    // you specify it when creating the generator:
```

```
40    let mut chacha_rng = rand::ChaChaRng::new_unseeded();
41    let random_chacha_num = chacha_rng.gen::<i32>();
42    println!("random_chacha_num: {}", random_chacha_num);
43  }
```

# How it works...

Before you can use `rand`, you have to tell Rust that you're using the `crate` by writing:

```
extern crate rand;
```

After that, `rand` will provide a random generator. We can access it by either calling `rand::random();` [6] or by accessing it directly with `rand::thread_rng();` [22].

If we go the first route, the generator will need to be told what type to generate. You can either explicitly state the type in the method call [6] or annotate the type of the resulting variable [8]. Both are equal and result in the exact same thing. Which one you use is up to you. In this book, we will use the first convention.

As you can see in lines [29 and 33], you need neither if the type is unambiguous in the called context.

The generated value will be between its type's MIN and MAX constants. In the case of `i32`, this would be `std::i32::MIN` and `std::i32::MAX`, or, in concrete numbers, -2147483648 and 2147483647. You can verify these numbers easily by calling the following:

```
println!("min: {}, max: {}", std::i32::MIN, std::i32::MAX);
```

As you can see, these are very big numbers. For most purposes, you will probably want to define custom limits. You can go the second route discussed earlier and use `rand::Rng` for that[22]. It has a `gen` method, which is actually implicitly called by `rand::random()`, but also a `gen_range()` that accepts a minimum and maximum value. Keep in mind that this range is non-inclusive, which means that the maximum value can never be reached. This is why in line [29], `rng.gen_range(0, 10)` will only generate the numbers 0, 1, 2, 3, 4, 5, 6, 7, 8, and 9, without the 10.

All of the described ways of generating random values use **uniform distribution**, which means that every number in the range has the same chance of being generated. In some contexts, it makes sense to use other distributions. You can specify a generator's distribution during its creation[40]. As of the time of publication, the rand crate supports the ChaCha and ISAAC distributions.

# There's more...

If you want to randomly populate an entire `struct`, you use the `rand_derive` helper crate in order to derive it from **Rand**. You can then generate your own `struct`, just as you would generate any other type.

# Querying with regexes

When parsing simple data formats, it is often easier to write regular expressions (or *regex* for short) than use a parser. Rust has pretty decent support for this through its `regex` crate.

# Getting ready

In order to really understand this chapter, you should be familiar with regexes. There are countless free online resources for this, like regexone (`https://www.regexone.com/`).

 This recipe will not conform to clippy, as we kept the regexes intentionally *too* simple because we want to keep the focus of the recipe on the code, not the regex. Some of the examples shown could have been rewritten to use `.contains()` instead.

# How to do it...

1. Open the `Cargo.toml` file that was generated earlier for you

2. Under `[dependencies]`, add the following line:

   ```
   regex = "0.2"
   ```

3. If you want, you can go to regex's crates.io page (`https://crates.io/crates/regex`) to check for the newest version and use that one instead

4. In the `bin` folder, create a file called `regex.rs`

5. Add the following code and run it with `cargo run --bin regex`:

   ```
   1    extern crate regex;
   2
   3    fn main() {
   ```

```
4    use regex::Regex;
5    // Beginning a string with 'r' makes it a raw string,
6    // in which you don't need to escape any symbols
7    let date_regex =
       Regex::new(r"^\d{2}.\d{2}.\d{4}$").expect("Failed
         to create regex");
8    let date = "15.10.2017";
9    // Check for a match
10   let is_date = date_regex.is_match(date);
11   println!("Is '{}' a date? {}", date, is_date);
12
13   // Let's use capture groups now
14   let date_regex = Regex::new(r"(\d{2}).(\d{2})
       .(\d{4})").expect("Failed to create regex");
15   let text_with_dates = "Alan Turing was born on 23.06.1912 and
         died on 07.06.1954. \
16     A movie about his life called 'The Imitation Game' came out
         on 14.11.2017";
17   // Iterate over the matches
18   for cap in date_regex.captures_iter(text_with_dates) {
19     println!("Found date {}", &cap[0]);
20     println!("Year: {} Month: {} Day: {}", &cap[3], &cap[2],
         &cap[1]);
21   }
22   // Replace the date format
23   println!("Original text:\t\t{}", text_with_dates);
24   let text_with_indian_dates =
       date_regex.replace_all(text_with_dates, "$1-$2-$3");
25   println!("In indian format:\t{}", text_with_indian_dates);
26
27   // Replacing groups is easier when we name them
28   // ?P<somename> gives a capture group a name
29   let date_regex = Regex::new(r"(?P<day>\d{2}).(?P<month>\d{2})
       .(?P<year>\d{4})")
30     .expect("Failed to create regex");
31   let text_with_american_dates =
       date_regex.replace_all(text_with_dates,
         "$month/$day/$year");
32   println!("In american format:\t{}",
     text_with_american_dates);
33   let rust_regex = Regex::new(r"(?i)rust").expect("Failed to
       create regex");
34   println!("Do we match RuSt? {}",
     rust_regex.is_match("RuSt"));
35   use regex::RegexBuilder;
36   let rust_regex = RegexBuilder::new(r"rust")
37     .case_insensitive(true)
38     .build()
```

```
39        .expect("Failed to create regex");
40    println!("Do we still match RuSt? {}",
          rust_regex.is_match("RuSt"));
41  }
```

# How it works...

You can construct a regex object by calling `Regex::new()` with a valid regex string[7]. Most of the time, you will want to pass a *raw string* in the form of `r"..."`. Raw means that all symbols in the string are taken at literal value without being escaped. This is important because of the backslash (\) character that is used in regex to represent a couple of important concepts, such as digits(\d) or whitespace (\s). However, Rust already uses the backslash to escape special *non-printable* symbols, such as the newline (\n) or the tab (\t)[23]. If we wanted to use a backslash in a normal string, we would have to escape it by repeating it ( \\). Or the regex on line [14] would have to be rewritten as:

```
"(\\d{2}).(\\d{2}).(\\d{4})"
```

Worse yet, if we wanted to match for the backslash itself, we would have to escape it as well because of regex. With normal strings, we would have to quadruple-escape it! ( \\\\) We can save ourselves the headache of missing readability and confusion by using raw strings and write our regex normally. In fact, it is considered good style to use raw strings in *every* regex, even when it doesn't have any backslashes [33]. This is a help for your future self if you notice down the line that you actually would like to use a feature that requires a backslash.

We can iterate over the results of our regex [18]. The object we get on every match is a collection of our capture groups. Keep in mind that the zeroeth index is always the entire capture [19]. The first index is then the string from our first capture group, the second index is the string of the second capture group, and so on. [20]. Unfortunately, we do not get a compile-time check on our index, so if we accessed `&cap[4]`, our program would compile but then crash during runtime.

When replacing, we follow the same concept: `$0` is the entire match, `$1` the result of the first capture group, and so on. To make our life easier, we can give the capture groups names by starting them with `?P<somename>`[29] and then use this name when replacing [31].

There are many flags that you can specify, in the form of (?flag), for fine-tuning, such as i, which makes the match case insensitive [33], or x, which ignores whitespace in the regex string. If you want to read up on them, visit their documentation (https://doc.rust-lang.org/regex/regex/index.html). Most of the time though, you can get the same result by using the RegexBuilder that is also in the regex crate [36]. Both of the rust_regex objects we generate in lines [33] and [36] are equivalent. While the second version is definitely more verbose, it is also way easier to understand at first glance.

## There's more...

The regexes work by compiling their strings into the equivalent Rust code on creation. For performance reasons, you are advised to reuse your regexes instead of creating them anew every time you use them. A good way of doing this is by using the lazy_static crate, which we will look at later in the book, in the Creating lazy static objects section in Chapter 5, *Advanced Data Structures*.

> Be careful not to overdo it with regexes. As they say, "When all you have is a hammer, everything looks like a nail." If you parse complicated data, regexes can quickly become an unbelievably complex mess. When you notice that your regex has become too big to understand at first glance, try to rewrite it as a parser.

## See also

- *Creating lazy static objects* recipe in Chapter 5, *Advanced Data Structures*

## Accessing the command line

Sooner or later, you'll want to interact with the user in some way or another. The most basic way to do this is by letting the user pass parameters while calling the application through the command line.

# How to do it...

1. In the `bin` folder, create a file called `cli_params.rs`

2. Add the following code and run it with `cargo run --bin cli_params some_option some_other_option`:

```
1   use std::env;
2
3   fn main() {
4     // env::args returns an iterator over the parameters
5     println!("Got following parameters: ");
6     for arg in env::args() {
7       println!("- {}", arg);
8     }
9
10    // We can access specific parameters using the iterator API
11    let mut args = env::args();
12    if let Some(arg) = args.nth(0) {
13      println!("The path to this program is: {}", arg);
14    }
15    if let Some(arg) = args.nth(1) {
16        println!("The first parameter is: {}", arg);
17    }
18    if let Some(arg) = args.nth(2) {
19        println!("The second parameter is: {}", arg);
20    }
21
22    // Or as a vector
23    let args: Vec<_> = env::args().collect();
24    println!("The path to this program is: {}", args[0]);
25    if args.len() > 1 {
26        println!("The first parameter is: {}", args[1]);
27    }
28    if args.len() > 2 {
29        println!("The second parameter is: {}", args[2]);
30    }
31  }
```

# How it works...

Calling `env::args()` returns an iterator over the provided parameters[6]. By convention, the first command-line parameter on most operating systems is the path to the executable itself [12].

We can access specific parameters in two ways: keep them as an iterator [11] or `collect` them into a collection such as `Vec`[23]. Don't worry, we are going to talk about them in detail in `Chapter 2`, *Working with Collections*. For now, it's enough for you to know that:

- Accessing an iterator forces you to check at compile time whether the element exists, for example, an `if let` binding [12]

- Accessing a vector checks the validity at runtime

This means that we could have executed lines [26] and [29] without checking for their validity first in [25] and [28]. Try it yourself, add the `&args[3];` line at the end of the program and run it.

 We check the length anyways because it is considered good style to check whether the expected parameters were provided. With the iterator way of accessing parameters, you don't have to worry about forgetting to check, as it forces you to do it. On the other hand, by using a vector, you can check for the parameters once at the beginning of the program and not worry about them afterward.

# There's more...

If you are building a serious command-line utility in the style of *nix tools, you will have to parse a lot of different parameters. Instead of reinventing the wheel, you should take a look at third-party libraries, such as clap (`https://crates.io/crates/clap`).

# Interacting with environment variables

According to the Twelve-Factor App (`https://12factor.net/`), you should store your configuration in the environment (`https://12factor.net/config`). This means that you should pass values that could change between deployments, such as ports, domains, or database handles, as environment variables. Many programs also use environment variables to communicate with each other.

## How to do it...

1. In the `bin` folder, create a file called `env_vars.rs`

2. Add the following code and run it with `cargo run --bin env_vars`:

```
1    use std::env;
2
3    fn main() {
4      // We can iterate over all the env vars for the current
       process
5      println!("Listing all env vars:");
6      for (key, val) in env::vars() {
7        println!("{}: {}", key, val);
8      }
9
10     let key = "PORT";
11     println!("Setting env var {}", key);
12     // Setting an env var for the current process
13     env::set_var(key, "8080");
14
15     print_env_var(key);
16
17     // Removing an env var for the current process
18     println!("Removing env var {}", key);
19     env::remove_var(key);
20
21     print_env_var(key);
22   }
23
24   fn print_env_var(key: &str) {
25     // Accessing an env var
26     match env::var(key) {
27       Ok(val) => println!("{}: {}", key, val),
28       Err(e) => println!("Couldn't print env var {}: {}", key,
```

```
       e),
29      }
30   }
```

# How it works...

With `env::vars()`, we can access an iterator over all the env var that were set for the current process at the time of execution [6]. This list is pretty huge though, as you'll see when running the code, and for the most part, irrelevant for us.

It's more practical to access a single env var with `env::var()` [26], which returns an `Err` if the requested var is either not present or doesn't contain valid Unicode. We can see this in action in line [21], where we try to print a variable that we just deleted.

Because your `env::var` returns a `Result`, you can easily set up default values for them by using `unwrap_or_default`. One real-life example of this, involving the address of a running instance of the popular Redis (`https://redis.io/`) key-value storage, looks like this:

```
redis_addr = env::var("REDIS_ADDR")
    .unwrap_or_default("localhost:6379".to_string());
```

Keep in mind that creating an env var with `env::set_var()` [13] and deleting it with `env::remove_var()` [19] both only change the env var for our current process. This means that the created env var are not going to be readable by other programs. It also means that if we accidentally remove an important env var, the rest of the operating system is not going to care, as it can still access it.

# There's more...

At the beginning of this recipe, I wrote about storing your configuration in the environment. The industry standard way to do this is by creating a file called `.env` that contains said config in the form of key-value-pairs, and loading it into the process at some point during the build. One easy way to do this in Rust is by using the dotenv (`https://crates.io/crates/dotenv`) third-party crate.

# Reading from stdin

If you want to create an interactive application, it's easy to prototype your functionality with the command line. For CLI programs, this will be all the interaction you need.

## How to do it...

1. In the src/bin folder, create a file called stdin.rs

2. Add the following code and run it with cargo run --bin stdin:

```
1    use std::io;
2    use std::io::prelude::*;
3
4    fn main() {
5      print_single_line("Please enter your forename: ");
6      let forename = read_line_iter();
7
8      print_single_line("Please enter your surname: ");
9      let surname = read_line_buffer();
10
11     print_single_line("Please enter your age: ");
12     let age = read_number();
13
14     println!(
15       "Hello, {} year old human named {} {}!",
16       age, forename, surname
17     );
18   }
19
20   fn print_single_line(text: &str) {
21     // We can print lines without adding a newline
22     print!("{}", text);
23     // However, we need to flush stdout afterwards
24     // in order to guarantee that the data actually displays
25     io::stdout().flush().expect("Failed to flush stdout");
26   }
27
28   fn read_line_iter() -> String {
29     let stdin = io::stdin();
30     // Read one line of input iterator-style
31     let input = stdin.lock().lines().next();
32     input
33       .expect("No lines in buffer")
```

```
34          .expect("Failed to read line")
35          .trim()
36          .to_string()
37   }
38
39   fn read_line_buffer() -> String {
40       // Read one line of input buffer-style
41       let mut input = String::new();
42       io::stdin()
43           .read_line(&mut input)
44           .expect("Failed to read line");
45       input.trim().to_string()
46   }
47
48   fn read_number() -> i32 {
49       let stdin = io::stdin();
50       loop {
51           // Iterate over all lines that will be inputted
52           for line in stdin.lock().lines() {
53               let input = line.expect("Failed to read line");
54               // Try to convert a string into a number
55               match input.trim().parse::<i32>() {
56                   Ok(num) => return num,
57                   Err(e) => println!("Failed to read number: {}", e),
58               }
59           }
60       }
61   }
```

# How it works...

In order to read from the standard console input, stdin, we first need to obtain a handle to it. We do this by calling io::stdin() [29]. Imagine the returned object as a reference to a global stdin object. This global buffer is managed by a Mutex, which means that only one thread can access it at a time (more on that later in the book, in the Parallelly accessing resources with Mutexes section in Chapter 7, *Parallelism and Rayon*). We get this access by locking (using lock()) the buffer, which returns a new handle [31]. After we have done this, we can call the lines method on it, which returns an iterator over the lines the user will write [31 and 52]. More on iterators in the *Accessing collections as Iterators* section in Chapter 2, *Working with Collections*.

Finally, we can iterate over as many submitted lines as we want until some kind of break condition is reached, otherwise the iteration would go on forever. In our example, we break the number-checking loop as soon as a valid number has been entered [56].

If we're not particularly picky about our input and just want the next line, we have two options:

- We can continue using the infinite iterator provided by `lines()`, but simply call next on it in order to just take the first one. This comes with an additional error check as, generally speaking, we cannot guarantee that there is a next element.

- We can use `read_line` in order to populate an existing buffer [43]. This doesn't require that we `lock` the handler first, as it is done implicitly.

Although they both result in the same end effect, you should choose the first option. It is more idiomatic as it uses iterators instead of a mutable state, which makes it more maintainable and readable.

On a side note, we are using `print!` instead of `println!` in some places in this recipe for aesthetic reasons [22]. If you prefer the look of newlines before user input, you can refrain from using them.

## There's more...

This recipe is written with the assumption that you want to use stdin for live interaction over the `cli`. If you plan on instead piping some data into it (for example, `cat foo.txt | stdin.rs` on *nix), you can stop treating the iterator returned by `lines()` as infinite and retrieve the individual lines, not unlike how you retrieved the individual parameters in the last recipe.

There are various calls to `trim()` in our recipe [35, 45 and 55]. This method removes leading and trailing whitespace in order to enhance the user-friendliness of our program. We are going to look at it in detail in the *Using a string* section in `Chapter 2`, *Working with Collections*.

# See also

- *Interacting with environment variables* recipe in `Chapter 1`, *Learning the Basics*
- *Using a string* and *Accessing collections as iterators* recipe in `Chapter 2`, *Working with Collections*
- *Parallelly accessing resources with Mutexes* recipe in `Chapter 7`, *Parallelism and Rayon*

# Accepting a variable number of arguments

Most of the time, when you want to operate on a dataset, you will design a function that takes a collection. In some cases, however, it is nice to have functions that just accept an unbound amount of parameters, like JavaScript's *rest parameters*. This concept is called **variadic functions** and is not supported by Rust. However, we can implement it ourselves by defining a recursive macro.

# Getting started

The code in this recipe might be small, but it will look like gibberish if you're not familiar with macros. If you have not yet learned about macros or need a refresh, I recommend that you take a quick look at the relevant chapter in the official Rust book (`https://doc.rust-lang.org/stable/book/first-edition/macros.html`).

# How to do it...

1. In the `src/bin` folder, create a file called `variadic.rs`

2. Add the following code and run it with `cargo run --bin variadic:`

```
1  macro_rules! multiply {
2      // Edge case
3      ( $last:expr ) => { $last };
4
5      ( $head:expr, $($tail:expr), +) => {
6          // Recursive call
7          $head * multiply!($($tail),+)
8      };
9  }
```

```
10
11  fn main() {
12      // You can call multiply! with
13      // as many parameters as you want
14      let val = multiply!(2, 4, 8);
15      println!("2*4*8 = {}", val)
16  }
```

# How it works...

Let's start with our intention: we want to create a macro called multiply that accepts an undefined amount of parameters and multiplies them all together. In macros, this is done via recursion. We begin every recursive definition with the **edge case**, that is, the parameters where the recursion should stop. Most of the time, this is where a function call stops making sense. In our case, this is the single parameter. Think about it, what should multiply!(3) return? It doesn't make sense to multiply it with anything, since we have no other parameter to multiply it with. Our best reaction is to simply return the parameter unmodified.

Our other condition is a match against more than one parameter, a $head and a comma-separated list of parameters inside of a $tail. Here, we just define the return value as the $head multiplied with the multiplication of the $tail. This will call multiply! with the $tail and without the $head, which means that on every call we process one parameter less until we finally reach our edge case, one single parameter.

# There's more...

Keep in mind that you should use this technique sparingly. Most of the time, it is clearer to just accept and operate on a slice instead. However, it makes sense to use this in combination with other macros and higher kinds of concepts where the analogy of *a graspable list of things* breaks down. Finding a good example for this is difficult since they tend to be extremely specific. You can find one of them at the end of the book though.

# See also

- *Composing functions* recipe in Chapter 10, *Using Experimental Nightly Features*

# Working with Collections

2

In this chapter, we will cover the following recipes:

- Using a vector
- Using a string
- Accessing collections as iterators
- Using a `VecDeque`
- Using a `HashMap`
- Using a `HashSet`
- Creating an own iterator
- Using a slab

# Introduction

**Rust** provides a very broad set of collections to use. We will look at most of them, see how they're used, discuss how they're implemented, and when to use and choose them. A big part of this chapter focuses on iterators. Much of Rust's flexibility comes from them, as all collections (and more!) can be used as iterators. Learning how to use them is crucial.

Throughout this chapter, we are going to use the *big O notation* to show how effective certain algorithms are. In case you don't know it yet, it is a way of telling how much longer an algorithm takes when working with more elements. Let's look at it briefly.

$O(1)$ means that an algorithm is going to take the same time, no matter how much data is stored in a collection. It doesn't tell us how fast exactly it is, just that it's not going to slow down with size. This is the realistic ideal for a function. A practical example for this is accessing the first number in an infinite list of numbers: no matter how many numbers there are, you're always going to be able to instantly pick out the first one.

$O(n)$ means that an algorithm is going to slow down by the same degree for every element. This is not good, but still okay. An example for this is printing all data in a `for` loop.

$O(n^2)$ is really bad. It tells us that an algorithm is going to be slower and slower with every element. An example of it would be accessing data in a `for` loop nested in another `for` loop over the same data.

# Using a vector

The most basic collection is the vector, or `Vec` for short. It is essentially a variable-length array with a very low overhead. As such, it is the collection that you will use most of the time.

# How to do it...

1. In the command line, jump one folder up with `cd ..` so you're not in `chapter-one` anymore. In the next chapters, we are going to assume that you always started with this step.
2. Create a Rust project to work on during this chapter with `cargo new chapter-two`.
3. Navigate into the newly-created `chapter-two` folder. For the rest of this chapter, we will assume that your command line is currently in this directory.
4. Inside the folder `src`, create a new folder called `bin`.
5. Delete the generated `lib.rs` file, as we are not creating a library.
6. In the folder `src/bin`, create a file called `vector.rs`.
7. Add the following code blocks to the file and run them with `cargo run --bin vector`:

```
1  fn main() {
2      // Create a vector with some elements
3      let fruits = vec!["apple", "tomato", "pear"];
```

```
4    // A vector cannot be directly printed
5    // But we can debug-print it
6    println!("fruits: {:?}", fruits);
7
8    // Create an empty vector and fill it
9    let mut fruits = Vec::new();
10    fruits.push("apple");
11   fruits.push("tomato");
12    fruits.push("pear");
13    println!("fruits: {:?}", fruits);
14
15    // Remove the last element
16    let last = fruits.pop();
17    if let Some(last) = last {
18        println!("Removed {} from {:?}", last, fruits);
19    }
20
21    // Insert an element into the middle of the vector
22    fruits.insert(1, "grape");
23    println!("fruits after insertion: {:?}", fruits);
24
25    // Swap two elements
26    fruits.swap(0, 1);
27    println!("fruits after swap: {:?}", fruits);
```

8. This is how you can access single elements in a vector:

```
29    // Access the first and last elements
30    let first = fruits.first();
31    if let Some(first) = first {
32      println!("First fruit: {}", first);
33    }
34    let last = fruits.last();
35    if let Some(last) = last {
36      println!("Last fruit: {}", last);
37    }
38
39    // Access arbitrary elements
40    let second = fruits.get(1);
41    if let Some(second) = second {
42      println!("Second fruit: {}", second);
43    }
44    // Access arbitrary elements without bonds checking
45    let second = fruits[1];
46    println!("Second fruit: {}", second);
```

9. The next few methods apply to the whole vector:

```
50      // Initialize the vector with a value
51      // Here, we fill our vector with five zeroes
52      let bunch_of_zeroes = vec![0; 5];
53      println!("bunch_of_zeroes: {:?}", bunch_of_zeroes);
54
55      // Remove some item and shift all that come after
56      // into place
57      let mut nums = vec![1, 2, 3, 4];
58      let second_num = nums.remove(1);
59      println!("Removed {} from {:?}", second_num, nums);
60
61      // Filter the vector in place
62      let mut names = vec!["Aaron", "Felicia", "Alex", "Daniel"];
63      // Only keep names starting with 'A'
64      names.retain(|name| name.starts_with('A'));
65      println!("Names starting with A: {:?}", names);
66
67      // Check if the vector contains an element
68      println!("Does 'names' contain \"Alex\"? {}",
            names.contains(&"Alex"));
69
70
71
72      // Remove consecutive(!) duplicates
73      let mut nums = vec![1, 2, 2, 3, 4, 4, 4, 5];
74      nums.dedup();
75      println!("Deduped, pre-sorted nums: {:?}", nums);
76
77      // Be careful if your data is not sorted!
78      let mut nums = vec![2, 1, 4, 2, 3, 5, 1, 2];
79      nums.dedup();
80      // Doens't print what you might expect
81      println!("Deduped, unsorted nums: {:?}", nums);
82
83      // Sort a vector
84      nums.sort();
85      println!("Manually sorted nums: {:?}", nums);
86      nums.dedup();
87      println!("Deduped, sorted nums: {:?}", nums);
88
89      // Reverse a vector
90      nums.reverse();
91      println!("nums after being reversed: {:?}", nums);
92
93      // Create a consuming iterator over a range
94      let mut alphabet = vec!['a', 'b', 'c'];
95      print!("The first two letters of the alphabet are: ");
96      for letter in alphabet.drain(..2) {
```

```
97        print!("{} ", letter);
98      }
99      println!();
100     // The drained elements are no longer in the vector
101     println!("alphabet after being drained: {:?}", alphabet);
102
103
104     // Check if a vector is empty
105     let mut fridge = vec!["Beer", "Leftovers", "Mayonaise"];
106     println!("Is the fridge empty {}", fridge.is_empty());
107     // Remove all elements
108     fridge.clear();
109     println!("Is the fridge now empty? {}", fridge.is_empty());
```

10. We can split a vector into two and combine them again:

```
111     // Split a vector into two pieces
112     let mut colors = vec!["red", "green", "blue", "yellow"];
113     println!("colors before splitting: {:?}", colors);
114     let half = colors.len() / 2;
115     let mut second_half = colors.split_off(half);
116     println!("colors after splitting: {:?}", colors);
117     println!("second_half: {:?}", second_half);
118
119     // Put two vectors together
120     colors.append(&mut second_half);
121     println!("colors after appending: {:?}", colors);
122     // This empties the second vector
123     println!("second_half after appending: {:?}", second_half);
```

11. You might remember the `splice` method from JavaScript:

```
127     let mut stuff = vec!["1", "2", "3", "4", "5", "6"];
128     println!("Original stuff: {:?}", stuff);
129     let stuff_to_insert = vec!["a", "b", "c"];
130     let removed_stuff: Vec<_> = stuff.splice(1..4,
          stuff_to_insert).collect();
131     println!("Spliced stuff: {:?}", stuff);
132     println!("Removed stuff: {:?}", removed_stuff);
```

12. If you are working with very big datasets, you can optimize the performance of your vector:

```
136   // Initialize the vector with a certain capacity
137   let mut large_vec: Vec<i32> = Vec::with_capacity(1_000_000);
138   println!("large_vec after creation:");
139   println!("len:\t\t{}", large_vec.len());
140   println!("capacity:\t{}", large_vec.capacity());
141
142   // Shrink the vector as close as possible to its length
143   large_vec.shrink_to_fit();
144   println!("large_vec after shrinking:");
145   println!("len:\t\t{}", large_vec.len());
146   println!("capacity:\t{}", large_vec.capacity());
147
148   // Remove some item, replacing it with the last
149   let mut nums = vec![1, 2, 3, 4];
150   let second_num = nums.swap_remove(1);
151   // This changes the order, but works in O(1)
152   println!("Removed {} from {:?}", second_num, nums);
153 }
```

# How it works...

This recipe is going to be a bit longer than the others, because:

- The vector is the most important collection
- Many of its core principles, like preallocation, apply to other collections as well
- It includes methods used on slices, which are also usable by many other collections

Let's start at the beginning.

A vector can be created [9] by using the constructor pattern we mentioned earlier (Chapter 1, *Learning the Basics, Using the Constructor Pattern*), and filled by calling push on it for every element we want to store [10]. Because this is such a common pattern, Rust provides you with a convenient macro called vec! [3]. While its end effect is the same, the macro is implemented with some nice performance optimizations.

Because of the convenience vec! provides, other Rustacians have implemented similar macros for the other collections, which you can find here: https://crates.io/crates/maplit.

If you want to initialize a vector by repeating an element over and over, you can use the special calling syntax described in line [52] to do so.

The opposite of `push` is `pop`: it removes the last element of the vector, and returns it if the vector wasn't empty before. Because of the memory layout of `Vec`, which we are going to look at in the next section, this operation is done in $O(1)$ complexity. If you don't know what that means, let me rephrase that: it's pretty fast. This is why vectors can be nicely used as **First In, Last Out (FILO)** stacks.

If you need to modify the contents of a vector, `insert`[22], `remove` [58], and `swap` [26] should be self-explanatory. Sometimes, though, you want to access a specific element in the vector. You can use `get` to borrow an element at an index [40], and `get_mut` to mutate it. Both return an `Option` that only contains `Some` element if the index was valid. Most times, though, this fine grade of error checking is unnecessary for vector access, as an out-of-bounds index is usually not recoverable, and will just be handled by unwrapping the `Option`. For this reason, Rust lets you call the `Index` operator, `[]`, on a `Vec` [45]. This will automatically deduce its mutability and perform an unwrap for you.

There are a bunch of methods that help us work with the entire vector at once. `retain` is a very useful one that is also implemented by most other collections [64]. It accepts a so-called **predicate**, which is a fancy word for a function that returns `true` or `false`. It applies that predicate to every element, and only keeps the ones where it returned `true`.

`dedup` removes all *consecutive* duplicates [74]. This means that for the vector `[1, 2, 2, 3, 2, 3]`, dedup would result in `[1, 2, 3, 2, 3]`, as only the duplicate 2s were consecutive. Always remember this when using it, as it can cause bugs that are hard to find. If you want to remove *all* duplicates, you need to make them consecutive by sorting the vector first. If your elements are comparable, this is as simple as calling `.sort()` [84].

Using `drain` creates a consuming iterator over your vector, accessing all elements and removing them in the process, leaving your vector empty [96]. This is useful when you have to *work through* your data and reuse your empty vector again afterwards to collect more work.

If you've never seen `splice` in another language, you're probably going to feel a bit confused at first about what it does. Let's take a look at it, shall we?

`splice` does three things:

- It takes a range. This range will be *removed* from the vector.
- It takes an iterator. This iterator will be *inserted* into the space left open by the removal from the last step.
- It *returns* the removed elements as an iterator.

How to handle the returned iterator is going to be the topic of the recipe in the *Access collections as iterators* section.

# There's more...

The vector should always be your go-to collection. Internally, it is implemented as a continuous chunk of memory stored on the heap:

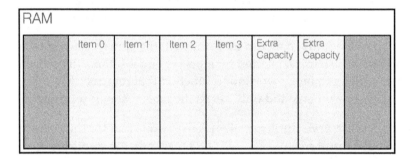

The important keyword here is *continuous*, which means that the memory is very cache-friendly. In other words, the vector is pretty fast! The vector even allocates a bit of extra memory in case you want to extend it. Be careful, though, when inserting a lot of data at the beginning of the vector: the entire stack will have to be moved.

At the end, you can see a bit of *extra capacity*. This is because `Vec` and many other collections preallocate a bit of extra memory each time you have to move the block, because it has grown too large. This is done in order to prevent as many reallocations as possible. You can check the exact amount of total space of a vector by calling `capacity`[140] on it. You can influence the preallocation by initializing your vector with `with_capacity`[137]. Use it when you have a rough idea about how many elements you plan on storing. This can be a big difference in capacity when working with big amounts of data.

The extra capacity doesn't go away when shortening the vector. If you had a vector with a length of 10,000 and a capacity of 100,000 and called `clear` on it, you would still have a capacity of 100,000 preallocated. When working on systems with memory limitations, like microcontrollers, this can become a problem. The solution is calling `shrink_to_fit` periodically on such vectors [143]. This will bring the capacity as close as possible to the length, but it is allowed to still leave a little bit of preallocated space ready.

Another way to optimize really big vectors is to call `swap_remove` [150]. Normally, when removing an element from a vector, all elements after it will be shifted to the left in order to preserve continuous memory. This is a lot of work when removing the first element in a big vector. If you don't care about the exact order of your vector, you can call `swap_remove` instead of `remove`. It works by swapping the element that is to be removed with the last element, and adjusting the length. This is great, because you don't create a *hole* that needs to be filled by shifting, and because swapping memory is a really fast operation in today's processors.

# Using a string

Rust provides an unusually large functionality for its string. Knowing it can save you quite some headache when dealing with raw user input.

# How to do it...

1. In the folder `src/bin`, create a file called `string.rs`.
2. Add the following code, and run it with `cargo run --bin string`:

```
1   fn main() {
2       // As a String is a kind of vector,
3       // you can construct them the same way
4       let mut s = String::new();
5       s.push('H');
6       s.push('i');
7       println!("s: {}", s);
8
9       // The String however can also be constructed
10      // from a string slice (&str)
11      // The next two ways of doing to are equivalent
12      let s = "Hello".to_string();
13      println!("s: {}", s);
14      let s = String::from("Hello");
15      println!("s: {}", s);
```

```
16
17    // A String in Rust will always be valid UTF-8
18    let s = "汉语 한글 Þjóðhildur 😉 🌐".to_string();
19    println!("s: {}", s);
20
21    // Append strings to each other
22    let mut s = "Hello ".to_string();
23    s.push_str("World");
24
25    // Iterate over the character
26    // A "character" is defined here as a
27    // Unicode Scalar Value
28    for ch in "Tubular".chars() {
29        print!("{}.", ch);
30    }
31    println!();
32    // Be careful though, a "character" might not
33    // always be what you expect
34    for ch in "ў".chars() {
35        // This does NOT print ў
36        print!("{} ", ch);
37    }
38    println!();
```

Use the following code to split a string in various ways:

```
42    // Split a string slice into two halves
43    let (first, second) = "HelloThere".split_at(5);
44    println!("first: {}, second: {}", first, second);
45
46    // Split on individual lines
47    let haiku = "\
48                she watches\n\
49                satisfied after love\n\
50                he lies\n\
51                looking up at nothing\n\
52                ";
53    for line in haiku.lines() {
54        println!("\t{}.", line);
55    }
56
57    // Split on substrings
58    for s in "Never;Give;Up".split(';') {
59        println!("{}", s);
60    }
61    // When the splitted string is at the beginning or end,
62    // it will result in the empty string
```

```
63    let s: Vec<_> = "::Hi::There::".split("::").collect();
64    println!("{:?}", s);
65
66    // If you can eliminate the empty strings at the end
67    // by using split_termitor
68    let s: Vec<_> = "Mr. T.".split_terminator('.').collect();
69    println!("{:?}", s);
70
71    // char has a few method's that you can use to split on
72    for s in "I'm2fast4you".split(char::is_numeric) {
73        println!("{}", s);
74    }
75
76    // Split only a certain amount of times
77    for s in "It's not your fault, it's mine".splitn(3,
        char::is_whitespace) {
78        println!("{}", s);
79    }
80
81    // Get only the substrings that match a pattern
82    // This is the opposite of splitting
83    for c in "The Dark Knight rises".matches(char::is_uppercase)
{
84        println!("{}", c);
85    }
86
87    // Check if a string starts with something
88    let saying = "The early bird gets the worm";
89    let starts_with_the = saying.starts_with("The");
90    println!(
        "Does \"{}\" start with \"The\"?: {}",
        saying,
        starts_with_the
    );
91    let starts_with_bird = saying.starts_with("bird");
92    println!(
        "Does \"{}\" start with \"bird\"?: {}",
        saying,
        starts_with_bird
    );
93
94    // Check if a string ends with something
95    let ends_with_worm = saying.ends_with("worm");
96    println!("Does \"{}\" end with \"worm\"?: {}", saying,
        ends_with_worm);
```

```
97
98      // Check if the string contains something somewhere
99      let contains_bird = saying.contains("bird");
100     println!("Does \"{}\" contain \"bird\"?: {}", saying,
           contains_bird);
```

## Remove whitespace:

```
105     // Splitting on whitespace might not result in what you
expect
106     let a_lot_of_whitespace = "   I   love spaaace     ";
107     let s: Vec<_> = a_lot_of_whitespace.split(' ').collect();
108     println!("{:?}", s);
109     // Use split_whitespace instead
110     let s: Vec<_> =
           a_lot_of_whitespace.split_whitespace().collect();
111     println!("{:?}", s);
112
113     // Remove leading and trailing whitespace
114     let username = "   P3ngu1n\n".trim();
115     println!("{}", username);
116     // Remove only leading whitespace
117     let username = "   P3ngu1n\n".trim_left();
118     println!("{}", username);
119     // Remove only trailing whitespace
120     let username = "   P3ngu1n\n".trim_right();
121     println!("{}", username);
122
123
124     // Parse a string into another data type
125     // This requires type annotation
126     let num = "12".parse::<i32>();
127     if let Ok(num) = num {
128       println!("{} * {} = {}", num, num, num * num);
129     }
```

## Modify the string:

```
133     // Replace all occurences of a pattern
134     let s = "My dad is the best dad";
135     let new_s = s.replace("dad", "mom");
136     println!("new_s: {}", new_s);
137
138     // Replace all characters with their lowercase
139     let lowercase = s.to_lowercase();
140     println!("lowercase: {}", lowercase);
141
142     // Replace all characters with their uppercase
```

```
143    let uppercase = s.to_uppercase();
144    println!("uppercase: {}", uppercase);
145
146    // These also work with other languages
147    let greek = "ὈΔΥΣΣΕΎΣ";
148    println!("lowercase greek: {}", greek.to_lowercase());
149
150    // Repeat a string
151    let hello = "Hello! ";
152    println!("Three times hello: {}", hello.repeat(3));
153 }
```

# How it works...

Essentially, being a kind of vector, a string can be created the same way by combining `new` and `push`; however, because this is really inconvenient, a `string`, which is an owned chunk of memory, can be created from a string slice (`&str`), which is either a borrowed string or a literal. Both of the ways to do it, that are shown in this recipe, are equivalent:

```
let s = "Hello".to_string();
println!("s: {}", s);
let s = String::from("Hello");
println!("s: {}", s);
```

Out of pure personal preference, we will use the first variant.

Before Rust `1.9`, `to_owned()` was the fastest way to create a string. Now, `to_string()` is equally performant and should be preferred, because it offers more clarity over what is done. We mention this because many old tutorials and guides have not been updated since then, and still use `to_owned()`.

All strings in Rust are valid Unicode in UTF-8 encoding. This can lead to some surprises, as a *character*, as we know it, is an inherently Latin invention. For instance, look at languages that have a modifier for a letter—is ä an own character, or is it merely a variation of a? What about languages that allow many combinations in extreme? What would that keyboard even look like? For this reason, Unicode lets you compose your *characters* from different *Unicode scalar values*. With `.chars()`, you can create an iterator that goes through these scalars [28]. If you work with non-Latin characters, you might get surprised by this when accessing composing characters —ÿ is not one, but two scalars, y and ˘ [36]. You can get around this by using the `Unicode-segmentation` crate, which supports iteration over graphemes: `https://crates.io/crates/unicode-segmentation`.

When splitting a string on a pattern that is at the beginning, is at the end, or occurs multiple times after each other, each instance gets split into an empty string " "[107]. This is especially nasty when splitting on spaces (' '). In this case, you should use `split_whitespace` instead [110]. Otherwise, `split_terminator` will remove the empty strings from the end of the string [68].

 By the way, when we talk about a *pattern* in this recipe, we mean one of three things:
- A character
- A string
- A predicate that takes one `char`

## There's more...

The implementation of `String` should not be much of a surprise—it's just a kind of vector:

| RAM | | | | | | |
|---|---|---|---|---|---|---|
| | char 0 | char 1 | char 2 | char 3 | Extra Capacity | Extra Capacity |

# Accessing collections as iterators

Welcome to one of the most flexible parts of the Rust standard library. Iterators are, as the name suggests, a way of applying actions of items in a collection. If you come from C#, you will already be familiar with iterators because of Linq. Rust's iterators are kind of similar, but come with a more functional approach to things.

Because they are an extremely fundamental part of the standard library, we are going to dedicate this recipe entirely to a showcase of all the different things you can do with them in isolation. For real-world use cases, you can simply continue reading the book, as a big portion of the other recipes features iterators in some way or another.

# How to do it...

1. In the folder `src/bin`, create a file called `iterator.rs`.
2. Add the following code, and run it with `cargo run --bin iterator`:

```
1   fn main() {
2     let names = vec!["Joe", "Miranda", "Alice"];
3     // Iterators can be accessed in many ways.
4     // Nearly all collections implement .iter() for this purpose
5     let mut iter = names.iter();
6     // A string itself is not iterable, but its characters are
7     let mut alphabet = "ABCDEFGHIJKLMNOPQRSTUVWXYZ".chars();
8     // Ranges are also (limited) iterators
9     let nums = 0..10;
10    // You can even create infinite iterators!
11    let all_nums = 0..;
12
13    // As the name says, you can iterate over iterators
14    // This will consume the iterator
15    for num in nums {
16        print!("{} ", num);
17    }
18    // nums is no longer usable
19    println!();
20
21    // Got the index of the current item
22    for (index, letter) in "abc".chars().enumerate() {
23      println!("#{}. letter in the alphabet: {}", index + 1,
            letter);
24    }
```

3. Access individual items:

```
26    // going through an iterator, step by step
27    if let Some(name) = iter.next() {
28        println!("First name: {}", name);
29    }
30    if let Some(name) = iter.next() {
31        println!("Second name: {}", name);
32    }
33    if let Some(name) = iter.next() {
34        println!("Third name: {}", name);
35    }
36    if iter.next().is_none() {
37        println!("No names left");
38    }
39
```

```
40      // Arbitrary access to an item in the iterator
41      let letter = alphabet.nth(3);
42      if let Some(letter) = letter {
43        println!("the fourth letter in the alphabet is: {}",
            letter);
44      }
45      // This works by consuming all items up to a point
46      let current_first = alphabet.nth(0);
47      if let Some(current_first) = current_first {
48        // This will NOT print 'A'
49        println!(
50          "The first item in the iterator is currently: {}",
51            current_first
52        );
53      }
54      let current_first = alphabet.nth(0);
55      if let Some(current_first) = current_first {
56        println!(
57          "The first item in the iterator is currently: {}",
58            current_first
59        );
60      }
61
62      // Accessing the last item; This will
63      // consume the entire iterator
64      let last_letter = alphabet.last();
65      if let Some(last_letter) = last_letter {
66        println!("The last letter of the alphabet is: {}",
            last_letter);
67      }
```

4. Collect the iterator into a collection:

```
69      // Collect iterators into collections
70      // This requires an anotation of which collection we want
71      // The following two are equivalent:
72      let nums: Vec<_> = (1..10).collect();
73      println!("nums: {:?}", nums);
74      let nums = (1..10).collect::<Vec<_>>();
75      println!("nums: {:?}", nums)
```

5. Change which items are being iterated over:

```
79    // Taking only the first n items
80    // This is often used to make an infinite iterator finite
81    let nums: Vec<_> = all_nums.take(5).collect();
82    println!("The first five numbers are: {:?}", nums);
83
84    // Skip the first few items
85    let nums: Vec<_> = (0..11).skip(2).collect();
86    println!("The last 8 letters in a range from zero to 10:
          {:?}", nums);
87
88    // take and skip accept predicates in the form of
89    // take_while and skip_while
90    let nums: Vec<_> = (0..).take_while(|x| x * x <
      50).collect();
91    println!(
92      "All positive numbers that are less than 50 when squared:
93        {:?}", nums
94    );
95
96    // This is useful to filter an already sorted vector
97    let names = ["Alfred", "Andy", "Jose", "Luke"];
98    let names: Vec<_> = names.iter().skip_while(|x|
        x.starts_with('A')).collect();
99    println!("Names that don't start with 'A': {:?}", names);
100
101   // Filtering iterators
102   let countries = [
103     "U.S.A.",
        "Germany",
        "France",
        "Italy",
        "India",
        "Pakistan",
        "Burma",
104   ];
105   let countries_with_i: Vec<_> = countries
106     .iter()
107     .filter(|country| country.contains('i'))
108     .collect();
109   println!(
110     "Countries containing the letter 'i': {:?}",
111     countries_with_i
112   );
```

6. Check if an iterator contains an element:

```
116    // Find the first element that satisfies a condition
117    if let Some(country) = countries.iter().find(|country|
118      country.starts_with('I')) {
119        println!("First country starting with the letter 'I':
             {}", country);
       }
120
121    // Don't get the searched item but rather its index
122    if let Some(pos) = countries
123      .iter()
124      .position(|country| country.starts_with('I'))
125      {
126        println!("It's index is: {}", pos);
127      }
128
129    // Check if at least one item satisfies a condition
130    let are_any = countries.iter().any(|country| country.len() ==
         5);
131    println!(
132      "Is there at least one country that has exactly five
           letters? {}",
133      are_any
134    );
135
136    // Check if ALL items satisfy a condition
137    let are_all = countries.iter().all(|country| country.len() ==
         5);
138    println!("Do all countries have exactly five letters? {}",
         are_all);
```

7. Useful operations for numeric items:

```
141    let sum: i32 = (1..11).sum();
142    let product: i32 = (1..11).product();
143    println!(
144      "When operating on the first ten positive numbers\n\
145        their sum is {} and\n\
146        their product is {}.",
147        sum, product
148    );
149
150    let max = (1..11).max();
151    let min = (1..11).min();
152    if let Some(max) = max {
153      println!("They have a highest number, and it is {}", max);
154    }
```

```
155   if let Some(min) = min {
156     println!("They have a smallest number, and it is {}", min);
157   }
```

## 8. Combine iterators:

```
161   // Combine an iterator with itself, making it infinite
162   // When it reaches its end, it starts again
163   let some_numbers: Vec<_> = (1..4).cycle().take(10).collect();
164   // Reader exercise: Try to guess what this will print
165   println!("some_numbers: {:?}", some_numbers);
166
167   // Combine two iterators by putting them after another
168   let some_numbers: Vec<_> = (1..4).chain(10..14).collect();
169   println!("some_numbers: {:?}", some_numbers);
170
171   // Zip two iterators together by grouping their first items
172   // together, their second items together, etc.
173   let swiss_post_codes = [8957, 5000, 5034];
174   let swiss_towns = ["Spreitenbach", "Aarau", "Suhr"];
175   let zipped: Vec<_> =
        swiss_post_codes.iter().zip(swiss_towns.iter()).collect();
176   println!("zipped: {:?}", zipped);
177
178   // Because zip is lazy, you can use two infine ranges
179   let zipped: Vec<_> = (b'A'..)
180     .zip(1..)
181     .take(10)
182     .map(|(ch, num)| (ch as char, num))
183     .collect();
184   println!("zipped: {:?}", zipped);
```

## 9. Apply functions to all items:

```
188   // Change the items' types
189   let numbers_as_strings: Vec<_> = (1..11).map(|x|
        x.to_string()).collect();
190   println!("numbers_as_strings: {:?}", numbers_as_strings);
191
192   // Access all items
193   println!("First ten squares:");
194   (1..11).for_each(|x| print!("{} ", x));
195   println!();
196
197   // filter and map items at the same time!
198   let squares: Vec<_> = (1..50)
199     .filter_map(|x| if x % 3 == 0 { Some(x * x) } else { None
      })
```

```
200       .collect();
201     println!(
202       "Squares of all numbers under 50 that are divisible by 3:
203         {:?}", squares
204     );
```

10. The real strength of iterators comes from combining them:

```
208     // Retrieve the entire alphabet in lower and uppercase:
209     let alphabet: Vec<_> = (b'A' .. b'z' + 1) // Start as u8
210       .map(|c| c as char) // Convert all to chars
211       .filter(|c| c.is_alphabetic()) // Filter only alphabetic
chars
212       .collect(); // Collect as Vec<char>
213     println!("alphabet: {:?}", alphabet);
214 }
```

# How it works...

*This recipe is incredibly important.* No matter what you do, or which library you use, it's going to use iterators somewhere. All of the operations presented can be used on any collection and all types that implement the `iterator` trait.

In the first section, we looked at different ways to create iterators. I mention that ranges are *limited* because, in order to be iterable, the range-type has to implement `Step`. `char` doesn't, so you wouldn't be able to use `'A'..'D'` as an iterator. For this reason, in line [209], we iterate over the characters as bytes:

```
let alphabet: Vec<_> = (b'A' .. b'z' + 1) // Start as u8
    .map(|c| c as char)            // Convert all to chars
    .filter(|c| c.is_alphabetic()) // Filter only alphabetic chars
    .collect(); // Collect as Vec<char>
```

We have to set the limit of the range to `b'z' + 1`, because ranges are non-inclusive. You might have noticed that this fact makes using ranges confusing sometimes. This is why, on the nightly compiler, you can use inclusive ranges (Chapter 10, *Using Experimental Nightly Features, Iterating over an inclusive range*).

Let's return to our recipe here, though. While iterating, you have the option to use `enumerate` in order to get an iteration counter [22]. This is the reason that Rust gets away with not supporting traditional, C-style `for` loop syntax. You most probably have seen some variation of the following C code in some language or another:

```
for (int i = 0; i < some_length; i++) {
    ...
}
```

Rust disallows this, because a range-based `for` loop is almost always cleaner to use, which you are going to know if you come from a Python background, as it pioneered this restriction. In fact, most programming languages have shifted their paradigm to promote range-based loops. In the rare cases where you really actually would like to know your iteration count, you can use `enumerate` to emulate this behavior.

When accessing single items with `nth`[41], you have to keep two things in mind:

- It accesses an item by going through all items until it reaches the one you want. In the worst case, this is an $O(n)$ access. If you can, use your collection's native access method (most of the time, this would be `.get()`).
- It consumes the iterator up to the specified index. This means that calling `nth` twice with the exact same parameters is going to result in two different returned values [54]. Don't let this catch you by surprise.

Another thing to take note of when using an iterator's various accessors is that they all return an `Option` that will be `None` if the iterator has no more items left.

When collecting an iterator into a collection, the following two forms of annotation are completely equivalent:

```
let nums: Vec<_> = (1..10).collect();
let nums = (1..10).collect::<Vec<_>>();
```

Just use the one that you like most. In this book, we stick to the first form because of personal preference. The second form, by the way, is called the *turbofish*. This is because `::<>` kinda looks like a certain family of fish. Cute, isn't it? Both forms are also able to deduce their exact type automatically, so you don't need to write `Vec<i32>`. The inner type can be omitted with an underscore (_), as shown.

`cycle` [163] takes an iterator and repeats it endlessly. `[1, 2, 3]` would become `[1, 2, 3, 1, 2, 3, 1, ...]`.

`zip` [175] takes two iterators and creates one out of them by putting items that are at the same index into a tuple, and then chaining them. If the iterators have different sizes, it just ignores the extra items of the longer one. For example, `[1, 2, 3]` zipped with `['a', 'b', 'c', 'd']` would become `[(1, 'a'), (2, 'b'), (3, 'c')]`, because `'d'` will be thrown away as it has no partner to zip with. If you zip two infinite ranges, you will have no problem, as `zip` is lazy, which means it will only actually start zipping your iterators when it's really necessary; for example, when using `take` to extract the first few tuples [81].

If you need to mutate all of your items, you can use `map`. It can also be used to change the underlying type of the iterator, as shown in line [182]. `for_each` is really similar, with one big difference: it doesn't return anything. It's basically the same as manually using a `for` loop on an iterator. The intended use case for it is situations in which you have a lot of chained method calls on an iterator, where it can be more elegant to chain `for_each` as well, as a kind of *consumer*.

Iterators are very often chained together to weave complex transformations together. If you find yourself calling many methods on a single iterator, don't worry, as this is exactly what you should be doing. On the other hand, when you see yourself doing a lot of complicated stuff in a `for` loop, you should probably rewrite that code with iterators.

When using `filter_map`[199], you can keep an item by returning it, wrapped in `Some`. If you want to filter it out, return `None`. Before that, you're allowed to change the item in whatever way you want, which is the `map` part of the deal.

# There's more...

`iter()` creates an iterator that *borrows* items. If you want to create an iterator that *consumes* items—for example, takes ownership of them by moving them – you can use `into_iter()`.

# See also

- *The Iterating over an inclusive range* recipe in `Chapter 10`, *Using Experimental Nightly Features*

# Using a VecDeque

When you need to insert or remove elements regularly into or from the beginning of the vector, your performance might take quite a hit, as it will force the vector to reallocate all data that comes after it. This is especially bothersome when implementing a queue. For this reason, Rust provides you with the VecDeque.

# How to do it...

1. In the folder src/bin, create a file called vecdeque.rs.
2. Add the following code, and run it with cargo run --bin vecdeque:

```
1    use std::collections::VecDeque;
2
3    fn main() {
4        // A VecDeque is best thought of as a
5        // First-In-First-Out (FIFO) queue
6
7        // Usually, you will use it to push_back data
8        // and then remove it again with pop_front
9        let mut orders = VecDeque::new();
10       println!("A guest ordered oysters!");
11       orders.push_back("oysters");
12
13       println!("A guest ordered fish and chips!");
14       orders.push_back("fish and chips");
15
16       let prepared = orders.pop_front();
17       if let Some(prepared) = prepared {
18           println!("{} are ready", prepared);
19       }
20
21       println!("A guest ordered mozarella sticks!");
22       orders.push_back("mozarella sticks");
23
24       let prepared = orders.pop_front();
25       if let Some(prepared) = prepared {
26           println!("{} are ready", prepared);
27       }
28
29       println!("A guest ordered onion rings!");
30       orders.push_back("onion rings");
31
32       let prepared = orders.pop_front();
```

```
33      if let Some(prepared) = prepared {
34        println!("{} are ready", prepared);
35      }
36
37      let prepared = orders.pop_front();
38      if let Some(prepared) = prepared {
39        println!("{} are ready", prepared);
40      }
41
42      // You can freely switch your pushing
43      // from front to back and vice versa
44      let mut sentence = VecDeque::new();
45      sentence.push_back("a");
46      sentence.push_front("had");
47      sentence.push_back("little");
48      sentence.push_front("Mary");
49      sentence.push_back("Lamb");
50      println!("sentence: {:?}", sentence);
51
52      // The same applies to popping data
53      sentence.pop_front();
54      sentence.push_front("Jimmy");
55      sentence.pop_back();
56      sentence.push_back("Cat");
57      println!("sentence: {:?}", sentence);
58
59
60      // The rest of the VecDeque's methods are
61      // pretty much the same as the vector's
62      // However, the VecDeque has additional options
63      // when swap removing!
64      let mut some_queue = VecDeque::with_capacity(5);
65      some_queue.push_back("A");
66      some_queue.push_back("B");
67      some_queue.push_back("C");
68      some_queue.push_back("D");
69      some_queue.push_back("E");
70      println!("some_queue: {:?}", some_queue);
71
72      // This is the same as Vec's swap_remove
73      some_queue.swap_remove_back(2);
74      println!("some_quere after swap_remove_back: {:?}",
          some_queue);
75
76      // This is the nearly the same, but swaps the removed
77      // element with the first one instead of the last one
78      some_queue.swap_remove_front(2);
79      println!("some_quere after swap_remove_front: {:?}",
```

```
                    some_queue);
      80      }
```

# How it works...

Most of the interface of `VecDeque` is identical to `Vec`. You can even optimize them the same way with `with_capacity` and its `swap_remove` equivalents. The differences come from the fact that `VecDeque` is more oriented around access from both ends. As such, multiple methods from `Vec` that implicitly affect the last element have two equivalents in `VecDeque`: one for the front, and one for the back. These are:

- `push`, which becomes `push_front` [46] and `push_back` [11]
- `pop`, which becomes `pop_front` [16] and `pop_back` [55]
- `swap_remove`, which becomes `remove_front` [78] and `remove_back` [73]

A `VecDeque` has the ability to freely append or remove elements from both ends in a performant way, which makes it an ideal candidate for a **First In, First Out** (**FIFO**) queue [24]. In fact, this is how it's nearly always used.

When you see yourself in a situation where you want to respond to any kind of requests in the order they arrive in and remove them again afterwards, a `VecDeque` is an ideal tool for the job.

# There's more...

Internally, the `VecDeque` is implemented as a *ring buffer*, also known as a *circular buffer*. It's called like this because it behaves like a circle: the end touches the beginning.

It works by allocating a continuous block of memory, like the `Vec`; however, where the `Vec` always leaves its extra capacity at the end of the block, the `VecDeque` has nothing against leaving spots inside the block empty. It follows that when you remove the first element, the `VecDeque` doesn't move all elements to the left, but simply leaves the first spot empty. If you then push an element into the beginning via `push_front`, it will take the spot freed earlier while leaving the elements after it untouched.

The circular catch in the story is that if you have some capacity in the front of the block but none in the back while using `push_back`, the `VecDeque` will simply use that space to allocate the extra element, leading to the following situation:

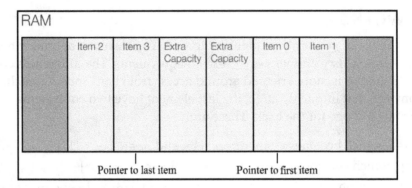

This is great, because you will not have to worry about this at all while using it, as its iterating methods hide the implementation by always showing you the *correct* order!

Like the vector, `VecDeque` will resize itself and move all its elements into a new block when its capacity runs out.

# Using a HashMap

If you imagine a `Vec` as a collection that assigns an index (0, 1, 2, and so on) to data, the `HashMap` is a collection that assigns any data to any data. It allows you to map arbitrary, hashable data to other arbitrary data. Hashing and mapping, that's where the name comes from!

# How to do it...

1. In the folder `src/bin`, create a file called `hashmap.rs`.
2. Add the following code, and run it with `cargo run --bin hashmap`:

```
1    use std::collections::HashMap;
2
3    fn main() {
4        // The HashMap can map any hashable type to any other
5        // The first type is called the "key"
6        // and the second one the "value"
```

```
7     let mut tv_ratings = HashMap::new();
8     // Here, we are mapping &str to i32
9     tv_ratings.insert("The IT Crowd", 8);
10    tv_ratings.insert("13 Reasons Why", 7);
11    tv_ratings.insert("House of Cards", 9);
12    tv_ratings.insert("Stranger Things", 8);
13    tv_ratings.insert("Breaking Bad", 10);
14
15    // Does a key exist?
16    let contains_tv_show = tv_ratings.contains_key("House of
        Cards");
17    println!("Did we rate House of Cards? {}", contains_tv_show);
18    let contains_tv_show = tv_ratings.contains_key("House");
19    println!("Did we rate House? {}", contains_tv_show);
20
21    // Access a value
22    if let Some(rating) = tv_ratings.get("Breaking Bad") {
23      println!("I rate Breaking Bad {} out of 10", rating);
24    }
25
26    // If we insert a value twice, we overwrite it
27    let old_rating = tv_ratings.insert("13 Reasons Why", 9);
28    if let Some(old_rating) = old_rating {
29      println!("13 Reasons Why's old rating was {} out of 10",
          old_rating);
30    }
31    if let Some(rating) = tv_ratings.get("13 Reasons Why") {
32      println!("But I changed my mind, it's now {} out of 10",
          rating);
33    }
34
35    // Remove a key and its value
36    let removed_value = tv_ratings.remove("The IT Crowd");
37    if let Some(removed_value) = removed_value {
38      println!("The removed series had a rating of {}",
          removed_value);
39    }
40
41    // Iterating accesses all keys and values
42    println!("All ratings:");
43    for (key, value) in &tv_ratings {
44      println!("{}\t: {}", key, value);
45    }
46
47    // We can iterate mutably
48    println!("All ratings with 100 as a maximum:");
49    for (key, value) in &mut tv_ratings {
50      *value *= 10;
```

```
51      println!("{}\t: {}", key, value);
52    }
53
54    // Iterating without referencing the HashMap moves its
         contents
55    for _ in tv_ratings {}
56    // tv_ratings is not usable anymore
```

If you don't need to access both keys and values at the same time, you can iterate over either individually:

```
58    // Like with the other collections, you can preallocate a
size
59    // to gain some performance
60    let mut age = HashMap::with_capacity(10);
61    age.insert("Dory", 8);
62    age.insert("Nemo", 5);
63    age.insert("Merlin", 10);
64    age.insert("Bruce", 9);
65
66    // Iterate over all keys
67    println!("All names:");
68    for name in age.keys() {
69      println!("{}", name);
70    }
71
72    // Iterate over all values
73    println!("All ages:");
74    for age in age.values() {
75      println!("{}", age);
76    }
77
78    // Iterate over all values and mutate them
79    println!("All ages in 10 years");
80    for age in age.values_mut() {
81      *age += 10;
82      println!("{}", age);
83    }
84
```

You can use the entry API to assign default values to keys if they're not yet in the
`HashMap`:

```
87    {
88        let age_of_coral = age.entry("coral").or_insert(11);
89        println!("age_of_coral: {}", age_of_coral);
90    }
91    let age_of_coral = age.entry("coral").or_insert(15);
92    println!("age_of_coral: {}", age_of_coral);
93 }
```

# How it works...

As mentioned earlier, a `HashMap` is a collection to map one type of data to another. You do
this by calling `insert`, and passing your key and its value [9]. If the key already had a
value, it will be overwritten. This is why `insert` returns an `Option`: if there was a value
before, it returns the old value [27], or otherwise `None`. If you want to make sure that you're
not overwriting anything, make sure to check the result of `contains_key` [16] before
inserting your value.

Both `get` and `remove` won't crash when called with an invalid key. Instead, they return a
`Result`. In the case of `remove`, said `Result` contains the removed value.

As with most collections, you have the options to iterate over your data, by borrowing the
key-value pairs[43], borrowing the keys while mutating the values [49], or moving them all
[55]. Due to its nature, `HashMap` additionally allows you three more options: borrowing all
values [74], mutating all values [80], or borrowing all keys [68]. You probably noticed that
one combination is missing: you cannot mutate a key. Ever. This is part of the contract you
sign when using a `HashMap`. Further down, where we explain how `HashMap` is
implemented, you're going to see that, because the key's hash is actually an index, mutating
a key is equivalent to deleting an entry and recreating it. This is reflected nicely in the
design choice of not letting you modify keys.

Last but not least, the `Entry` API lets you access an abstraction of a value that might or
might not be there. Most of the time, it's used while being paired with `or_insert` in order
to insert a default value if the key was not found [88]. If you want to insert a default value
based on a closure, you can use `or_insert_with`. Another use for the entry object is to
match it against its variants: `Occupied`, or `Vacant`. This results in the same thing as calling
`get` directly on a key. Note that in our example, we had to scope the entry access like so:

```
    {
        let age_of_coral = age.entry("coral").or_insert(11);
```

```
        println!("age_of_coral: {}", age_of_coral);
    }
    let age_of_coral = age.entry("coral").or_insert(15);
    println!("age_of_coral: {}", age_of_coral);
```

This is because `or_insert` returns a mutable reference to a value. If we had omitted the scope, the second call of `entry` would have borrowed our `age` object at the same time as a mutable reference to it existed, which is an error in Rust's borrowing concept in order to guarantee data race-free access to resources.

If you need to fine-tune your `HashMap` for performance, you can call your usual friends —`with_capacity` [60], `shrink_to_fit`, and `reserve` are also available for it, and work the same way as in other collections.

## There's more...

Internally, you can imagine the `HashMap` as being implemented as two vectors: a table, and a buffer. Of course, we're simplifying here; there are actually no vectors in the implementation. But this analogy is accurate enough.

 If you want to look at the actual implementation, feel free to do so, as Rust is completely open source: `https://github.com/rust-lang/rust/blob/master/src/libstd/collections/hash/table.rs`.

In the background, the buffer stores our values in a sequential fashion. In the front, we have a table storing buckets that don't do much more than point to the element they stand for. When you insert a key-value pair, what happens is:

1. The value gets put in the buffer.
2. The key goes through a hashing function and becomes an index.
3. The table creates a bucket at said index that points to the actual value:

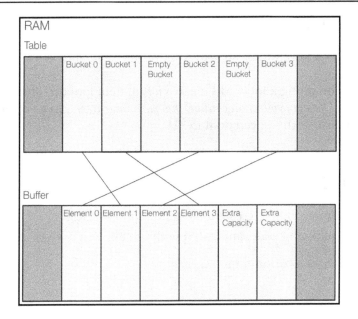

Rust's hashing algorithm doesn't actually generate unique indices, for performance reasons. Instead, Rust uses a clever way to handle hash collisions called **Robin Hood bucket stealing** (http://codecapsule.com/2013/11/11/robin-hood-hashing/).

The default hashing algorithm of the standard library has been chosen specifically to protect you from HashDoS attacks (https://cryptanalysis.eu/blog/2011/12/28/effective-dos-attacks-against-web-application-plattforms-hashdos/). If you want to squeeze out every bit of performance, you can do that, of your HashMap without caring about this particular risk, or you can specify a custom hasher by constructing it with with_hasher.

Many people have already implemented various hashers on crates.io, so make sure to check them out before rolling with your own solution.

# Using a HashSet

The best way to describe a HashSet is by describing how it's implemented: HashMap<K, ()>. It's just a HashMap without any values!

The two best reasons to choose a `HashSet` are:

- You don't want to deal with duplicate values at all, as it doesn't even include them.
- You plan on doing a lot (and I mean a *lot*) of item lookup - that is the question, *Does my collection contain this particular item?*. In a vector, this is done in $O(n)$, while a `HashSet` can do it in $O(1)$.

# How to do it...

1. In the folder `src/bin`, create a file called `hashset.rs`.
2. Add the following code, and run it with `cargo run --bin hashset`:

```
1    use std::collections::HashSet;
2
3    fn main() {
4      // Most of the interface of HashSet
5      // is the same as HashMap, just without
6      // the methods that handle values
7      let mut books = HashSet::new();
8      books.insert("Harry Potter and the Philosopher's Stone");
9      books.insert("The Name of the Wind");
10     books.insert("A Game of Thrones");
11
12     // A HashSet will ignore duplicate entries
13     // but will return if an entry is new or not
14     let is_new = books.insert("The Lies of Locke Lamora");
15     if is_new {
16       println!("We've just added a new book!");
17     }
18
19     let is_new = books.insert("A Game of Thrones");
20     if !is_new {
21       println!("Sorry, we already had that book in store");
22     }
23
24     // Check if it contains a key
25     if !books.contains("The Doors of Stone") {
26       println!("We sadly don't have that book yet");
27     }
28
29     // Remove an entry
30     let was_removed = books.remove("The Darkness that comes
            before");
```

```
31    if !was_removed {
32      println!("Couldn't remove book; We didn't have it to begin
          with");
33    }
34    let was_removed = books.remove("Harry Potter and the
        Philosopher's Stone");
35    if was_removed {
36      println!("Oops, we lost a book");
37    }
```

3. Compare different HashSets:

```
41    let one_to_five: HashSet<_> = (1..6).collect();
42    let five_to_ten: HashSet<_> = (5..11).collect();
43    let one_to_ten: HashSet<_> = (1..11).collect();
44    let three_to_eight: HashSet<_> = (3..9).collect();
45
46    // Check if two HashSets have no elements in common
47    let is_disjoint = one_to_five.is_disjoint(&five_to_ten);
48    println!(
49      "is {:?} disjoint from {:?}?: {}",
50        one_to_five,
51        five_to_ten,
52        is_disjoint
53    );
54    let is_disjoint = one_to_five.is_disjoint(&three_to_eight);
55    println!(
56      "is {:?} disjoint from {:?}?: {}",
57        one_to_five,
58        three_to_eight,
59        is_disjoint
60    );
61
62    // Check if a HashSet is fully contained in another
63    let is_subset = one_to_five.is_subset(&five_to_ten);
64    println!(
65      "is {:?} a subset of {:?}?: {}",
66        one_to_five,
67        five_to_ten,
68        is_subset
69    );
70    let is_subset = one_to_five.is_subset(&one_to_ten);
71    println!(
72      "is {:?} a subset of {:?}?: {}",
73        one_to_five,
74        one_to_ten,
75        is_subset
76    );
```

```
77
78   // Check if a HashSet fully contains another
79   let is_superset = three_to_eight.is_superset(&five_to_ten);
80   println!(
81     "is {:?} a superset of {:?}?: {}",
82     three_to_eight,
83     five_to_ten,
84     is_superset
85   );
86   let is_superset = one_to_ten.is_superset(&five_to_ten);
87   println!(
88   "is {:?} a superset of {:?}?: {}",
89     one_to_ten,
90     five_to_ten,
91     is_superset
92   );
```

4. Join two `HashSet`s in various ways:

```
96   // Get the values that are in the first HashSet
97   // but not in the second
98   let difference = one_to_five.difference(&three_to_eight);
99   println!(
100    "The difference between {:?} and {:?} is {:?}",
101      one_to_five,
102      three_to_eight,
103      difference
104  );
105
106  // Get the values that are in either HashSets, but not in
both
107  let symmetric_difference =
       one_to_five.symmetric_difference(&three_to_eight);
108  println!(
109    "The symmetric difference between {:?} and {:?} is {:?}",
110      one_to_five,
111      three_to_eight,
112      symmetric_difference
113  );
114
115  // Get the values that are in both HashSets
116  let intersection = one_to_five.intersection(&three_to_eight);
117  println!(
118    "The intersection difference between {:?} and {:?} is
{:?}",
119      one_to_five,
120      three_to_eight,
121      intersection
```

```
122    );
123
124    // Get all values in both HashSets
125    let union = one_to_five.union(&three_to_eight);
126    println!(
127      "The union difference between {:?} and {:?} is {:?}",
128        one_to_five,
129        three_to_eight,
130        union
131    );
132 }
```

# How it works...

As a HashSet is a kind of HashMap, most of its interface is pretty similar. The major difference is that the methods that would return a key's value in the HashMap instead simply return a bool on the HashSet in order to tell if a key already existed or not [14].

Additionally, HashSet brings a few methods for analyzing two sets [46 to 92] and joining them [96 to 131]. If you've ever heard of set theory or Venn diagrams, or done a bit of SQL, you're going to recognize it all. Otherwise, I advise you to run the example, and study the outputs in combination with the relevant comments.

Some illustrations might help you. For the analytical methods, the dark green part is the object of reference:

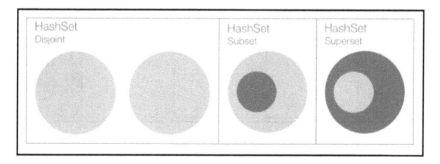

For the selecting methods, the dark green part is the one that is returned:

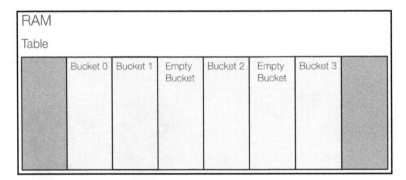

# There's more...

No big surprises in the implementation of the HashSet, since it's exactly the same as the HashMap, just without any values!

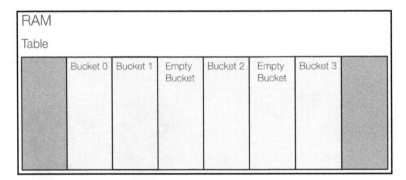

# Creating an own iterator

When you create an infinitely applicable algorithm or a collection-like structure, it's really nice to have the dozens of methods that an iterator provides at your disposal. For this, you will have to know how to tell Rust to implement them for you.

# How to do it...

1. In the folder src/bin, create a file called own_iterator.rs.
2. Add the following code, and run it with cargo run --bin own_iterator:

```
1  fn main() {
2    let fib: Vec<_> = fibonacci().take(10).collect();
3    println!("First 10 numbers of the fibonacci sequence: {:?}",
         fib);
4
5    let mut squared_vec = SquaredVec::new();
6    squared_vec.push(1);
7    squared_vec.push(2);
8    squared_vec.push(3);
9    squared_vec.push(4);
10   for (index, num) in squared_vec.iter().enumerate() {
11     println!("{}^2 is {}", index + 1, num);
12   }
13 }
14
15
16 fn fibonacci() -> Fibonacci {
17   Fibonacci { curr: 0, next: 1 }
18 }
19 struct Fibonacci {
20 curr: u32,
21 next: u32,
22 }
23 // A custom iterator has to implement
24 // only one method: What comes next
25 impl Iterator for Fibonacci {
26   type Item = u32;
27   fn next(&mut self) -> Option<u32> {
28     let old = self.curr;
29     self.curr = self.next;
30     self.next += old;
31     Some(old)
32   }
33 }
34
35
36 use std::ops::Mul;
37 struct SquaredVec<T>
38 where
39 T: Mul + Copy,
40 {
41   vec: Vec<T::Output>,
```

```
42  }
43  impl<T> SquaredVec<T>
44  where
45  T: Mul + Copy,
46  {
47    fn new() -> Self {
48    SquaredVec { vec: Vec::new() }
49  }
50  fn push(&mut self, item: T) {
51    self.vec.push(item * item);
52  }
53  }
54
55  // When creating an iterator over a collection-like struct
56  // It's best to just allow it to be convertible into
57  // a slice of your underlying type.
58  // This way you automatically implemented a bunch of methods
59  // and are flexible enough to change your implementation later
       on
60  use std::ops::Deref;
61  impl<T> Deref for SquaredVec<T>
62  where
63  T: Mul + Copy,
64  {
65    type Target = [T::Output];
66    fn deref(&self) -> &Self::Target {
67    &self.vec
68  }
69  }
```

# How it works...

In our little example here, we are going to look at two different uses for an iterator:

- fibonacci(), which returns an infinite range of the **Fibonacci sequence**
- SquaredVec, which implements a (very) small subset of a Vec with a twist: it squares all items

 The Fibonacci sequence is defined as a series of numbers, starting from 0 and 1, where the next number is the sum of the last two. It starts like this: 0, 1, 1, 2, 3, 5, 8, 13, 21, and so on.
The first two are 0 and 1 per definition. The next one is their sum — *0 + 1 = 1*. After that comes *1 + 1 = 2*. Then *2 + 1 = 3. 3 + 2 = 5*. Repeat ad infinitum.

An algorithm can be turned into an iterator by implementing the Iterator trait. This is pretty simple, as it only expects you to provide the type you're iterating over and a single method, next, which fetches the next item. If the iterator doesn't have any items left, it should return None, otherwise Some. Our Fibonacci iterator always returns Some item, which makes it an infinite iterator [31].

Our SquaredVec, on the other hand, is more of a collection than an algorithm. In lines [37] to [53], we wrap the minimum of the Vec interface — we can create a SquaredVec, and we can fill it. Our type constraints Mul + Copy mean that the item the user wants to store has to be able to be copied and to be multiplied. We need this in order to square it, but it's not relevant for the iterator. T::Output is just the type that a multiplication would return, which most of the time is going to be T itself.

We could implement the Iterator trait again, but there's an easier option that will provide you with even more methods. We can allow our struct to be implicitly convertible into a slice [T], which will not only implement Iterator for you, but also a whole bunch of other methods. Because Vec implements it already, you can just return it like that [67]. If your underlying collection didn't provide a slice conversion, you could still go the same way as before and implement the Iterator trait manually.

## There's more...

If you have a lot of complex logic to perform in the iterator and want to separate it a bit from your collection, you can do so by providing your collection with the IntoIterator trait instead. This would allow you to return a struct specifically made for your iteration, which itself provides the Iterator trait.

## Using a slab

Some algorithms require you to hold access tokens to data that may or may not exist. This could be solved in Rust by using Vec<Option<T>>, and treating the index of your data as a token. But we can do better! slab is an optimized abstraction of exactly this concept.

While it is not meant as a general-purpose collection, slab can help you a lot if you use it in the right places.

# How to do it...

1. Open the `Cargo.toml` file that has been generated earlier for you.

2. Under `[dependencies]`, add the following line:

   ```
   slab = "0.4.0"
   ```

3. If you want, you can go to slab's crates.io page (`https://crates.io/crates/slab`) to check for the newest version, and use that one instead.

4. In the folder `bin`, create a file called `slab.rs`.

5. Add the following code, and run it with `cargo run --bin slab`:

```
1    extern crate slab;
2    use slab::{Slab, VacantEntry};
3
4    fn main() {
5      // A slab is meant to be used as a limited buffer
6      // As such, you should initialize it with a pre-
7      // defined capacity
8      const CAPACITY: usize = 1024;
9      let mut slab = Slab::with_capacity(CAPACITY);
10
11     // You cannot simply access a slab's entry by
12     // index or by searching it. Instead, every
13     // insert gives you a key that you can use to
14     // access its entry
15     let hello_key = slab.insert("hello");
16     let world_key = slab.insert("world");
17
18     println!("hello_key -> '{}'", slab[hello_key],);
19     println!("world_key -> '{}'", slab[world_key],);
20
21
22     // You can pass an "empty spot" around
23     // in order to be filled
24     let data_key = {
25     let entry = slab.vacant_entry();
26       fill_some_data(entry)
27     };
28     println!("data_key -> '{}'", slab[data_key],);
29
30     // When iterating, you get a key-value pair
31     for (key, val) in &slab {
```

```
32        println!("{} -> {}", key, val);
33    }
34
35    // If you want to keep your slab at a constant
36    // capacity, you have to manually check its
37    // length before inserting data
38    if slab.len() != slab.capacity() {
39      slab.insert("the slab is not at capacity yet");
40    }
41  }
42
43
44  fn fill_some_data(entry: VacantEntry<&str>) -> usize {
45    let data = "Some data";
46    // insert() consumes the entry
47    // so we need to get the key before
48    let key = entry.key();
49    entry.insert(data);
50    key
51  }
```

# How it works...

A slab is very similar to a vector, with one quintessential difference: you don't get to choose your index. Instead, when inserting data [15], you receive the data's index as a kind of *key* that you can use to access it again. It is your responsibility to store this key somewhere; otherwise, the only way to retrieve your data is by iterating over your slab. The flipside is that you don't have to provide any key either. In contrast to a HashMap, you don't need any hashable objects at all.

A situation in which this is useful is in a connection pool: if you have multiple clients who want to access individual resources, you can store said resources in a slab and provide the clients with their key as a kind of token.

This example suits the second use case of a slab really well. Suppose you only accept a certain amount of connections at a given time. When accepting a connection, you don't care about the exact index, or the way it is stored. Instead, you care only that it is stored in a retrievable way, and that it doesn't exceed your limit. This fits the bill of the slab quite nicely, which is why most of the time you won't be creating a slab with Slab::new(), but with with_capacity, set to a constant upper limit [9].

The slab, however, does not impose this limit by itself, as it behaves exactly like the vector in the way it handles capacity: as soon as the length exceeds the capacity, the slab reallocates all objects to a bigger block of memory and ups the capacity. This is why, when dealing with upper bonds, you should insert your data with some kind of variation of line [38]:

```
if slab.len() != slab.capacity() {
    slab.insert("the slab is not at capacity yet");
}
```

Other valid approaches would be to wrap an insertion in a function that returns a `Result`, or an `Option`.

## There's more...

A slab is backed by a `Vec<Entry>`. You might remember the `Entry` from our recipe about the `HashMap` earlier. It is the same as an `Option`, with the difference that its variants are not called `Some(...)` and `None`, but `Occupied(...)` and `Vacant`. This means that, in a nutshell, a slab is implemented as a vector with holes in it:

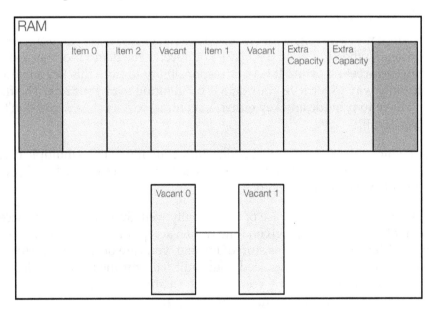

Additionally, in order to guarantee fast occupation of vacant spots, the slab keeps a linked list of all vacant entries.

# 3
# Handling Files and the Filesystem

In this chapter, we will cover the following recipes:

- Working with text files
- Handling bytes
- Working with binary files
- Compressing and decompressing data
- Traversing the filesystem
- Finding files with glob patterns

## Introduction

In these times of big data, machine learning, and cloud services, you cannot rely on having all of your data always in memory. Rather, you need to be able to effectively inspect and traverse the filesystem and manipulate its content at your leisure.

Examples of things you will be able to do after reading this chapter include configuring files in subdirectories with different naming variations, saving your data in efficient binary formats, reading protocols generated by other programs, and compressing your data in order to send it over the internet at fast speeds.

# Working with text files

In this recipe, we will learn how to read, write, create, truncate, and append text files. Armed with this knowledge, you will be able to apply all other recipes to files instead of in-memory strings.

# How to do it...

1. Create a Rust project to work on during this chapter with `cargo new chapter-three`.
2. Navigate into the newly created `chapter-three` folder. For the rest of this chapter, we will assume that your command line is currently in this directory.
3. Inside the `src` folder, create a new folder called `bin`.
4. Delete the generated `lib.rs` file, as we are not creating a library.
5. In the `src/bin` folder, create a file called `text_files.rs`.
6. Add the following code and run it with `cargo run --bin text_files`:

```
1    use std::fs::{File, OpenOptions};
2    use std::io::{self, BufReader, BufWriter, Lines, Write};
3    use std::io::prelude::*;
4
5    fn main() {
6        // Create a file and fill it with data
7        let path = "./foo.txt";
8        println!("Writing some data to '{}'", path);
9        write_file(path, "Hello World!\n").expect("Failed to write
to
         file");
10       // Read entire file as a string
11       let content = read_file(path).expect("Failed to read file");
12       println!("The file '{}' contains:", path);
13       println!("{}", content);
14
15       // Overwrite the file
16       println!("Writing new data to '{}'", path);
17       write_file(path, "New content\n").expect("Failed to write to
         file");
18       let content = read_file(path).expect("Failed to read file");
19       println!("The file '{}' now contains:", path);
20       println!("{}", content);
21
22       // Append data to the file
```

```
23      println!("Appending data to '{}'", path);
24      append_file(path, "Some more content\n").expect("Failed to
          append to file");
25      println!("The file '{}' now contains:", path);
26      // Read file line by line as an iterator
27      let lines = read_file_iterator(path).expect("Failed to read
          file");
28      for line in lines {
29        println!("{}", line.expect("Failed to read line"));
30      }
31
32      append_and_read(path, "Last line in the file,
          goodbye").expect("Failed to read and write file");
        }
```

7. These are the functions called by the `main()` function:

```
37    fn read_file(path: &str) -> io::Result<String> {
38      // open() opens the file in read-only mode
39      let file = File::open(path)?;
40      // Wrap the file in a BufReader
41      // to read in an efficient way
42      let mut buf_reader = BufReader::new(file);
43      let mut content = String::new();
44      buf_reader.read_to_string(&mut content)?;
45      Ok(content)
46    }
47
48    fn read_file_iterator(path: &str) ->
          io::Result<Lines<BufReader<File>>> {
49      let file = File::open(path)?;
50      let buf_reader = BufReader::new(file);
51      // lines() returns an iterator over lines
52      Ok(buf_reader.lines())
53    }
54
55
56    fn write_file(path: &str, content: &str) -> io::Result<()> {
57      // create() opens a file with the standard options
58      // to create, write and truncate a file
59      let file = File::create(path)?;
60      // Wrap the file in a BufReader
61      // to read in an efficient way
62      let mut buf_writer = BufWriter::new(file);
63      buf_writer.write_all(content.as_bytes())?;
64      Ok(())
65    }
66
```

```
67    fn append_file(path: &str, content: &str) -> io::Result<()> {
68        // OpenOptions lets you set all options individually
69        let file = OpenOptions::new().append(true).open(path)?;
70        let mut buf_writer = BufWriter::new(file);
71        buf_writer.write_all(content.as_bytes())?;
72        Ok(())
73    }
```

8. Reading and writing on the same handle:

```
76    fn append_and_read(path: &str, content: &str) -> io::Result<()
      {
          let file =
77            OpenOptions::new().read(true).append(true).open(path)?;
78        // Passing a reference of the file will not move it
79        // allowing you to create both a reader and a writer
80        let mut buf_reader = BufReader::new(&file);
81        let mut buf_writer = BufWriter::new(&file);
82
83        let mut file_content = String::new();
84        buf_reader.read_to_string(&mut file_content)?;
85        println!("File before appending:\n{}", file_content);
86
87        // Appending will shift your positional pointer
88        // so you have to save and restore it
89        let pos = buf_reader.seek(SeekFrom::Current(0))?;
90        buf_writer.write_all(content.as_bytes())?;
91        // Flushing forces the write to happen right now
92        buf_writer.flush()?;
93        buf_reader.seek(SeekFrom::Start(pos))?;
94
95        buf_reader.read_to_string(&mut file_content)?;
96        println!("File after appending:\n{}", file_content);
97
98        Ok(())
99    }
```

# How it works...

Our `main` function is split into three parts:

1. Creating a file.
2. Overwriting a file, which in this context is called *truncating*.
3. Appending to a file.

In the first two parts, we load the entire content of the file into a single `String` and display it [11 and 18]. In the last one, we iterate over the individual lines in the file and print them [28].

`File::open()` opens a file in read-only mode and returns you a handle to it [39]. Because this handle implements the `Read` trait, we could now just directly read it into a string with `read_to_string`. However, in our examples, we wrap it first in a `BufReader`[42]. This is because a dedicated reader can greatly improve the performance of their resource access by collecting read instructions, which is called *buffering*, and executing them in big batches. For the first reading example, `read_file`[37], this doesn't make any difference whatsoever, as we read it all in one go anyway. We still use it because it is a good practice, as it allows us to flexibly change the exact reading mechanisms of our function later on without worrying about performance. If you want to see a function where a `BufReader` actually does something, look a little further down, to `read_file_iterator`[48]. It appears to read the file line by line. This would be a very inefficient operation when dealing with a large file, which is why a `BufReader` actually reads a large chunk of the file in one go and then returns that segment line by line. The result is optimized file reading without us even noticing or caring what is going on in the background, which is pretty convenient.

`File::create()` creates a new file if it doesn't exist, otherwise it truncates the file. In any case, it returns the same kind of `File` handle like `File::open()` did before. Another similarity is the `BufWriter` we wrap around it. Just like with the `BufReader`, we would be able to access our underlying file without it, but use it to optimize future accesses as well.

There are more options than just opening a file in read-only or truncation mode. We can use them by creating our file handle with `OpenOptions`[69], which use the builder pattern we explored in the *Using the builder pattern* section in `Chapter 1`, *Learning the Basics*. In our example, we are interested in the `append` mode, which lets us add content to a file instead of overwriting it on every access.

 For a full list of all available options, see the OpenOption documentation: `https://doc.rust-lang.org/std/fs/struct.OpenOptions.html`.

We can read and write on the same file handle. For this, when creating the `ReadBuf` and `WriteBuf`, we pass a reference to the file instead of moving it, as the buffers would otherwise consume the handle, making sharing impossible:

```
let mut buf_reader = BufReader::new(&file);
let mut buf_writer = BufWriter::new(&file);
```

When doing this, be careful when appending and reading the same handle. The internal pointer that stored the current reading position might get shifted when appending. If you want to first read, then append, and then continue reading, you should save the current position before writing and then restore it afterward.

We can access our current position in the file by calling `seek(SeekFrom::Current(0))`[89]. `seek` moves our pointer by a certain amount of bytes and returns its new position. `SeekFrom::Current(0)` means that the distance we want to move is exactly zero bytes away from where we are right now. Because of this, as we don't move at all, `seek` will return our current position.

Then, we append our data using `flush`[92]. We have to call this method, as a `BufWriter` would normally wait for the actual writing until it is dropped, that is, it is no longer in scope. As we want to read before that happens, we use `flush` to force a write.

Finally, we get ready to read again by restoring our position from before, seeking it again:

```
buf_reader.seek(SeekFrom::Start(pos))?;
```

I invite you to run the code, look at the results, and then compare them with the output after commenting this line out.

# There's more...

Instead of opening up a new file handle in every function, we could open one single handle at the beginning of the program and pass it around to every function that needs it. This is a trade-off—we get more performance if we don't repeatedly lock and unlock a file. In turn, we disallow other processes to access our file while our program is running.

# See also

- *Using the builder pattern* recipe in Chapter 1, *Learning the Basics*

# Handling bytes

When designing your own protocol or using existing ones, you have to be able to comfortably move around and manipulate binary buffers. Luckily, the extended standard library ecosystem provides the `byteorder` crate to fulfill all your binary needs with various bits and pieces of reading and writing functionality.

# Getting ready

In this chapter, we are going to talk about *endianness*. It is a way of describing how the values in a buffer are ordered. There are two ways to order them:

- Put the smallest one first (*Little Endian*)
- Put the biggest one first (*Big Endian*)

Let's try an example. Suppose we wanted to save the hexadecimal value `0x90AB12CD`. We first have to split it into bits of `0x90`, `0xAB`, `0x12`, and `0xCD`. We now can either store them with the biggest value first (Big Endian), `0x90 - 0xAB - 0x12 - 0xCD`, or we could write the smallest number first (Little Endian), `0xCD - 0x12 - 0xAB - 0x90`.

As you can see, it's the exact same set of values, but flipped. If this short explanation left you confused, I advise you to look at this excellent explanation by the University of Maryland's Department of Computer Science: `https://web.archive.org/web/20170808042522/http://www.cs.umd.edu/class/sum2003/cmsc311/Notes/Data/endian.html`.

There is no *better* endianness. Both are used in different domains: microprocessors, such as Intel, use Little Endian, and internet protocols, such as TCP, IPv4, IPv6, and UDP, use Big Endian. This is not a rule but rather a convention maintained to be backward compatible. As such, there are exceptions.

When designing your own protocol, orient yourself on the endianness of similar protocols, choose one and simply stick to it.

# How to do it...

Follow these steps:

1. Open the `Cargo.toml` file that was generated earlier for you.

2. Under `[dependencies]`, add the following line:

   ```
   byteorder = "1.1.0"
   ```

3. If you want, you can go to `byteorder`'s crates.io page (`https://crates.io/crates/byteorder`) to check for the newest version and use that one instead.

4. In the `bin` folder, create a file called `bytes.rs`.

5. Add the following code and run it with `cargo run --bin bytes`:

```rust
1    extern crate byteorder;
2    use std::io::{Cursor, Seek, SeekFrom};
3    use byteorder::{BigEndian, LittleEndian, ReadBytesExt,
     WriteBytesExt};
4
5    fn main() {
6      let binary_nums = vec![2, 3, 12, 8, 5, 0];
7      // Wrap a binary collection in a cursor
8      // to provide seek functionality
9      let mut buff = Cursor::new(binary_nums);
10     let first_byte = buff.read_u8().expect("Failed to read
          byte");
11     println!("first byte in binary: {:b}", first_byte);
12
13     // Reading advances the internal position,
14     // so now we read the second
15     let second_byte_as_int = buff.read_i8().expect("Failed to
          read byte as int");
16     println!("second byte as int: {}", second_byte_as_int);
17
18     // Overwrite the current position
19     println!("Before: {:?}", buff);
20     buff.write_u8(123).expect("Failed to overwrite a byte");
21     println!("After: {:?}", buff);
22
23
24     // Set and get the current position
25     println!("Old position: {}", buff.position());
26     buff.set_position(0);
27     println!("New position: {}", buff.position());
```

```
28
29      // This also works using the Seek API
30      buff.seek(SeekFrom::End(0)).expect("Failed to seek end");
31      println!("Last position: {}", buff.position());
32
33      // Read and write in specific endianness
34      buff.set_position(0);
35      let as_u32 = buff.read_u32::<LittleEndian>()
36        .expect("Failed to read bytes");
37      println!(
38        "First four bytes as u32 in little endian order:\t{}",
39        as_u32
40      );
41
42      buff.set_position(0);
43      let as_u32 = buff.read_u32::<BigEndian>().expect("Failed to
          read bytes");
44      println!("First four bytes as u32 in big endian order:\t{}",
          as_u32);
45
46      println!("Before appending: {:?}", buff);
47      buff.seek(SeekFrom::End(0)).expect("Failed to seek end");
48      buff.write_f32::<LittleEndian>(-33.4)
49        .expect("Failed to write to end");
50      println!("After appending: {:?}", buff);
51
52      // Read a sequence of bytes into another buffer
53      let mut read_buffer = [0; 5];
54      buff.set_position(0);
55      buff.read_u16_into::<LittleEndian>(&mut read_buffer)
56        .expect("Failed to read all bytes");
57      println!(
58        "All bytes as u16s in little endian order: {:?}",
59        read_buffer
60      );
61    }
```

# How it works...

First things first, we need a binary source. In our example, we simply use a vector. Then, we wrap it into a `Cursor`, as it provides us with a `Seek` implementation and some methods for our convenience.

The `Cursor` has an internal position count that keeps track of which byte we are accessing at the moment. As expected, it starts at zero. With `read_u8` and `read_i8`, we can read the current byte as an unsigned or signed number. This will advance the position by one. Both do the same thing, but return a different type.

Did you notice that we printed the returned byte by using `{:b}` as the formatting parameter [11]?

```
println!("first byte in binary: {:b}", first_byte);
```

By doing so, we tell the underlying `format!` macro to interpret our byte as binary, which is why it will print `10` instead of `2`. If you want to, try replacing `{}` in our other printing calls with `{:b}` and compare the results.

The current position can be read with `position()` [25] and set with `set_position()`. You can also manipulate your position with the more verbose `Seek` API we introduced in the last recipe [30]. When using `SeekFrom::End`, keep in mind that this will *not* count backward from the end. For example, `SeekFrom::End(1)` will point to one byte *after* the end of the buffer and not before. The behavior is defined in this way because, maybe somewhat surprisingly, it is legal to seek past a buffer. This can be useful when writing, as it will simply pad the space between the end of the buffer and the cursor position with zeros.

When dealing with more then one byte, you will need to specify the endianness of the bytes via type annotation. Reading or writing will then advance the position by the number of bytes read or written, which is why, in our example code, we need to frequently reset the position with `set_position(0)`. Note that when you write past the end, you will always simply extend the buffer [48].

If you know that you want to read a very specific amount of bytes, like when parsing a well-defined protocol, you can do so by providing a fixed-size array and filling it by post-fixing your `read` with `_into`, like this:

```
// Read exactly five bytes
let mut read_buffer = [0; 5];
buff.read_u16_into::<LittleEndian>(&mut read_buffer).expect("Failed to
fill buffer");
```

When doing so, the read will return an error if the buffer was not filled completely, in which case its contents are undefined.

# There's more...

There are various aliases in the byte order crate to ease your endianness annotation. The BE alias, for Big Endian, and the LE alias, for Little Endian, are useful if you don't want to type as much. On the other hand, if you keep forgetting which endianness is used where, you can use NativeEndian, which sets itself to the default endianness of your operating system, and NetworkEndian, for Big Endian.

To use them, you will have to drag them into scope like this:

```
use byteorder::{BE, LE, NativeEndian, NetworkEndian};
```

# Working with binary files

We are now going to combine what we learned in the last two chapters in order to parse and write binary files. This will prove essential when you plan on implementing custom, manual processing of file types such as PDFs, torrents, and ZIPs. It will also come in handy when designing custom file types for your own use cases.

# How to do it...

1. If you haven't done it already in the last chapter, open the Cargo.toml file that was generated earlier for you.

2. Under [dependencies], add the following line:

```
byteorder = "1.1.0"
```

3. If you want, you can go to byteorder's crates.io page (https://crates.io/crates/byteorder) to check for the newest version and use that one instead.

4. In the bin folder, create a file called binary_files.rs.

5. Add the following code and run it with cargo run --bin binary_files:

```
1    extern crate byteorder;
2    use byteorder::{ByteOrder, ReadBytesExt, WriteBytesExt, BE,
     LE};
3    use std::fs::File;
4    use std::io::{self, BufReader, BufWriter, Read};
5    use std::io::prelude::*;
```

```
6
7
8    fn main() {
9      let path = "./bar.bin";
10     write_dummy_protocol(path).expect("Failed write file");
11     let payload = read_protocol(path).expect("Failed to read
          file");
12     print!("The protocol contained the following payload: ");
13     for num in payload {
14       print!("0x{:X} ", num);
15     }
16     println!();
17   }
```

6. Create a binary file:

```
19     // Write a simple custom protocol
20     fn write_dummy_protocol(path: &str) -> io::Result<()> {
21       let file = File::create(path)?;
22       let mut buf_writer = BufWriter::new(file);
23
24       // Let's say our binary file starts with a magic string
25       // to show readers that this is our protocoll
26       let magic = b"MyProtocol";
27       buf_writer.write_all(magic)?;
28
29       // Now comes another magic value to indicate
30       // our endianness
31       let endianness = b"LE";
32       buf_writer.write_all(endianness)?;
33
34       // Let's fill it with two numbers in u32
35       buf_writer.write_u32::<LE>(0xDEAD)?;
36       buf_writer.write_u32::<LE>(0xBEEF)?;
37
38       Ok(())
39     }
```

7. Read and parse the file:

```
42     fn read_protocol(path: &str) -> io::Result<Vec<u32>> {
43       let file = File::open(path)?;
44       let mut buf_reader = BufReader::new(file);
45
46       // Our protocol has to begin with a certain string
47       // Namely "MyProtocol", which is 10 bytes long
48       let mut start = [0u8; 10];
49       buf_reader.read_exact(&mut start)?;
```

```
50      if &start != b"MyProtocol" {
51        return Err(io::Error::new(
52          io::ErrorKind::Other,
53          "Protocol didn't start with the expected magic string",
54        ));
55      }
56
57      // Now comes the endianness indicator
58      let mut endian = [0u8; 2];
59      buf_reader.read_exact(&mut endian)?;
60      match &endian {
61        b"LE" => read_protocoll_payload::<LE, _>(&mut buf_reader),
62        b"BE" => read_protocoll_payload::<BE, _>(&mut buf_reader),
63        _ => Err(io::Error::new(
64          io::ErrorKind::Other,
65          "Failed to parse endianness",
66        )),
67      }
68    }
69
70  // Read as much of the payload as possible
71  fn read_protocoll_payload<E, R>(reader: &mut R) ->
        io::Result<Vec<u32>>
72  where
73  E: ByteOrder,
74  R: ReadBytesExt,
75  {
76    let mut payload = Vec::new();
77    const SIZE_OF_U32: usize = 4;
78    loop {
79    let mut raw_payload = [0; SIZE_OF_U32];
80    // Read the next 4 bytes
81    match reader.read(&mut raw_payload)? {
82    // Zero means we reached the end
83    0 => return Ok(payload),
84    // SIZE_OF_U32 means we read a complete number
85    SIZE_OF_U32 => {
86      let as_u32 = raw_payload.as_ref().read_u32::<E>()?;
87      payload.push(as_u32)
88    }
89    // Anything else means the last element was not
90    // a valid u32
91    _ => {
92      return Err(io::Error::new(
93      io::ErrorKind::UnexpectedEof,
94        "Payload ended unexpectedly",
95      ))
96    }
```

```
97    }
98   }
99 }
```

# How it works...

To demonstrate how to read and write a binary file, we will create a little custom binary protocol. It will start with what is called a *magic number*, that is, a certain hardcoded value. Our magic number will be the binary representation of the MyProtocol string. We can put a b before the string to tell Rust that we want the text to be represented as a binary slice (&[u8]) instead of a string slice(&str) [26].

 Many protocols and files start with magic numbers to indicate what they are. For example, the internal headers of .zip files start with the magic hex numbers 0x50 and 0x4B. These represent the initials *PH* in ASCII, which is short for the name of its creator Phil Katz. Another example would be PDF; it starts with 0x25, 0x50, 0x44, and 0x46, which stands for PDF%, followed by a version number.

Afterward, we follow it by the binary representation of either LE or BE to tell the reader the endianness of the rest of the data [31]. Finally, we have the payload, which is just an arbitrary amount of u32 numbers, encoded in the aforementioned endianness [35 and 36]. By putting 0x in front of our number, we tell Rust to treat it as a hexadecimal number and convert it into decimal for us. As such, Rust treats 0xDEAD as the same value as 57005.

Let's put it all together and write a binary file containing MyProtocolLE5700548879. Other files we could have created in accordance with our protocol would be MyProtocolBE92341739241842518425 or MyProtocolLE0000, and so on.

If you read the previous recipes, write_dummy_protocol should be easy to understand. We use a combination of good old write_all from the standard library to write our binary texts and write_u32 from byteorder to write the values that require an endianness.

The reading of the protocol is split into the read_protocol and read_protocol_payload functions. The first verifies the validity of the protocol by reading the magic numbers and then calls the latter, which reads the remaining numbers as the payload.

We validate the magic numbers as follows:

1. As we know the exact size of the magic numbers used, prepare buffers of those exact sizes.
2. Fill them with just as many bytes.
3. Compare the bytes with the expected magic number.
4. If they don't match, return an error.

After parsing both magic numbers, we can parse the actual *data* contained in the payload. Remember, we defined it as an arbitrary amount of 32 bit (= 4 bytes) long, unsigned numbers. To parse them, we are going to repeatedly read up to four bytes into a buffer called `raw_payload`. We are then going to examine the amount of bytes that were actually read. This number can have three forms in our case, as demonstrated nicely by our `match`.

The first value we are interested in is zero, which means that there are no more bytes to read, that is, we have reached the end. In this case, we can return our payload:

```
// Zero means we reached the end
0 => return Ok(payload),
```

The second value is `SIZE_OF_U32`, which we have previously defined as four. Receiving this value means that our reader has successfully read four bytes into a four-byte-long buffer. This means that we have successfully read a value! Let's parse it into a `u32` and push it into our `payload` vector:

```
// SIZE_OF_U32 means we read a complete number
SIZE_OF_U32 => {
    let as_u32 = raw_payload.as_ref().read_u32::<E>()?;
    payload.push(as_u32)
}
```

We have to call `as_ref()` on our buffer because a fixed-size array doesn't implement `Read`. Since a slice does implement said trait and a reference to an array is implicitly convertible into a slice, we work on a reference to `raw_payload` instead.

The third and last value we can expect is everything other than zero or four. In this case, the reader was not able to read four bytes, which means that our buffer ended in something other than a `u32` and is malformed. We can react to this by returning an error:

```
    // Anything else means the last element was not
    // a valid u32
    _ => {
        return Err(io::Error::new(
            io::ErrorKind::UnexpectedEof,
            "Payload ended unexpectedly",
        ))
    }
}
```

# There's more...

When reading a malformed protocol, we reuse `io::ErrorKind` to show what exactly went wrong. In the recipes of `Chapter 6`, *Handling Errors*, you will learn how to provide your own error to better separate your areas of failure. If you want, you could read them now and then return here to improve our code.

The errors that need to be pushed into an own variant are:

- `InvalidStart`
- `InvalidEndianness`
- `UnexpectedEndOfPayload`

Another improvement to the code would be to put all of our strings, namely `MyProtocol`, `LE`, and `BE`, into their own constants, as in the following line:

```
    const PROTOCOL_START: &[u8] = b"MyProtocol";
```

The provided code in this recipe and some others doesn't use many constants, as they proved to be somewhat harder to understand in printed form. In real code bases, however, be sure to always put strings that you find yourself copy-pasting into own constants!

# See also

- *Providing user-defined error types* recipes in `Chapter 6`, *Handling Errors*

# Compressing and decompressing data

In today's age of bloated websites and daily new web frameworks, many sites feel way more sluggish than they used (and ought) to. One way to mitigate this is by compressing your resources before sending them and then decompressing them when received. This has become the (often ignored) standard on the web. For this purpose, this recipe will teach you how to compress and decompress any kind of data with different algorithms.

# How to do it...

Follow these steps:

1. Open the `Cargo.toml` file that was generated earlier for you.

2. Under `[dependencies]`, add the following line:

    1. `flate2 = "0.2.20"`

    If you want, you can go to `flate2`'s crates.io page (`https://crates.io/crates/flate2`) to check for the newest version and use that one instead.

2. In the `bin` folder, create a file called `compression.rs`.

3. Add the following code and run it with `cargo run --bin compression`:

```
1    extern crate flate2;
2
3    use std::io::{self, SeekFrom};
4    use std::io::prelude::*;
5
6    use flate2::{Compression, FlateReadExt};
7    use flate2::write::ZlibEncoder;
8    use flate2::read::ZlibDecoder;
9
10   use std::fs::{File, OpenOptions};
```

```
11   use std::io::{BufReader, BufWriter, Read};
12
13   fn main() {
14     let bytes = b"I have a dream that one day this nation will
          rise up, \
15     and live out the true meaning of its creed";
16     println!("Original: {:?}", bytes.as_ref());
17     // Conpress some bytes
18     let encoded = encode_bytes(bytes.as_ref()).expect("Failed to
          encode bytes");
19     println!("Encoded: {:?}", encoded);
20     // Decompress them again
21     let decoded = decode_bytes(&encoded).expect("Failed to
decode
          bytes");
22     println!("Decoded: {:?}", decoded);
23
24     // Open file to compress
25     let original = File::open("ferris.png").expect("Failed to
          open file");
26     let mut original_reader = BufReader::new(original);
27
28     // Compress it
29     let data = encode_file(&mut original_reader).expect("Failed
        to encode file");
30
31     // Write compressed file to disk
32     let encoded = OpenOptions::new()
33       .read(true)
34       .write(true)
35       .create(true)
36       .open("ferris_encoded.zlib")
37       .expect("Failed to create encoded file");
38     let mut encoded_reader = BufReader::new(&encoded);
39     let mut encoded_writer = BufWriter::new(&encoded);
40     encoded_writer
41       .write_all(&data)
42       .expect("Failed to write encoded file");
43
44
45     // Jump back to the beginning of the compressed file
46     encoded_reader
47       .seek(SeekFrom::Start(0))
48       .expect("Failed to reset file");
49
50     // Decompress it
51     let data = decode_file(&mut encoded_reader).expect("Failed
to
```

```
                decode file");
52
53      // Write the decompressed file to disk
54      let mut decoded =
          File::create("ferris_decoded.png").expect("Failed to
create
            decoded file");
55      decoded
56        .write_all(&data)
57        .expect("Failed to write decoded file");
58  }
```

5. These are the functions doing the actual encoding and decoding:

```
61  fn encode_bytes(bytes: &[u8]) -> io::Result<Vec<u8>> {
62    // You can choose your compression algorithm and it's
          efficiency
63    let mut encoder = ZlibEncoder::new(Vec::new(),
          Compression::Default);
64    encoder.write_all(bytes)?;
65    encoder.finish()
66  }
67
68  fn decode_bytes(bytes: &[u8]) -> io::Result<Vec<u8>> {
69    let mut encoder = ZlibDecoder::new(bytes);
70    let mut buffer = Vec::new();
71    encoder.read_to_end(&mut buffer)?;
72    Ok(buffer)
73  }
74
75
76  fn encode_file(file: &mut Read) -> io::Result<Vec<u8>> {
77    // Files have a built-in encoder
78    let mut encoded = file.zlib_encode(Compression::Best);
79    let mut buffer = Vec::new();
80    encoded.read_to_end(&mut buffer)?;
81    Ok(buffer)
82  }
83
84  fn decode_file(file: &mut Read) -> io::Result<Vec<u8>> {
85    let mut buffer = Vec::new();
86    // Files have a built-in decoder
87    file.zlib_decode().read_to_end(&mut buffer)?;
88    Ok(buffer)
89  }
```

# How it works...

A lot of the `main` function work is just repetition for you from the last few chapters. The real deal happens below it. In `encode_bytes`, you can see how to use *encoders*. You can write to it as much as you want and call `finish` when you're done.

`flate2` gives you several compression options. You can choose your compression strength through the passed `Compression` instance:

```
let mut encoder = ZlibEncoder::new(Vec::new(), Compression::Default);
```

`Default` is a compromise between speed and size. Your other options are `Best`, `Fast`, and `None`. Additionally, you can specify the encoding algorithm used. `flate2` supports zlib, which we use in this recipe, gzip, and plain deflate. If you want to use an algorithm other than zlib, simply replace every mention of it with another supported algorithm. For instance, if you wanted to rewrite the preceding code to use gzip instead, it would look like this:

```
use flate2::write::GzEncoder;
let mut encoder = GzEncoder::new(Vec::new(), Compression::Default);
```

For a full list of how the specific encoders are called, visit `flate2`'s documentation at `https://docs.rs/flate2/`.

Because people would often prefer to compress or decompress whole files instead of byte buffers, there are some convenient methods for that. In fact, they are implemented on every type that implements `Read`, which means that you can also use them on a `BufReader` and many other types. `encode_file` and `decode_file` use them with `zlib` in the form of the following lines:

```
let mut encoded = file.zlib_encode(Compression::Best);
file.zlib_decode().read_to_end(&mut buffer)?;
```

The same applies to the `gzip` and `deflate` algorithms.

In our example, we are compressing and decompressing `ferris.png`, which is an image of Rust's mascot:

You can find it in the GitHub repository at `https://github.com/SirRade/rust-standard-library-cookbook` or you can use any other file you want. If you feel like verifying the compression, you can take a look at the original, compressed, and decompressed files to check how much smaller the compressed one is, and that the original and decompressed ones are identical.

# There's more...

The current `encode_something` and `decode_something` functions are designed to be as simple to use as possible. However, they waste some performance by allocating `Vec<u8>` even though we could pipe the data directly into a writer. When writing a library, it would be nice to give the user both possibilities by adding methods in this way:

```
use std::io::Write;
fn encode_file_into(file: &mut Read, target: &mut Write) ->
io::Result<()> {
    // Files have a built-in encoder
    let mut encoded = file.zlib_encode(Compression::Best);
    io::copy(&mut encoded, target)?;
    Ok(())
}
```

The user could call them like this:

```
// Compress it
encode_file_into(&mut original_reader, &mut encoded_writer)
    .expect("Failed to encode file");
```

# Traversing the filesystem

Up until now, we always provided our code with the static location of a certain file. Alas, the real world is seldom so predictable, and some digging is going to be necessary when dealing with data scattered throughout different folders.

walkdir helps us with this by abstracting away the intricacies and inconsistencies of operating systems' representation of the filesystem by unifying them under one common API, which we are going to learn about in this recipe.

# Getting ready

This recipe makes heavy use of iterators to manipulate streams of data. If you are not yet familiar with them or need a quick refresher, you should read the *Access collections as Iterators* section in Chapter 2, *Working with Collections*, before continuing.

# How to do it...

1. Open the Cargo.toml file that was generated earlier for you.

2. Under [dependencies], add the following line:

   walkdir = "2.0.1"

3. If you want, you can go to walkdir's crates.io page (https://crates.io/crates/walkdir) to check for the newest version and use that one instead.

4. In the bin folder, create a file called traverse_files.rs.

5. Add the following code and run it with cargo run --bin traverse_files:

```
1    extern crate walkdir;
2    use walkdir::{DirEntry, WalkDir};
3
4    fn main() {
5      println!("All file paths in this directory:");
6      for entry in WalkDir::new(".") {
7        if let Ok(entry) = entry {
8          println!("{}", entry.path().display());
9        }
10     }
```

```
11
12      println!("All non-hidden file names in this directory:");
13      WalkDir::new("../chapter_three")
14        .into_iter()
15        .filter_entry(|entry| !is_hidden(entry)) // Look only at
          non-hidden enthries
16        .filter_map(Result::ok) // Keep all entries we have access
to
17        .for_each(|entry| {
18          // Convert the name returned by theOS into a Rust string
19          // If there are any non-UTF8 symbols in it, replace them
              with placeholders
20          let name = entry.file_name().to_string_lossy();
21            println!("{}", name)
22        });
23
24      println!("Paths of all subdirectories in this
directory:");
25      WalkDir::new(".")
26        .into_iter()
27        .filter_entry(is_dir) // Look only at directories
28        .filter_map(Result::ok) // Keep all entries we have
          access to
29        .for_each(|entry| {
30          let path = entry.path().display();
31          println!("{}", path)
32        });
33
34      let are_any_readonly = WalkDir::new("..")
35        .into_iter()
36        .filter_map(Result::ok) // Keep all entries we have
          access to
37        .filter(|e| has_file_name(e, "vector.rs")) // Get the
          ones with a certain name
38        .filter_map(|e| e.metadata().ok()) // Get metadata if
the
          OS allows it
39        .any(|e| e.permissions().readonly()); // Check if at
          least one entry is readonly
40      println!(
41        "Are any the files called 'vector.rs' readonly? {}",
42          are_any_readonly
43      );
44
45      let total_size = WalkDir::new(".")
46        .into_iter()
47        .filter_map(Result::ok) // Keep all entries we have
access
```

```
            to
48          .filter_map(|entry| entry.metadata().ok()) // Get
metadata
            if supported
49          .filter(|metadata| metadata.is_file()) // Keep all files
50          .fold(0, |acc, m| acc + m.len()); // Accumulate sizes
51
52       println!("Size of current directory: {} bytes",
total_size);
53    }
```

6. Now, come to the predicates used in this recipe:

```
55    fn is_hidden(entry: &DirEntry) -> bool {
56      entry
57        .file_name()
58        .to_str()
59        .map(|s| s.starts_with('.'))
60        .unwrap_or(false) // Return false if the filename is
           invalid UTF8
61    }
62
63    fn is_dir(entry: &DirEntry) -> bool {
64      entry.file_type().is_dir()
65    }
66
67    fn has_file_name(entry: &DirEntry, name: &str) -> bool {
68      // Check if file name contains valid unicode
69      match entry.file_name().to_str() {
70      Some(entry_name) => entry_name == name,
71      None => false,
72    }
73 }
```

# How it works...

`walkdir` consists of three important types:

- `WalkDir`: A builder (see the *Using the builder pattern* section in Chapter 1, *Learning the Basics*) for your directory walker
- `IntoIter`: The iterator created by the builder
- `DirEntry`: Represents a single folder or file

If you just want to operate on a list of all entries under a root folder, such as in the first example in line [6], you can implicitly use WalkDir directly as an iterator over different instances of DirEntry:

```
for entry in WalkDir::new(".") {
    if let Ok(entry) = entry {
        println!("{}", entry.path().display());
    }
}
```

As you can see, the iterator doesn't directly give you a DirEntry, but a Result. This is because there are some cases where accessing a file or folder might prove difficult. For instance, the OS could prohibit you from reading the contents of a folder, hiding the files in it. Or a symlink, which you could enable by calling follow_links(true) on the WalkDir instance, could point back to a parent directory, potentially resulting in an endless loop.

Our solution strategy for the errors in this recipe is simple—we just ignore them and carry on with the rest of the entries that didn't report any issues.

When you extract the actual entry, it can tell you a lot about itself. One of those things is its path. Keep in mind, though, that .path() [8] doesn't just return the path as a string. Actually, it returns a native Rust Path struct that could be used for further analysis. You could, for example, read a file path's extension by calling .extension() on it. Or you could get its parent directory by calling .parent(). Feel free to explore the possibilities by exploring the Path documentation at https://doc.rust-lang.org/std/path/struct.Path.html. In our case, we are only going to display it as a simple string by calling .display() on it.

When we explicitly convert WalkDir into an iterator with into_iter(), we can access a special method that no other iterator has: filter_entry. It is an optimization over filter in that it gets called during the traversal. When its predicate returns false on a directory, the walker won't go into the directory at all! This way, you can gain a lot of performance when traversing big filesystems. In the recipe, we use it while looking for non-hidden files [15]. If you need to operate only on files and never on directories, you should use plain old filter instead.

 We define *hidden files*, by Unix convention, as all directories and files that start with a dot. For this reason, they are sometimes also called *dotfiles*.

In both cases, your filtering requires a predicate. They are usually put in their own function for simplicity and reusability.

Note that `walkdir` doesn't just give us the filename as a normal string. Instead, it returns an `OsStr`. This is a special kind of string that Rust uses when talking directly to the operating system. The type exists because some operating systems allow invalid UTF-8 in their filenames. When looking at such files in Rust, you have two choices—let Rust try to convert them into UTF-8 and replace all invalid characters with the Unicode Replacement Character (◆), or instead handle the error yourself. You can go the first route by calling `to_string_lossy` on an `OsStr` [20]. The second route is accessible by calling `to_str` and checking the returned `Option`, like we did in `has_file_name`, where we simply discard invalid names.

In this recipe, you can see a splendid example of when to choose a `for_each` method call (discussed in the *Access collections as Iterators* section in `Chapter 1`, *Learning the Basics, Working with collections*) over a `for` loop—most of our iterator calls are chained together, and so a `for_each` call can naturally be chained into the iterator as well.

## There's more...

If you plan on publishing your application on Unix and Unix only, you can access additional permissions on an entry over its `.metadata().unwrap().permissions()` call. Namely, you can see the exact `st_mode` bits by calling `.mode()` and change them by calling `set_mode()` with a new set of bits.

## See also

- *Using the builder pattern* recipe in `Chapter 1`, *Learning the Basics*
- *Access collections as iterators* recipe in `Chapter 2`, *Working with Collections*

# Finding files with glob patterns

As you may have noticed, using `walkdir` to filter files based on their name can be a bit clunky at times. Luckily, you can greatly simplify this by using the `glob` crate, which brings you its titular patterns, known from Unix, right into Rust.

# How to do it...

Follow these steps:

1. Open the `Cargo.toml` file that was generated earlier for you.

2. Under `[dependencies]`, add the following line:

   ```
   glob = "0.2.11"
   ```

3. If you want, you can go to glob's crates.io page (`https://crates.io/crates/glob`) to check for the newest version and use that one instead.

4. In the `bin` folder, create a file called `glob.rs`.

5. Add the following code and run it with `cargo run --bin glob`:

```
1     extern crate glob;
2     use glob::{glob, glob_with, MatchOptions};
3
4     fn main() {
5         println!("All all Rust files in all subdirectories:");
6         for entry in glob("**/*.rs").expect("Failed to read glob
          pattern") {
7             match entry {
8                 Ok(path) => println!("{:?}", path.display()),
9                 Err(e) => println!("Failed to read file: {:?}", e),
10            }
11        }
12
13        // Set the glob to be case insensitive and ignore hidden
              files
14        let options = MatchOptions {
15            case_sensitive: false,
16            require_literal_leading_dot: true,
17            ..Default::default()
18        };
19
20
21        println!(
22            "All files that contain the word \"ferris\" case
              insensitive \
23            and don't contain an underscore:"
24        );
25        for entry in glob_with("*Ferris[!_]*",
          &options).expect("Failed to read glob pattern") {
26            if let Ok(path) = entry {
```

```
27              println!("{:?}", path.display())
28          }
29      }
30  }
```

# How it works...

This crate is pretty small and simple. With `glob(...)`, you can create an iterator over all matching files by specifying a `glob` pattern. If you aren't familiar with them but remember the regex recipe from earlier (in the *Querying with regexes* section in Chapter 1, *Learning the Basics*), think of them as very simplified regexes used primarily for filenames. Its syntax is nicely described on Wikipedia: https://en.wikipedia.org/wiki/Glob_(programming).

As with `WalkDir` before, the `glob` iterator returns a `Result` because the program might not have the permissions to read a filesystem entry. Inside the `Result` sits a `Path`, which we also touched on in the last recipe. If you want to read the contents of the file, refer to the first recipe in this chapter, which deals with file manipulation.

With `glob_with`, you can specify a `MatchOptions` instance to change the way `glob` searches for files. The most useful options you can toggle are:

- `case_sensitive`: This is enabled per default and controls whether lowercase letters (abcd) and uppercase letters (ABCD) should be treated differently or not.
- `require_literal_leading_dot`: This is disabled per default and, when set, prohibits wildcards from matching a leading dot in a filename. This is used when you want to ignore a user's hidden files.

You can view the rest of the options in the documentation of `MatchOption`: https://doc. rust-lang.org/glob/glob/struct.MatchOptions.html.

If you have set the options you care about, you can leave the rest at their default by using the `..Default::default()` *update syntax* discussed in the *Providing a default implementation* section in Chapter 1, *Learning the Basics*.

# See also

- *Querying with Regexes* and *Providing a default implementation* recipes in Chapter 1, *Learning the Basics*

# Serialization **4**

In this chapter, we will cover the following recipes:

- Working with CSV
- Serialization basics with Serde
- Working with TOML
- Working with JSON
- Building JSON dynamically

## Introduction

Reinventing the wheel doesn't make sense. A great deal of functionality has already been provided by many programs that are more than happy to interact with your program. Of course, this offer is worthless if you're not able to communicate with them.

In this chapter, we are going to look at the most important formats in the Rust ecosystem in order to enable you to comfortably speak with other services.

## Working with CSV

A nice and simple way to store uncomplicated and small datasets is CSV. This format is also of interest if you're working with spreadsheet applications such as Microsoft Excel, as they have excellent support for importing and exporting various flavors of CSV.

# Getting started

You probably already know what a CSV is, but a little refresher won't hurt.

The idea of the format is to take a table of values and write all rows down as *records*. Inside a record, every column item is written down and separated by a comma. That's where the format's name comes from—comma-separated values.

Let's do an example. In the following code, we are going to write a CSV comparing various planets in the solar system to our own. A radius, distance from the sun, and gravity of 1 means *exactly as on earth*. Written as a table, our values look like this:

| name | radius | distance_from_sun | gravity |
| --- | --- | --- | --- |
| Mercury | 0.38 | 0.47 | 0.38 |
| Venus | 0.95 | 0.73 | 0.9 |
| Earth | 1 | 1 | 1 |
| Mars | 0.53 | 1.67 | 0.38 |
| Jupiter | 11.21 | 5.46 | 2.53 |
| Saturn | 9.45 | 10.12 | 1.07 |
| Uranus | 4.01 | 20.11 | 0.89 |
| Neptune | 3.88 | 30.33 | 1.14 |

Take every row, separate the values by commas, put them each on a separate line, and you end up with the CSV file:

```
name,radius,distance_from_sun,gravity
Mercury,0.38,0.47,0.38
Venus,0.95,0.73,0.9
Earth,1,1,1
Mars,0.53,1.67,0.38
Jupiter,11.21,5.46,2.53
Saturn,9.45,10.12,1.07
Uranus,4.01,20.11,0.89
Neptune,3.88,30.33,1.14
```

As you can see, the heading (`planet,radius,distance_from_sun,gravity`) is simply written as the first record.

# How to do it...

1. Create a Rust project to work on during this chapter with `cargo new chapter_four`.
2. Navigate into the newly-created `chapter_four` folder. For the rest of this chapter, we will assume that your command line is currently in this directory.
3. Inside the `src` folder, create a new folder called `bin`.
4. Delete the generated `lib.rs` file, as we are not creating a library.
5. Open the `Cargo.toml` file that was generated earlier for you.

6. Under `[dependencies]`, add the following line:

   ```
   csv = "1.0.0-beta.5"
   ```

7. If you want, you can go to `csv`'s crates.io page (`https://crates.io/crates/csv`) to check for the newest version and use that one instead.
8. In the `src/bin` folder, create a file called `csv.rs`.
9. Add the following code and run it with `cargo run --bin csv`:

   ```
    1    extern crate csv;
    2
    3    use std::io::{BufReader, BufWriter, Read, Seek, SeekFrom,
       Write};
    4    use std::fs::OpenOptions;
    5
    6    fn main() {
    7      let file = OpenOptions::new()
    8        .read(true)
    9        .write(true)
   10        .create(true)
   11        .open("solar_system_compared_to_earth.csv")
   12        .expect("failed to create csv file");
   13
   14      let buf_writer = BufWriter::new(&file);
   15      write_records(buf_writer).expect("Failed to write csv");
   16
   17      let mut buf_reader = BufReader::new(&file);
   18      buf_reader
   19        .seek(SeekFrom::Start(0))
   20        .expect("Failed to jump to the beginning of the csv");
   21      read_records(buf_reader).expect("Failed to read csv");
   22    }
   23
   24    fn write_records<W>(writer: W) -> csv::Result<()>
   ```

```
25    where
26    W: Write,
27    {
28       let mut wtr = csv::Writer::from_writer(writer);
29
30       // The header is just a normal record
31       wtr.write_record(&["name", "radius", "distance_from_sun",
32       "gravity"])?;
33
34       wtr.write_record(&["Mercury", "0.38", "0.47", "0.38"])?;
35       wtr.write_record(&["Venus", "0.95", "0.73", "0.9"])?;
36       wtr.write_record(&["Earth", "1", "1", "1"])?;
37       wtr.write_record(&["Mars", "0.53", "1.67", "0.38"])?;
38       wtr.write_record(&["Jupiter", "11.21", "5.46", "2.53"])?;
39       wtr.write_record(&["Saturn", "9.45", "10.12", "1.07"])?;
40       wtr.write_record(&["Uranus", "4.01", "20.11", "0.89"])?;
41       wtr.write_record(&["Neptune", "3.88", "30.33", "1.14"])?;
42       wtr.flush()?;
43       Ok(())
44    }
45
46    fn read_records<R>(reader: R) -> csv::Result<()>
47    where
48    R: Read,
49    {
50       let mut rdr = csv::Reader::from_reader(reader);
51       println!("Comparing planets in the solar system with the
52       earth");
53       println!("where a value of '1' means 'equal to earth'");
54       for result in rdr.records() {
55          println!("-------");
56          let record = result?;
57          if let Some(name) = record.get(0) {
58             println!("Name: {}", name);
59          }
60          if let Some(radius) = record.get(1) {
61             println!("Radius: {}", radius);
62          }
63          if let Some(distance) = record.get(2) {
64             println!("Distance from sun: {}", distance);
65          }
66          if let Some(gravity) = record.get(3) {
67             println!("Surface gravity: {}", gravity);
68          }
69       }
70       Ok(())
71    }
```

# How it works...

First of all, we prepare our file[9] and its `OpenOptions` so that we have both `read` and `write` access on the file. You will remember this from `Chapter 3`, *Handling Files and the Filesystem; Working with text files*.

Then we write the CSV. We do this by wrapping any kind of `Write` in a `csv::Writer`[30]. You can then use `write_record` on it to write any data type that can be represented as an iterator over `&[u8]`. Most of the time, this will simply be an array of strings.

While reading, we similarly wrap a `Read` in a `csv::Read`. The `records()` method returns an iterator over `Result` of `StringRecord`. This way, you get to decide how to handle a malformed record. In our example, we simply skip it. Lastly, we call `get()` on a record to get a certain field. If there was no entry at the specified index or if it was out of bounds, this would return `None`.

# There's more...

If you need to read or write a custom CSV format, like one that uses tabs instead of commas as a delimiter, you can use `WriterBuilder` and `ReaderBuilder` to customize the expected format. Remember this well if you're planning on using Microsoft Excel, as it has the annoying tendency to be regionally inconsistent in its choice of delimiters (`https://stackoverflow.com/questions/10140999/csv-with-comma-or-semicolon`).

 When working with CSV and Microsoft Excel, be careful and sanitize your data before handing it to Excel. Even though CSV is defined as plain data with no control identifiers, Excel will interpret and execute macros when importing CSV. For examples of possible attack vectors opened by this, see `http://georgemauer.net/2017/10/07/csv-injection.html`.

This is also useful if a Windows application refuses to accept the `\n` terminator that `csv` uses as per default. In this case, simply specify the following code in the builder to use the Windows-native `\r\n` terminator:

```
.terminator(csv::Terminator::CRLF)
```

The `csv` crate allows you to manipulate your data much more than what is shown in this recipe. You can, for example, insert new fields on the fly into a `StringRecord`. We deliberately don't explore these possibilities in detail as the CSV format is not meant for these kinds of data manipulation. If you need to do more than simple import/export, you should use a more suitable format, such as JSON, which we will explore in this chapter as well.

## See also

- *Using the builder pattern* recipe in `Chapter 1`, *Learning the Basics*
- *Working with text files* recipe in `Chapter 3`, *Handling Files and the Filesystem*

# Serialization basics with Serde

The *de facto* standard for all things serialization in Rust is the Serde framework. All the other recipes in this chapter are going to use it to some extent. In order to make you familiar with the Serde way of doing things, we are going to rewrite the last recipe using it. Later in the chapter, we will learn in detail how Serde works in order to implement idiomatic deserialization into a homemade format.

## How to do it...

1. Open the `Cargo.toml` file that was generated earlier for you.

2. Under `[dependencies]`, add the following lines:

   ```
   serde = "1.0.24"
   serde_derive = "1.0.24"
   ```

3. If you haven't done so already in the last recipe, add the following line as well:

   ```
   csv = "1.0.0-beta.5"
   ```

4. If you want, you can go to the crates.io web pages for Serde (`https://crates.io/crates/serde`), serde_derive (`https://crates.io/crates/serde_derive`), and CSV (`https://crates.io/crates/csv`) to check for the newest versions and use those ones instead.

5. In the `bin` folder, create a file called `serde_csv.rs`.

4. Add the following code and run it with `cargo run --bin serde_csv`:

```
1    extern crate csv;
2    extern crate serde;
3    #[macro_use]
4    extern crate serde_derive;
5
6    use std::io::{BufReader, BufWriter, Read, Seek, SeekFrom,
     Write};
7    use std::fs::OpenOptions;
8
9    #[derive(Serialize, Deserialize)]
10   struct Planet {
11     name: String,
12     radius: f32,
13     distance_from_sun: f32,
14     gravity: f32,
15   }
16
17   fn main() {
18     let file = OpenOptions::new()
19       .read(true)
20       .write(true)
21       .create(true)
22       .open("solar_system_compared_to_earth.csv")
23       .expect("failed to create csv file");
24
25     let buf_writer = BufWriter::new(&file);
26     write_records(buf_writer).expect("Failed to write csv");
27
28     let mut buf_reader = BufReader::new(&file);
29     buf_reader
30       .seek(SeekFrom::Start(0))
31       .expect("Failed to jump to the beginning of the csv");
32     read_records(buf_reader).expect("Failed to read csv");
33   }
34
35   fn write_records<W>(writer: W) -> csv::Result<()>
36   where
37   W: Write,
38   {
39     let mut wtr = csv::Writer::from_writer(writer);
40
41     // No need to specify a header; Serde creates it for us
42     wtr.serialize(Planet {
43       name: "Mercury".to_string(),
44       radius: 0.38,
```

```
45          distance_from_sun: 0.47,
46          gravity: 0.38,
47      })?;
48      wtr.serialize(Planet {
49        name: "Venus".to_string(),
50        radius: 0.95,
51        distance_from_sun: 0.73,
52        gravity: 0.9,
53      })?;
54      wtr.serialize(Planet {
55        name: "Earth".to_string(),
56        radius: 1.0,
57        distance_from_sun: 1.0,
58        gravity: 1.0,
59      })?;
60      wtr.serialize(Planet {
61        name: "Mars".to_string(),
62        radius: 0.53,
63        distance_from_sun: 1.67,
64        gravity: 0.38,
65      })?;
66      wtr.serialize(Planet {
67        name: "Jupiter".to_string(),
68        radius: 11.21,
69        distance_from_sun: 5.46,
70        gravity: 2.53,
71      })?;
72      wtr.serialize(Planet {
73        name: "Saturn".to_string(),
74        radius: 9.45,
75        distance_from_sun: 10.12,
76        gravity: 1.07,
77      })?;
78      wtr.serialize(Planet {
79        name: "Uranus".to_string(),
80        radius: 4.01,
81        distance_from_sun: 20.11,
82        gravity: 0.89,
83      })?;
84      wtr.serialize(Planet {
85        name: "Neptune".to_string(),
86        radius: 3.88,
87        distance_from_sun: 30.33,
88        gravity: 1.14,
89      })?;
90      wtr.flush()?;
91      Ok(())
92  }
```

```
 93
 94   fn read_records<R>(reader: R) -> csv::Result<()>
 95   where
 96   R: Read,
 97   {
 98     let mut rdr = csv::Reader::from_reader(reader);
 99     println!("Comparing planets in the solar system with the
       earth");
100     println!("where a value of '1' means 'equal to earth'");
101     for result in rdr.deserialize() {
102       println!("-------");
103       let planet: Planet = result?;
104       println!("Name: {}", planet.name);
105       println!("Radius: {}", planet.radius);
106       println!("Distance from sun: {}",
       planet.distance_from_sun);
107       println!("Surface gravity: {}", planet.gravity);
108     }
109     Ok(())
110   }
```

# How it works...

The code in this recipe reads and writes the exact same CSV as the last recipe. The only difference is how we treat a single record. Serde helps us by enabling us to use plain old Rust structures for this. The only thing we need to do is derive our Planet structure from Serialize and Deserialize [9]. The rest is taken care of automatically by Serde.

Because we now use actual Rust structures to represent a planet, we create a record by calling serialize with a structure instead of write_record as before [42]. Looks way more readable, doesn't it? If you think that the example became a little bit too verbose, you could hide the actual object creation behind a constructor, as described in Chapter 1, *Learning the Basics; Using the Constructor Pattern.*

When reading a CSV, we also no longer have to manually access the fields of a StringRecord. Instead, deserialize() returns an iterator over a Result of an already deserialized Planet object. Again, look how much more readable this has become.

As you may have already guessed, you should use Serde whenever you can, as it helps you catch possible errors early by providing you with readability and compile-time type safety.

# There's more...

Serde gives you the ability to tweak the serialization process somewhat by annotating your fields. For example, you can give a field a standard value if it wasn't able to be parsed by writing #[serde(default)] above its declaration. In a struct, it would look like this:

```
#[derive(Serialize, Deserialize)]
struct Foo {
    bar: i32,
    #[serde(default)]
    baz: i32,
}
```

If baz hasn't been parsed, its Default::default value (See Chapter 1, *Learning the Basics*; Providing a default implementation) will be used. Another useful thing you can do with annotations is changed the expected case convention. By default, Serde will expect Rust's snake_case, however, you can change this by annotating a struct or enum with #[serde(rename_all = "PascalCase")]. You can use it on a struct like this:

```
#[derive(Serialize, Deserialize)]
#[serde(rename_all = "PascalCase")]
struct Stats {
    number_of_clicks: i32,
    total_time_played: i32,
}
```

This would, instead of parsing number_of_clicks and total_time_played, expect the NumberOfClicks and TotalTimePlayed keys to be called. Other possible case conventions than PascalCase that Serde supports are lowercase, *camelCase*, and *SCREAMING_SNAKE_CASE*.

There are many different and useful attributes. If you want to, you can familiarize yourself with them at https://serde.rs/attributes.html.

You can use Serde to provide idiomatic serialization and deserialization, however, discussing all best practices would cover an entire chapter on its own. If you want to delve into such things, Serde has a nice write-up on how to do it at https://serde.rs/data-format.html.

# See also

- *Using the constructor pattern* and *Providing a default implementation* recipes in `Chapter 1`, *Learning the Basics*
- *Working with text files* recipe in `Chapter 3`, *Handling Files and the Filesystem*

# Working with TOML

Do you like the simplicity of INI files but wish they were formally specified and had a few more features? So did Tom Preston-Werner, founder of services such as GitHub and Gravatar. He created Tom's Obvious, Minimal Language, or TOML for short. This relatively new format is seeing increasing adoption in new projects. In fact, you have used it multiple times by now as well: Cargo's dependencies are specified in every project's `Cargo.toml` file!

# Getting started

At its heart, TOML is all about *key-value* pairs. This is the simplest TOML file you can create:

```
message = "Hello World"
```

Here, the key message has the `"Hello World"` value. A value can also be an array:

```
messages: ["Hello", "World", "out", "there"]
```

A group of key-values is called a *table*. The following TOML lets the `smileys` table contain the `happy` key with the `":)"` value and the `sad` key with the `":("` value:

```
[smileys]
happy = ":)"
sad = ":("
```

A particularly small table can be *inlined,* that is, written in one line. The last example is the exact same as the following:

```
smileys = { happy = ":)", sad = ":(" }
```

Tables can be nested by separating their names with a dot:

```
[servers]
  [servers.production]
  ip = "192.168.0.1"
  [servers.beta]
  ip = "192.169.0.2"
  [servers.testing]
  ip = "192.169.0.3"
```

A nice property of TOML is that you can convert any key into a table if you need to specify additional information. For example, Cargo itself expects this when declaring dependency versions. For example, if you wanted to use `rocket_contrib`, a helper crate of the popular `rocket` web framework for Rust, at version 0.3.3, you would write this:

```
[dependencies]
rocket_contrib = 0.3.3
```

However, if you wanted to specify the exact features to be included in `rocket_contrib`, you would need to instead write it as a sub-table of `dependencies`. The following TOML would tell `Cargo` to use its JSON serialization feature:

```
[dependencies]
[dependencies.rocket_contrib]
version = "0.3.3"
default-features = false
features = ["json"]
```

Another nice thing TOML brings to the table is that its whitespace is not significant, that is, you can indent a file however you want. You can even add comments by beginning a line with the following:

```
# some comment
```

If you want to explore the format further, the entirety of the TOML syntax is specified at `https://github.com/toml-lang/toml`.

# How to do it...

1. Open the `Cargo.toml` file that was generated earlier for you

2. Under `[dependencies]`, add the following line:

```
toml = "0.4.5"
```

3. If you haven't done so already, add the following lines as well:

```
serde = "1.0.24"
serde_derive = "1.0.24"
```

4. If you want, you can go to the crates.io web pages for TOML (`https://crates.io/crates/toml`), Serde (`https://crates.io/crates/serde`), and serde_derive (`https://crates.io/crates/serde_derive`) to check for the newest versions and use those ones instead

5. In the `bin` folder, create a file called `toml.rs`

6. Add the following code and run it with `cargo run --bin toml`:

```
1   #[macro_use]
2   extern crate serde_derive;
3   extern crate toml;
4
5   use std::io::{BufReader, BufWriter, Read, Seek, SeekFrom,
    Write};
6   use std::fs::OpenOptions;
```

7. These are the structures we are going to use throughout the recipe:

```
8   #[derive(Serialize, Deserialize)]
9   struct Preferences {
10    person: Person,
11    language: Language,
12    privacy: Privacy,
13  }
14
15  #[derive(Serialize, Deserialize)]
16  struct Person {
17    name: String,
18    email: String,
19  }
20
21  #[derive(Serialize, Deserialize)]
22  struct Language {
23    display: String,
24    autocorrect: Option<Vec<String>>,
25  }
26
```

```
27   #[derive(Serialize, Deserialize)]
28   struct Privacy {
29     share_anonymous_statistics: bool,
30     public_name: bool,
31     public_email: bool,
32   }
```

8. Prepare a new file and call the other functions:

```
34   fn main() {
35     let file = OpenOptions::new()
36      .read(true)
37      .write(true)
38      .create(true)
39      .open("preferences.toml")
40      .expect("failed to create TOML file");
41
42     let buf_writer = BufWriter::new(&file);
43     write_toml(buf_writer).expect("Failed to write TOML");
44
45     let mut buf_reader = BufReader::new(&file);
46     buf_reader
47       .seek(SeekFrom::Start(0))
48       .expect("Failed to jump to the beginning of the TOML
             file");
49     read_toml(buf_reader).expect("Failed to read TOML");
50   }
```

9. Save our structures as a TOML file:

```
52   type SerializeResult<T> = Result<T, toml::ser::Error>;
53   fn write_toml<W>(mut writer: W) -> SerializeResult<()>
54   where
55   W: Write,
56   {
57     let preferences = Preferences {
58       person: Person {
59         name: "Jan Nils Ferner".to_string(),
60         email: "jn_ferner@hotmail.de".to_string(),
61       },
62       language: Language {
63         display: "en-GB".to_string(),
64         autocorrect: Some(vec![
65           "en-GB".to_string(),
66           "en-US".to_string(),
67           "de-CH".to_string(),
68         ]),
69       },
```

```
70        privacy: Privacy {
71          share_anonymous_statistics: false,
72          public_name: true,
73          public_email: true,
74        },
75      };
76
77      let toml = toml::to_string(&preferences)?;
78      writer
79        .write_all(toml.as_bytes())
80        .expect("Failed to write file");
81      Ok(())
82    }
```

10. Read the TOML file we just created:

```
84    type DeserializeResult<T> = Result<T, toml::de::Error>;
85    fn read_toml<R>(mut reader: R) -> DeserializeResult<()>
86    where
87    R: Read,
88    {
89      let mut toml = String::new();
90      reader
91        .read_to_string(&mut toml)
92        .expect("Failed to read TOML");
93      let preferences: Preferences = toml::from_str(&toml)?;
94
95      println!("Personal data:");
96      let person = &preferences.person;
97      println!(" Name: {}", person.name);
98      println!(" Email: {}", person.email);
99
100     println!("\nLanguage preferences:");
101     let language = &preferences.language;
102     println!(" Display language: {}", language.display);
103     println!(" Autocorrect priority: {:?}",
          language.autocorrect);
104
105
106     println!("\nPrivacy settings:");
107     let privacy = &preferences.privacy;
108     println!(
109       " Share anonymous usage statistics: {}",
110         privacy.share_anonymous_statistics
111     );
112     println!(" Display name publically: {}",
          privacy.public_name);
113     println!(" Display email publically: {}",
```

```
                          privacy.public_email);
          114
          115      Ok(())
          116  }
```

## How it works...

As always with Serde, we first need to declare the structures we plan on using [8 to 32].

While serializing, we can directly call Serde's `to_string` method with a structure as TOML re-exports them [77]. This returns a `String` that we can then write into a file [79]. The same is true of Serde's `from_str`, which, when type-annotated, takes a `&str` and converts it into a structure.

## There's more...

You might have noticed that we are not using the try-operator (?) while reading or writing in this recipe. This is because the function's expected error types, `se::Error` [77] and `de::Error`[93], are incompatible with `std::io::Error`. In Chapter 6, *Handling Errors; Providing user-defined Error types,* we will explore how to avoid this by returning our own error type that encompasses the other ones mentioned.

The TOML crate used in this recipe is the same one that Cargo itself uses. If you are interested in how Cargo parses its own `Cargo.toml` file, you can check out `https://github.com/rust-lang/cargo/blob/master/src/cargo/util/toml/mod.rs`.

## See also

- *Working with* text *files* recipe in Chapter 3, *Handling Files and the Filesystem*
- *Providing user-defined error types* recipe in Chapter 6, *Handling Errors*

# Working with JSON

Most Web APIs and many native APIs speak JSON nowadays. It should be your format of choice when designing data meant for consumption by other programs, as it is lightweight, simple, easy to use and understand, and has excellent library support across programming languages, most notably JavaScript, of course.

# Getting ready

JSON was created at a time when most web communication was done by sending XML over browser plugins such as Java or Flash. This was cumbersome and made the exchanged information quite bloated. Douglas Crockford, the creator of JSLint and author of the famous *JavaScript: The Good Parts*, decided in the early 2000s that it was time for a lightweight format that was easily integrated with JavaScript. He oriented himself on a small subset of JavaScript, namely the way it defined objects, and extended it a little bit to form the JavaScript Object Notation or JSON. Yes, you've read that right; JSON is *not* a subset of JavaScript, as it accepts things that JavaScript doesn't. You can read more about that at `http://timelessrepo.com/json-isnt-a-javascript-subset`.

> The sad irony of the story is that today we have gone full-circle: our best practices for web development include a labyrinth of task runners, frameworks, and transpilers, which are all quite nice in theory but end up being a giant bloated mess in the end. But that is a story for another time.

JSON is built upon two structures:

- A group of key-value pairs surrounded by { and }, which is called an *object* and can be a value itself
- A list of values surrounded by [ and ] called an *array*

This might remind you a bit of the TOML syntax we discussed earlier, and you might ask yourself when you should prefer one over the other. The answer is that JSON is a good format when your data is going to be read automatically by a tool, while TOML is excellent when your data is meant to be read and modified manually by a human.

Take note that one thing that JSON *doesn't* allow is comments. This makes sense, as comments are not readable by tools anyway.

An example of a JSON object with values, sub-objects, and arrays could be the following:

```
{
  name: "John",
  age: 23,
  pets: [
    {
      name: "Sparky",
      species: "Dog",
      age: 2
    },
    {
      name: "Speedy",
      species: "Turtle",
      age: 47,
      colour: "Green"
    },
    {
      name: "Meows",
      species: "Cat",
      colour: "Orange"
    }
  ]
}
```

We are going to write and read this exact example in the following code. The definitions of the pets are intentionally inconsistent because many web APIs omit certain keys in some situations.

## How to do it...

1. Open the `Cargo.toml` file that has been generated earlier for you

2. Under `[dependencies]`, add the following line:

   ```
   serde_json = "1.0.8"
   ```

3. If you haven't done so already, add the following lines as well:

   ```
   serde = "1.0.24"
   serde_derive = "1.0.24"
   ```

4. If you want, you can go to the crates.io web pages for `serde_json` (https://crates.io/crates/serde_json), Serde (https://crates.io/crates/serde), and serde_derive (https://crates.io/crates/serde_derive) to check for the newest versions and use those ones instead

5. In the `bin` folder, create a file called `json.rs`

6. Add the following code and run it with `cargo run --bin json`:

```
1    extern crate serde;
2    extern crate serde_json;
3
4    #[macro_use]
5    extern crate serde_derive;
6
7    use std::io::{BufReader, BufWriter, Read, Seek, SeekFrom,
     Write};
8    use std::fs::OpenOptions;
```

7. These are the structures we are going to use throughout the recipe:

```
10   #[derive(Serialize, Deserialize)]
11   struct PetOwner {
12     name: String,
13     age: u8,
14     pets: Vec<Pet>,
15   }
16
17   #[derive(Serialize, Deserialize)]
18   struct Pet {
19     name: String,
20     species: AllowedSpecies,
21     // It is usual for many JSON keys to be optional
22     age: Option<u8>,
23     colour: Option<String>,
24   }
25
26   #[derive(Debug, Serialize, Deserialize)]
27   enum AllowedSpecies {
28     Dog,
29     Turtle,
30     Cat,
31   }
```

8. Prepare a new file and call the other functions:

```
33  fn main() {
34    let file = OpenOptions::new()
35      .read(true)
36      .write(true)
37      .create(true)
38      .open("pet_owner.json")
39      .expect("failed to create JSON file");
40
41    let buf_writer = BufWriter::new(&file);
42    write_json(buf_writer).expect("Failed to write JSON");
43
44    let mut buf_reader = BufReader::new(&file);
45    buf_reader
46      .seek(SeekFrom::Start(0))
47      .expect("Failed to jump to the beginning of the JSON
            file");
48    read_json(buf_reader).expect("Failed to read JSON");
49  }
```

9. Save our structures as a JSON file:

```
52  fn write_json<W>(mut writer: W) -> serde_json::Result<()>
53  where
54  W: Write,
55  {
56    let pet_owner = PetOwner {
57      name: "John".to_string(),
58      age: 23,
59      pets: vec![
60        Pet {
61          name: "Waldo".to_string(),
62          species: AllowedSpecies::Dog,
63          age: Some(2),
64          colour: None,
65        },
66        Pet {
67          name: "Speedy".to_string(),
68          species: AllowedSpecies::Turtle,
69          age: Some(47),
70          colour: Some("Green".to_string()),
71        },
72        Pet {
73          name: "Meows".to_string(),
74          species: AllowedSpecies::Cat,
75          age: None,
76          colour: Some("Orange".to_string()),
```

```
77          },
78        ],
79      };
80
81      let json = serde_json::to_string(&pet_owner)?;
82      writer
83        .write_all(json.as_bytes())
84        .expect("Failed to write file");
85      Ok(())
86    }
```

10. Read the JSON file we just created:

```
88    fn read_json<R>(mut reader: R) -> serde_json::Result<()>
89    where
90    R: Read,
91    {
92      let mut json = String::new();
93      reader
94        .read_to_string(&mut json)
95        .expect("Failed to read TOML");
96      let pet_owner: PetOwner = serde_json::from_str(&json)?;
97
98      println!("Pet owner profile:");
99      println!(" Name: {}", pet_owner.name);
100     println!(" Age: {}", pet_owner.age);
101
102     println!("\nPets:");
103     for pet in pet_owner.pets {
104       println!(" Name: {}", pet.name);
105       println!(" Species: {:?}", pet.species);
106       if let Some(age) = pet.age {
107         println!(" Age: {}", age);
108       }
109       if let Some(colour) = pet.colour {
110         println!(" Colour: {}", colour);
111       }
112       println!();
113     }
114     Ok(())
115   }
```

# How it works...

Notice how this recipe looks nearly identical to the last one? Except for the structures, the only significant difference is that we called `serde_json::to_string()` [81] instead of `toml::to_string()`, and `serde_json::from_str()` [96] instead of `toml::from_str()`. This is the beauty of a well-thought-out framework like Serde: the custom serialization and deserialization code are hidden behind trait definitions and we can use the same API without caring about internal implementation details.

Other than that, there is nothing to say that hasn't been said in the previous recipe, which is why we are not going to go over any other formats. All important formats support Serde, so you can use them the exact same way you use the other formats in this chapter. For a full list of all supported formats, see `https://docs.serde.rs/serde/index.html`.

# There's more...

JSON has no concept of something resembling an `enum`. As many languages *do* work with them, however, multiple conventions on how to handle the conversion from JSON into `enum` have emerged over the years. Serde allows you to support these conventions with annotations on your enums. For a full list of supported conversions, visit `https://serde.rs/enum-representations.html`.

# See also

- *Working with text files* recipe in `Chapter 3`, *Handling Files and the Filesystem*
- *Providing user-defined error types* recipe in `Chapter 6`, *Handling Errors*

# Building JSON dynamically

When a JSON API is designed with a poorly-thought-out schema and inconsistent objects, you might end up with giant structures where most members are an `Option`. If you find yourself only sending data to such a service, it might be a bit easier to dynamically build your JSON property by property.

# How to do it...

1. Open the `Cargo.toml` file that was generated earlier for you

2. Under `[dependencies]`, if you haven't done so already, add the following line:

    ```
    serde_json = "1.0.8"
    ```

3. If you want, you can go to the `serde_json` crates.io web page (`https://crates.io/crates/serde_json`) to check for the newest version and use that one instead

4. In the `bin` folder, create a file called `dynamic_json.rs`

5. Add the following code and run it with `cargo run --bin dynamic_json`:

```
1    #[macro_use]
2    extern crate serde_json;
3
4    use std::io::{self, BufRead};
5    use std::collections::HashMap;
6
7    fn main() {
8      // A HashMap is the same as a JSON without any schema
9      let mut key_value_map = HashMap::new();
10     let stdin = io::stdin();
11     println!("Enter a key and a value");
12     for input in stdin.lock().lines() {
13       let input = input.expect("Failed to read line");
14       let key_value: Vec<_> =
input.split_whitespace().collect();
15       let key = key_value[0].to_string();
16       let value = key_value[1].to_string();
17
18       println!("Saving key-value pair: {} -> {}", key, value);
19       // The json! macro lets us convert a value into its JSON
              representation
20       key_value_map.insert(key, json!(value));
21       println!(
22         "Enter another pair or stop by pressing '{}'",
23         END_OF_TRANSMISSION
24       );
25     }
26     // to_string_pretty returns a JSON with nicely readable
          whitespace
27     let json =
28     serde_json::to_string_pretty(&key_value_map).expect("Failed
```

```
               to convert HashMap into JSON");
29             println!("Your input has been made into the following
               JSON:");
30             println!("{}", json);
31         }
32
33         #[cfg(target_os = "windows")]
34         const END_OF_TRANSMISSION: &str = "Ctrl Z";
35
36         #[cfg(not(target_os = "windows"))]
37         const END_OF_TRANSMISSION: &str = "Ctrl D";
```

# How it works...

In this example, the user can enter any number of key-value pairs until they decide to stop, at which point they receive their input back in the form of JSON. Some example input you could enter could include:

```
name abraham
age 49
fav_colour red
hello world
(press 'Ctrl Z' on Windows or 'Ctrl D' on Unix)
```

Use `#[cfg(target_os = "some_operating_system")]` to handle operating system specific circumstances. In this recipe, we use this to conditionally compile the `END_OF_TRANSMISSION` constant differently on Windows than on Unix. This key combination tells the OS to stop the current input stream.

This program begins with the idea that a JSON object without a clearly defined schema is nothing but a `HashMap<String, String>`[9]. Now, `serde_json` doesn't accept a `String` as a value, as that would not be general enough. Instead, it wants a `serde_json::Value`, which you can easily construct by calling the `json!` macro on pretty much any type [20].

When we are done, we don't call `serde_json::to_string()` as before, but use `serde_json::to_string_pretty()` instead [28], as this results in a less efficient but much more readable JSON. Remember, JSON is not supposed to be primarily read by humans, which is why the default way Serde serialized it is without any whitespace whatsoever. If you're curious about the exact difference, feel free to go ahead and change `to_string_pretty()` to `to_string()` and compare the results.

# See also

- *Reading from stdin* recipe in Chapter 1, *Learning the Basics*
- *Access collections as Iterators* and *Using a HashMap* recipe in Chapter 2, *Working with Collections*

# Advanced Data Structures

**5**

In this chapter, we will cover the following recipes:

- Creating lazy static objects
- Working with bit fields
- Providing custom derives
- Converting types into each other
- Boxing data
- Sharing ownership with smart pointers
- Working with interior mutability

## Introduction

So far, we have primarily looked at techniques that were all useful in their own right. Of course, we are continuing that trend, but the recipes shown in this chapter truly shine when combined with other code. You can imagine them as the *glue* holding a nice Rust program together, as they are primarily oriented toward new enabling ways in which different components of your crate can work together.

# Creating lazy static objects

Big objects, especially constant ones, should be reused instead of rebuilt. The lazy_static! macro helps you with this by extending Rust's normal static functionality, which normally requires your objects to be constructable at compile-time, with the ability to create lazy objects that are initialized during runtime.

# How to do it...

1. Create a Rust project to work on during this chapter with cargo new chapter_five.
2. Navigate into the newly created chapter_five folder. For the rest of this chapter, we will assume that your command line is currently in this directory.
3. Inside the src folder, create a new folder called bin.
4. Delete the generated lib.rs file, as we are not creating a library.
5. Open the Cargo.toml file that was generated earlier for you.

6. Under [dependencies], add the following lines:

   ```
   lazy_static = "1.0"
   regex = "0.2"
   ```

   If you want, you can go to the crates.io web pages for lazy_static (https://crates.io/crates/lazy_static) and regex (https://crates.io/crates/regex) to check for the newest version and use that one instead.

7. In the src/bin folder, create a file called lazy_static.rs
8. Add the following code and run it with cargo run --bin lazy_static:

   ```
   1    #[macro_use]
   2    extern crate lazy_static;
   3    extern crate regex;
   4
   5    use regex::Regex;
   6    use std::collections::HashMap;
   7    use std::sync::RwLock;
   8
   9    // Global immutable static
   10   lazy_static! {
   11     static ref CURRENCIES: HashMap<&'static str, &'static str> =
          {
   12       let mut m = HashMap::new();
   ```

```
13        m.insert("EUR", "Euro");
14        m.insert("USD", "U.S. Dollar");
15        m.insert("CHF", "Swiss Francs");
16        m
17      };
18    }
19
20    // Global mutable static
21    lazy_static! {
22      static ref CLIENTS: RwLock<Vec<String>> =
      RwLock::new(Vec::new());
23    }
24
25    // Local static
26    fn extract_day(date: &str) -> Option<&str> {
27      // lazy static objects are perfect for
28      // compiling regexes only once
29      lazy_static! {
30        static ref RE: Regex =
31        Regex::new(r"(\d{2}).(\d{2}).(\d{4})")
32          .expect("Failed to create regex");
33      }
34      RE.captures(date)
35        .and_then(|cap| cap.get(1).map(|day| day.as_str()))
36    }
37
38    fn main() {
39      // The first access to CURRENCIES initializes it
40      let usd = CURRENCIES.get("USD");
41      if let Some(usd) = usd {
42        println!("USD stands for {}", usd);
43      }
44
45      // All accesses will now refer to the same,
46      // already constructed object
47      if let Some(chf) = CURRENCIES.get("CHF") {
48        println!("CHF stands for {}", chf);
49      }
50
51      // Mutable the global static
52      CLIENTS
53        .write()
54        .expect("Failed to unlock clients for writing")
55        .push("192.168.0.1".to_string());
56
57      // Get an immutable reference to the global static
58      let clients = CLIENTS
59        .read()
```

```
60              .expect("Failed to unlock clients for reading");
61          let first_client = clients.get(0).expect("CLIENTS is
            empty");
62          println!("The first client is: {}", first_client);
63
64          let date = "12.01.2018";
65          // The static object is nicely hidden inside
66          // the definition of extract_day()
67          if let Some(day) = extract_day(date) {
68            println!("The date \"{}\" contains the day \"{}\"", date,
              day);
69          }
70      }
```

# How it works...

By invoking the `lazy_static!` macro [10, 21 and 29], we define a lazily initialized object in the current scope. *Lazy* here means *created only the first time it is used*.

Contrary to a `let` binding, its scope can also be the global scope [10]. A realistic example for this is creating a collection with a known content that is used by many functions, as the alternative would be to create it once and pass it around endlessly.

If your `lazy_static` consists of a `Vec` with content that is known at compile time, you can instead use a `const` array, as its construction is constant. In terms of code, this means you don't need to use this:

```
lazy_static!{
    static ref FOO: Vec<&'static str> = vec!["a", "b", "c"];
}
```

Instead, you can use the following:

```
const FOO: [&str; 3] = ["a", "b", "c"];
```

Remember when, in `Chapter 1`, *Learning the Basics; Querying with Regexes*, we talked about how compiling Regexes is expensive and should be avoided? `lazy_static!` is ideal for this. In fact, the pattern of creating a local `static` regex in a function is so widespread that we included it in this example [29]:

```
fn extract_day(date: &str) -> Option<&str> {
    lazy_static! {
        static ref RE: Regex =
            Regex::new(r"(\d{2}).(\d{2}).(\d{4})")
            .expect("Failed to create regex");
    }
    RE.captures(date)
        .and_then(|cap| cap.get(1).map(|day| day.as_str()))
}
```

Lastly, you can also create a global mutable state with `lazy_static` objects [21]. As mentioned in earlier chapters, the excessive state is the root of many evils in software development and should be treated with care. There are very few cases where having such an object is justifiable, as it is almost always better to pass the object around. There are exceptions, however. Sometimes a program revolves around the manipulation of one specific dataset in memory and all involved actors want to access it. In these cases, it can be very cumbersome to pass an object to literally every function in your code. One possible, but still very rare, an example where this might happen, is when dealing exclusively with a list of active connections [21]:

```
lazy_static! {
    static ref CLIENTS: RwLock<Vec<String>> = RwLock::new(Vec::new());
}
```

Note that, as the borrow checker is disabled for objects with `'static` lifetimes (see the following *There's more...* section), we need to wrap our `static` in a parallel lock, such as `RwLock` or `Mutex`, to guarantee thread safety. You can read more about that in `Chapter 7`, *Parallelism and Rayon; Access resources in parallel with RwLocks.*

# There's more...

People coming from other languages might wonder what `lazy_static` offers that can't already be done by a normal `static` object. The difference between them is as follows.

In Rust, a `static` variable is a variable that lives for the entire duration of the program, which is why they get their own, special lifetime, `'static`. The catch is that the variable has to be built in a constant way, that is, a way that is known at compile time. In our example, we cannot replace CURRENCIES [11] with a normal `static` because `HashMap::new()` returns a newly constructed `HashMap` sitting somewhere in the memory during runtime. As this requires it to live in memory, it's impossible to build a `HashMap` during compile time, so its constructor is not `constant`.

Another catch with `static` variables is that, because they have a global lifetime, the borrow checker cannot make sure that their access is thread-safe. As a consequence, any access on a `static mut` variable will always be `unsafe`.

 The convention for `static` variables is to write them in ALL_CAPS, just like `const` variables. This is because they are very closely linked. In fact, a `const` is nothing but an inlined `static` that can never be `mut`.

`lazy_static` gets around these restrictions by wrapping your object in a newly created `struct` that can be implicitly dereferenced into your object. This means that you never actually access your object directly. `lazy_static` stresses this by demanding that you write `ref` during the declaration of the `static`, as this makes you mentally treat the variable as a reference rather than an actual object:

```
lazy_static! {
    static ref foo: Foo = Foo::new();
}
```

While dereferencing, the wrapper `struct` works with a `static mut` pointer in your dynamically created object. All it does then is wrap the `unsafe` calls in a safe way.

 If you come from a modern C++ background, you can view a normal `static` Rust as a `static constexpr` C++ and a `lazy_static` Rust as a `static` C++ local.

# See also

- *Querying with Regexes* recipe in Chapter 1, *Learning the Basics*
- *Access resources in parallel with RwLocks* recipe in Chapter 7, *Parallelism and Rayon*

# Working with bit fields

Programs written in C don't have the possibility to use the Builder Pattern (Chapter 1, *Learning the Basics; Using the builder pattern*) to provide users with combinable options. Instead, they have to rely on bit fields. As C has historically become the *lingua franca* of system languages, you will have to interact with a lot of C code if you plan on wrapping existing programs in a Rust interface or vice versa. Because of this, you will sooner or later come in contact with bit fields. As Rust's enum is way more complex than a C enum, you have to instead rely on the bitflags crate to provide you with all of the necessary functionality to comfortably handle bit fields.

## Getting started

This chapter assumes that you know what a bit field is. Explaining it here doesn't make sense, as it would also incorporate an explanation of binary arithmetic and is not that relevant in your day-to-day Rust experience. For a good introduction to bit fields, check out this forum post and tutorial: http://forum.codecall.net/topic/56591-bit-fields-flags-tutorial-with-example/ and https://www.tutorialspoint.com/cprogramming/c_bit_fields.htm, respectively.

## How to do it...

1. Open the Cargo.toml file that was generated earlier for you.

2. Under [dependencies], add the following lines:

```
bitflags = "1.0"
```

3. If you want, you can go to bitflags' crates.io page (https://crates.io/crates/bitflags) to check for the newest version and use that one instead.

4. In the bin folder, create a file called bit_fields.rs.

5. Add the following code and run it with cargo run --bin bit_fields:

```
1    #[macro_use]
2    extern crate bitflags;
3
4    bitflags! {
5       struct Spices: u32 {
```

```
6      const SALT    = 0b0000_0001;
7      const PEPPER  = 0b0000_0010;
8      const CHILI   = 0b0000_0100;
9      const SAFFRON = 0b0000_1000;
10     const ALL     = Self::SALT.bits
11                   | Self::PEPPER.bits
12                   | Self::CHILI.bits
13                   | Self::SAFFRON.bits;
14   }
15 }
16
17 impl Spices {
18   // Implementing a "clear" method can be useful
19   pub fn clear(&mut self) -> &mut Self {
20     self.bits = 0;
21     self
22   }
23 }
24
25 fn main() {
26   let classic = Spices::SALT | Spices::PEPPER;
27   let spicy = Spices::PEPPER | Spices::CHILI;
28   // Bit fields can nicely be printed
29   println!("Classic: {:?}", classic);
30   println!("Bits: {:08b}", classic.bits());
31   println!("Spicy: {:?}", spicy);
32   println!("Bits: {:08b}", spicy.bits());
33
34   println!();
35
36   // Use set operations
37   println!("Union: {:?}", classic | spicy);
38   println!("Intersection: {:?}", classic & spicy);
39   println!("Difference: {:?}", classic - spicy);
40   println!("Complement: {:?}", !classic);
41
42   // Interact with flags in a bit field
43   let mut custom = classic | spicy;
44   println!("Custom spice mix: {:?}", custom);
45   custom.insert(Spices::SAFFRON);
46   // Note that ALL is now also contained in the bit field
47   println!("Custom spice after adding saffron: {:?}", custom);
48   custom.toggle(Spices::CHILI);
49   println!("Custom spice after toggling chili: {:?}", custom);
50   custom.remove(Spices::SALT);
51   println!("Custom spice after removing salt: {:?}", custom);
52
53   // This could be user input
```

```
54      let wants_salt = true;
55      custom.set(Spices::SALT, wants_salt);
56      if custom.contains(Spices::SALT) {
57        println!("I hope I didn't put too much salt in it");
58      }
59
60      // Read flags from raw bits
61      let bits = 0b0000_1101;
62      if let Some(from_bits) = Spices::from_bits(bits) {
63        println!("The bits {:08b} represent the flags {:?}", bits,
          from_bits);
64      }
65
66      custom.clear();
67      println!("Custom spice mix after clearing: {:?}", custom);
68    }
```

# How it works...

The `bitflags!` macro lets you define all of your flags and their underlying type (in our case, this is `u32`)[4 to 15]. They are written in `ALL_CAPS` because they are constants. We can also define collections of flags this way, as we did with `ALL`[10]. We could have added additional combinations, for example:

```
const SPICY = Self::PEPPER.bits | Self::CHILI.bits;
```

The macro then creates a struct with the specified members for you and implements a bunch of traits for it in order to enable the familiar `|`, `&`, `-`, and `!` notations [37 to 40] and pretty printing. You can still access the raw `bits` used in the background directly over the member of the same name.

Note that, when printing, flag combinations will be listed separately. For instance, look at the output in line [47]. After setting all possible flags in the field to active, it will pretty print itself as the following:

```
Custom spice after adding saffron: SALT | PEPPER | CHILI | SAFFRON |
ALL
```

A useful method to additionally define on a bit field is `clear()` [19]. This hides the underlying `bits` from the user and is nicely readable.

With the aforementioned binary operators, you can perform *set operations* on your bit field [37 to 40]. These are the same operations as the ones you can perform on a `HashSet` and are explained with a nice diagram in `Chapter 2`, *Working with Collections; Using a HashSet*.

Working with single flags in the bit field is also very easy. `insert()` sets a flag in the field to active [45], `remove()` sets it to inactive [50], and `toggle` flips it from active to inactive and vice versa [48]. If you don't yet know whether you're going to `insert` or `remove` a flag, as is the case with unpredictable user input, you can use `set()` to explicitly set the activation of a flag to either `true` or `false` [55].

You can check whether a certain flag is active by calling `contains()` [56]. This also works for another bit field or a flag combination. This means that the following is also valid:

```
if custom.contains(Spices::SALT | Spices::PEPPER) {
    println!("The custom spice contains both salt and pepper");
}
```

Additionally, you can use `intersects()` to check whether *any* flags in two-bit fields match.

Last but not least, you can deserialize raw bytes into your generated bit field struct by calling `from_bits()` on it [62]. This will check whether every bit actually corresponds to a flag and return `None` otherwise. You can skip the error checking and simply ignore invalid bits with `from_bits_truncate()` if you're absolutely 100% sure that the data has to be valid.

## See also

- *Using a HashSet* recipe in `Chapter 2`, *Working with Collections*

# Providing custom derives

You might have looked at `#[derive(Debug)]` and assumed it's some weird compiler magic. It is not. It is a so-called *procedural macro*, that is, a macro that doesn't simply expand at compile time but instead *runs* at compile time. This way, you can inject code into the actual compilation process. The most useful application for this is creating custom derives, with which you can generate new code based on the analysis of existing code.

# Getting started

This recipe will operate with an *Abstract Syntax Tree*, or AST. It is a tree-like representation of a language's elements in relation to each other. In this recipe, we (that is, a cool crate called `syn`) will parse our entire program into a single deep `struct`.

# How to do it...

1. Create a new sub-crate for the custom derive with `cargo new chapter-five-derive`.

2. Open the newly generated `chapter-five-derive/Cargo.toml`.

3. Add this directly above the `[dependencies]` section of the file in order to mark the crate as a procedural macro crate:

   ```
   [lib]
   proc-macro = true
   ```

4. Under `[dependencies]`, add the following lines:

   ```
   syn = "0.11.11"
   quote = "0.3.15"
   ```

   If you want, you can go to the crates.io web pages for `syn` (`https://crates.io/crates/syn`) and `quote` (`https://crates.io/crates/quote`) to check for the newest version and use that one instead.

5. In the `chapter-five-derive/src/lib.rs` file, delete the generated code and add the following:

   ```
   1    extern crate proc_macro;
   2    #[macro_use]
   3    extern crate quote;
   4    extern crate syn;
   5
   6    use proc_macro::TokenStream;
   7
   8    // HelloWorld is the name for the derive
   9    // hello_world_name is the name of our optional attribute
   10   #[proc_macro_derive(HelloWorld, attributes(hello_world_name))]
   11   pub fn hello_world(input: TokenStream) -> TokenStream {
   12       // Construct a string representation of the type definition
   13       let s = input.to_string();
   ```

```
14      // Parse the string representation into an abstract syntax
           tree
15      let ast = syn::parse_derive_input(&s).expect("Failed to
        parse the source into an AST");
16
17      // Build the implementation
18      let gen = impl_hello_world(&ast);
19
20      // Return the generated implementation
21      gen.parse()
22        .expect("Failed to parse the AST generated from deriving
           from HelloWorld")
23    }
24
25    fn impl_hello_world(ast: &syn::DeriveInput) -> quote::Tokens {
26      let identifier = &ast.ident;
27      // Use the name provided by the attribute
28      // If there is no attribute, use the identifier
29      let hello_world_name =
        get_name_attribute(ast).unwrap_or_else(||
        identifier.as_ref());
30      quote! {
31        // Insert an implementation for our trait
32        impl HelloWorld for #identifier {
33          fn hello_world() {
34            println!(
35              "The struct or enum {} says: \"Hello world from
                 {}!\"",
36              stringify!(#identifier),
37              #hello_world_name
38            );
39          } //end of fn hello_world()
40        } //end of impl HelloWorld
41      } //end of quote
42    } //end of fn impl_hello_world
43
44    fn get_name_attribute(ast: &syn::DeriveInput) -> Option<&str>
      {
45      const ATTR_NAME: &str = "hello_world_name";
46
47      // Go through all attributes and find one with our name
48      if let Some(attr) = ast.attrs.iter().find(|a| a.name() ==
        ATTR_NAME) {
49        // Check if it's in the form of a name-value pair
50        if let syn::MetaItem::NameValue(_, ref value) = attr.value
           {
51          // Check if the value is a string
52          if let syn::Lit::Str(ref value_as_str, _) = *value {
```

```
53              Some(value_as_str)
54            } else {
55                panic!(
56                  "Expected a string as the value of {}, found {:?}
                     instead",
57                   ATTR_NAME, value
58                );
59            }
60        } else {
61            panic!(
62              "Expected an attribute in the form #[{} = \"Some
                 value\"]",
63               ATTR_NAME
64            );
65        }
66    } else {
67        None
68    }
69  }
```

6. In the original `Cargo.toml` file of this chapter, add the following to the `[dependencies]`:

   ```
   custom-derive = { path = "custom-derive" }
   ```

7. In the `bin` folder, create a file called `custom_derive.rs`.

8. Add the following code and run it with `cargo run --bin custom_derive`:

```
1   #[macro_use]
2   extern crate chapter_five_derive;
3
4   // trait definitions have to be in "consumer" crate
5   trait HelloWorld {
6     // This method will send a friendly greeting
7     fn hello_world();
8   }
9
10  // thanks to the code in the custom_derive crate
11  // we can derive from HelloWorld in order to provide
12  // an automatic implementation for the HelloWorld trait
13  #[derive(HelloWorld)]
14  struct Switzerland;
15
16  #[derive(HelloWorld)]
17  struct Britain;
18
19  #[derive(HelloWorld)]
```

```
20    // We can use an optional attribute to change the message
21    #[hello_world_name = "the Land Down Under"]
22    struct Australia;
23
24    fn main() {
25      Switzerland::hello_world();
26      Britain::hello_world();
27      Australia::hello_world();
28    }
```

# How it works...

The instructions for this recipe are a bit more complex than the others, as we need to manage two separate crates. If your code doesn't compile, compare your version with the one used in the book at https://github.com/SirRade/rust-standard-library-cookbook/tree/master/chapter_five. We need to separate the code into two crates because providing a custom derive requires creating a procedural macro, as indicated by all of the instances of proc_macro in the code. A procedural macro is Rust code that runs alongside the compiler and interacts directly with it. Because of the special nature and unique restrictions of such code, it needs to be in a separate crate that is annotated with the following:

```
[lib]
proc-macro = true
```

This crate is typically named after the main crate with the _derive suffix added. In our example, the main crate is called chapter_five, so the crate providing the procedural macro is called chapter_five_derive.

In our example, we are going to create a derived version of good, old Hello World: a struct or enum deriving from HelloWorld will implement the HelloWorld trait, providing a hello_world() function with a friendly greeting containing its own name. Additionally, you can specify a HelloWorldName attribute to alter the message.

The code in custom.rs should be self-explanatory. We begin by importing our derivation crate [2] where we need to include the #[macro_use] attribute in order to actually import the procedural macros. We then define our HelloWorld trait [5] and proceed to derive it on a bunch of structures [13, 16 and 19], just like we would with built-in derives such as Debug or Clone. Australia gets a custom message via the HelloWorldName attribute. Lastly, in the main function, we call the generated hello_world() function.

Let's take a look at `chapter-five-derive/src/lib.rs` now. Procedural macro crates typically begin by importing the `proc_macro`, `quote`, and `syn` crates. Attentive readers will have noticed that we didn't add the `proc_macro` to our `[dependencies]` section in the crate's `Cargo.toml`. We didn't need to because this special support crate is provided by the standard Rust distribution.

The `quote` crate provides the `quote!` macro, which lets us translate Rust code into tokens that the compiler can use. The really useful feature of this macro is that it supports code interpolation of a variable by writing a # in front of it. This means that when we write the following, the value inside the `struct_name` variable is interpreted as Rust code:

```
impl HelloWorld for #struct_name { ... }
```

If `struct_name` has the `Switzerland` value, the following code will be generated:

```
impl HelloWorld for Switzerland { ... }
```

The `syn` crate is a Rust parser built upon the `nom` parser combinator framework (`https://github.com/Geal/nom`), which you should check out as well if you're thinking about writing a parser. In fact, some of the crates used in `Chapter 4`, *Serialization*, are written with `nom`, too. Back on track, `syn` parses the code annotated by your custom attributes or derives and lets you work with the generated abstract syntax tree.

The convention for a custom derive is to create a function with the name of the derive in `snake_case` (`pub fn hello_world`, in our case) that parses the annotated code and then calls a function that generates the new code. The second function typically has the name of the first one, prefixed with `impl`. In our code, this is `fn impl_hello_world`.

In a `proc_macro` crate, only functions tagged with `proc_macro_derive` are allowed to be published. The consequence of this is, by the way, that we are not able to move our `HelloWorld` trait into this crate; it wouldn't be allowed to be `pub`.

The `proc_macro_derive` annotation requires you to specify which name will be used for the derive (`HelloWorld` for us) and which attributes it allows. If we didn't want to accept the `HelloWorldName` attribute, we could simply omit the entire attributes section and annotate our function like this:

```
#[proc_macro_derive(HelloWorld)]
```

Because `hello_world` hooks itself directly into the compiler, it both accepts and returns a `TokenStream`, which is the compiler-internal representation of Rust code. We start by turning the `TokenStream` back into a `String` in order to be parsed again by `syn`. This is not an expensive action, as the `TokenStream` we receive from the compiler is not the entire program, but only the part annotated by our custom derive. For example, the `String` behind the `TokenStream` of the first `struct` annotated by `HelloWorld` is simply the following:

```
struct Switzerland;
```

We then parse the said string with `syn::parse_derive_input(&s)`, which basically tells `syn` that the code we want to parse is a `struct` or `enum` that is deriving something.

We then generate the code with the following:

```
let gen = impl_hello_world(&ast);
```

Then we convert it back into a `TokenStream` with this:

```
gen.parse()
```

The `TokenStream` is then injected back into the code by the compiler. As you can see, a procedural macro cannot change existing code, but only analyze it and generate additional code.

Here is the process described in `hello_world`:

1. Convert the `TokenStream` into a `String`
2. Parse the `String` with `syn`
3. Generate an implementation of another method
4. Parse the implementation back into a `TokenStream`

It is very typical for a custom derive. You can reuse the code presented in nearly all basic procedural macros.

Let's move on to `impl_hello_world` now. With the help of the `ast` passed, we can analyze the annotated structure. The `ident` member, which stands for *identifier*, tells us the name of the `struct` or `enum`. For instance, in the first struct that derives from `HelloWorld`, this is the "Switzerland" string.

We then decide which name to use in the greeting with the help of
the `get_name_attribute` little helper function, which we will look at in a moment. It
returns the value of the `HelloWorldName` attribute if it has been set. If not, we default to
the `identifier`, converted to a string via `as_ref`[29]. How this is done is explained in the
next recipe.

Finally, we create some `quote::Tokens` by writing the implementation and surrounding it
with `quote!`. Notice again how we interpolate variables into the code by writing # in front
of it. Additionally, while printing, we surround `#identifier` with `stringify!`, which
turns an identifier into a string. We don't need to do this with `#hello_world_identifier`
because it already holds a string. To understand why this is needed, let's look at the code
that would be generated for the `Switzerland` struct if we *didn't* include `stringify!`:

```
impl HelloWorld for Switzerland {
    fn hello_world() {
        println!(
            "The struct or enum {} says: \"Hello world from {}!\"",
            Switzerland,
            "Switzerland"
        );
    }
}
```

Try it out for yourself, and you will be greeted with an error message stating that
something along the lines of "`Switzerland` cannot be formatted with the
default formatter". This is because we are not printing the "`Switzerland`" string, but
instead trying to print the concept of the `Switzerland` struct itself, which is clearly
nonsense. To fix this, we just need to make sure that the interpolated variable is surrounded
by quotes ("), which is exactly what `stringify!` does.

Let's look at the final piece of the puzzle now: `get_name_attribute`. This function might
look a little intimidating at first. Let's go through it step by step:

```
if let Some(attr) = ast.attrs.iter().find(|a| a.name() == ATTR_NAME) {
... }
```

Here we'll go through all available attributes and search for one named
"`HelloWorldName`". If we don't find any, the function call already ends by returning `None`.
Otherwise, we continue with the following line:

```
if let syn::MetaItem::NameValue(_, ref value) = attr.value { ... }
```

`syn::MetaItem` is simply how `syn` calls attributes. This line is necessary because there are many ways to write attributes in Rust. For example, a `syn::MetaItem::Word` can be written like `#[foo]`. An example for `syn::MetaItem::List` is `#[foo(Bar, Baz, Quux)]`. `#[derive(...)]` itself also a `syn::MetaItem::List`. We, however, are only interested in `syn::MetaItem::NameValue`, which is an attribute in the form of `#[foo = Bar]`. If the `HelloWorldName` attribute is not in this form, we `panic!` with a message explaining what the problem is. A `panic` in procedural macro results in a compiler error. You can verify this by replacing `#[HelloWorldName = "the Land Down Under"` in `custom.rs` with `#[HelloWorldName]`.

Contrary to normal programs, because of procedural macros `panic!` at compile time, it's okay for them to `panic!` often. When doing so, remember that errors originating from other crates are very nasty to debug, doubly so in any kind of macros, so it's incredibly important to write the error messages as explicitly as possible.

The last check we need to do is on the value of `HelloWorldName`. As we are going to print it, we want to accept only strings:

```
if let syn::Lit::Str(ref value_as_str, _) = *value { ... }
```

On success, we return the string. Otherwise, we again `panic!` with an error message detailing the problem.

# There's more...

If you ran into trouble while running this recipe, you can use David Tolney's `cargo-expand` (`https://github.com/dtolnay/cargo-expand`) to show you how the compiler expanded your `proc_macros`. It's a really useful tool to debug your macros, so be sure to check it out.

The reason behind the two-crate restriction is historical and only temporary. In the beginning, there was only one way to define macros, `macro_rules!`. People with exotic needs, who were ready to put in the effort, were (and still are) able to extend their programs by directly hooking into the Rust compiler itself. Crates written this way are called *compiler plugins*. Of course, this is incredibly unstable because every minor Rust release can break your plugin, but people kept on doing it because it gave them one big advantage, custom derives. The core team reacted to the increased demand for language extensibility by deciding to launch `macros2.0` at some point in the future, bringing an overhaul to the entire macro system and many additional features, such as namespacing macros.

As they saw that most of the plugins were used only for custom derives, they also decided to bridge the time until `macros2.0` with `macros1.1`, which are also called *procedural macros*. Stabilizing the small subset of the compiler that is needed to create custom derives. The only problem was that crates now had parts that ran normally and parts that ran at compile time instead. Mixing them proved difficult to implement and a bit chaotic, so the two-crate system of moving all procedural macro code into a `-derive` crate was created. This is the system used in this recipe, as at the time of writing, `macros2.0` has not been stabilized yet. I encourage you to take a look at the current progress: `https://github.com/rust-lang/rust/issues/39412`.

If by the time you read this book, `macros2.0` has been released, you should update your knowledge about how to write modern custom derives.

# Converting types into each other

Having dedicated types is great, but true flexibility can only come when these types can easily be converted from and into each other. Luckily, Rust provides this functionality quite literally through the `From` and `Into` traits, along with some friends.

# How to do it...

1. In the `bin` folder, create a file called `conversion.rs`.

2. Add the following code and run it with `cargo run --bin conversion`:

```
1    use std::ops::MulAssign;
2    use std::fmt::Display;
3
4    // This structure doubles all elements it stores
5    #[derive(Debug)]
6    struct DoubleVec<T>(Vec<T>);
7
8
9    // Allowing conversion from a Vec<T>,
10   // where T is multipliable with an integer
11   impl<T> From<Vec<T>> for DoubleVec<T>
12   where
13   T: MulAssign<i32>,
14   {
15       fn from(mut vec: Vec<T>) -> Self {
```

```
16        for elem in &mut vec {
17          *elem *= 2;
18        }
19        DoubleVec(vec)
20      }
21   }
22
23   // Allowing conversion from a slice of Ts
24   // where T is again multipliable with an integer
25   impl<'a, T> From<&'a [T]> for DoubleVec<T>
26   where
27   T: MulAssign<i32> + Clone,
28   {
29     fn from(slice: &[T]) -> Self {
30       // Vec<T: MulAssign<i32>> automatically
31       // implements Into<DoubleVec<T>>
32       slice.to_vec().into()
33     }
34   }
35
36   // Allowing conversion from a &DoubleVec<T> to a &Vec<T>
37   impl<T> AsRef<Vec<T>> for DoubleVec<T> {
38     fn as_ref(&self) -> &Vec<T> {
39       &self.0
40     }
41   }
42
43
44   fn main() {
45     // The following three are equivalent
46     let hello_world = "Hello World".to_string();
47     let hello_world: String = "Hello World!".into();
48     let hello_world = String::from("Hello World!");
49
50     // Vec<u8> implements From<&str>
51     // so hello_world_bytes has the value b"Hello World!"
52     let hello_world_bytes: Vec<u8> = "Hello World!".into();
53     let hello_world_bytes = Vec::<u8>::from("Hello World!");
54
55     // We can convert a Vec<T: MulAssign<i32>> into a DoubleVec
56     let vec = vec![1, 2, 3];
57     let double_vec = DoubleVec::from(vec);
58     println!("Creating a DoubleVec from a Vec: {:?}",
             double_vec);
59
60     // Vec<T: MulAssign<i32>> automatically implements
            Into<DoubleVec<T>>
61     let vec = vec![1, 2, 3];
```

```
62      let double_vec: DoubleVec<_> = vec.into();
63      println!("Converting a Vec into a DoubleVec: {:?}",
        double_vec);
64
65      // A reference to DoubleVec can be converted to a reference
            to Vec
66      // Which in turn dereferences to a slice
67      print_elements(double_vec.as_ref());
68
69      // The standard library provides From<T> for Option<T>
70      // You can design your API in an ergonomic way thanks to
this
71      easy_public_func(Some(1337), Some(123), None);
72      ergonomic_public_func(1337, 123, None);
73   }
74
75
76   fn print_elements<T>(slice: &[T])
77   where
78   T: Display,
79   {
80     for elem in slice {
81       print!("{} ", elem);
82     }
83     println!();
84   }
85
86
87   // Easily written but cumbersome to use
88   fn easy_public_func(foo: Option<i32>, bar: Option<i32>, baz:
     Option<i32>) {
89     println!(
90       "easy_public_func = foo: {:?}, bar: {:?}, baz: {:?}",
91        foo,
92        bar,
93        baz
94     );
95   }
96
97
98   // This is quite some extra typing, so it's only worth to do
         for
99   // public functions with many optional parameters
100  fn ergonomic_public_func<Foo, Bar, Baz>(foo: Foo, bar: Bar,
     baz: Baz)
101  where
102  Foo: Into<Option<i32>>,
103  Bar: Into<Option<i32>>,
```

```
104   Baz: Into<Option<i32>>,
105   {
106     let foo: Option<i32> = foo.into();
107     let bar: Option<i32> = bar.into();
108     let baz: Option<i32> = baz.into();
109
110     println!(
111       "ergonomic_public_func = foo: {:?}, bar: {:?}, baz: {:?}",
112       foo,
113       bar,
114       baz
115     );
116   }
```

# How it works...

The most important trait for conversion is From. Implementing it means defining how to obtain a type *from* another.

We present this on the example of DoubleVec[6]. Its concept is simple, when you construct it out of a Vec, it doubles all its elements. For this purpose, we implement From<Vec<T>> [11] with a where clause specifying T: MulAssign<i32>[13], which means that the trait will be implemented for all types that can be assigned to the result of a multiplication with an integer. Or, in terms of code, all types that allow the following, assuming the t variable is of the T type:

```
t *= 2;
```

The actual implementation should be self-explanatory, we simply multiply every element in the vector by two and wrap it in our DoubleVec[19]. Afterwards, we implement From as well for slices of the same type [25].

It is considered good practice to extend all of your trait definitions that work with vectors ( Vec<T> ) to also work with slices (&[T]). This way, you gain generality and performance, as you can operate on direct references to arrays (such as &[1, 2, 3]) and ranges of other vectors (vec[1..3]) without converting them first. This best practice carries over to functions as well, where you should always accept a slice of your type (as shown with print_elements()), if possible, for the same reasons.

In this implementation, however, we see something interesting:

```
fn from(slice: &[T]) -> Self {
    slice.to_vec().into()
}
```

`slice.to_vec()` simply converts the slice into a vector. But what's up with `.into()`? Well, it comes from the `Into` trait, which is the opposite of the `From` trait, it converts a type *into* another. But how does a `Vec` know how to turn into a `DoubleVec`?

Let's take a look at the standard library's implementation of `Into` at `https://github.com/rust-lang/rust/blob/master/src/libcore/convert.rs`, where we find the following lines:

```
// From implies Into
impl<T, U> Into<U> for T where U: From<T>
{
    fn into(self) -> U {
        U::from(self)
    }
}
```

Aha! According to this, every `T` type that implements `From` for `U` automatically lets `U` implement `Into` for `T`. And sure enough because we implemented `From<Vec<T>>` for `DoubleVec<T>`, we automatically also implemented `Into<DoubleVec<T>>` for `Vec<T>`. Let's look at our code from before again:

```
fn from(slice: &[T]) -> Self {
    slice.to_vec().into()
}
```

The slice gets turned into a `Vec`, which implements `Into` for `DoubleVec`, among many others. Because our function signature says that we return `Self`, Rust knows which `Into` implementation to use, as only one of them returns `DoubleVec` as well.

Another useful trait for type conversion is `AsRef`. Its only function, `as_ref`, is nearly identical to `into`, but instead of moving itself into another type, it takes a reference to itself and returns a reference to another type. In a way, it *translates* references. You can expect this operation to be cheap in most cases, as it typically just returns a reference to an internal object. In fact, you have already used this method in the last recipe:

```
let hello_world_name = get_name_attribute(ast).unwrap_or_else(||
identifier.as_ref());
```

`identifier` internally holds a `String` of its name. The compiler knows that `hello_world_name` has to be a `&str`, as the return type of `get_name_attribute(ast)` is `Option<&str>` and we are trying to unwrap it with a default value. Based on this information, `as_ref()` tries to return a `&str`, which it can, as the only implementation of `AsRef` for `identifier` that returns a `&str` is the one that returns a reference to the aforementioned `String` that holds its name.

We are only implementing `AsRef` for `Vec`, and not for a slice, because of a reference to a vector (`&Vec<T>`) with automatically deref-coerce into a slice (`&[T]`), which means we automatically implement it. You can read more about the concept of deref coercion at `https://doc.rust-lang.org/book/second-edition/ch15-02-deref.html#implicit-deref-coercions-with-functions-and-methods`.

`AsRef` also has a brother called `AsMut`, which is identical but operates on mutable references. We intentionally didn't implement it in this example, as we don't want users messing with the internal state of `DoubleVec`. In general, you should be very conservative with this trait as well, as excessive access to the internals of anything can quickly become very chaotic.

The `main` function contains some examples of converting types. A popular example is the conversion from `&str` to `String` in lines [46 to 48]. Interestingly, `&str` can also be converted into a vector of its underlying bytes [52 and 53]. Let's look at how our `DoubleVec` can be converted in the same way.

The next line showcases how the `&Vec<i32>` returned by `double_vec.as_ref()` seamlessly behaves like an `&[i32]`, as `print_elements()` only accepts slices [67]:

```
print_elements(double_vec.as_ref());
```

The last part of the recipe is about API design. There is a little implementation of `From` in the standard library that reads:

```
impl<T> From<T> for Option<T> {
    fn from(val: T) -> Option<T> {
        Some(val)
    }
}
```

This means that every type can be converted into an `Option`. You can use this trick, as showcased in the implementation of `ergonomic_public_func` [100], to make functions with multiple parameters of the `Option` type easier to use and look at, as you can see by comparing the following two function calls [71 and 72]:

```
easy_public_func(Some(1337), Some(123), None);
ergonomic_public_func(1337, 123, None);
```

However, because some extra typing is required to achieve this, it's okay if you only do this on functions that are part of your API, that is, available to users of your crate. If you want to read some more tips about clean API design in Rust, check out Rust core developer Pascal Hertleif's excellent blog entry: `https://deterministic.space/elegant-apis-in-rust.html`.

# Boxing data

The first smart pointer we are going to look at is the `Box`. This very special type is the analogue to C++'s `unique_ptr`, a pointer to data stored on the heap that deletes said data automatically when it's out of scope. Because of the shift from stack to heap, `Box` can allow you some flexibility by intentionally losing type information.

# How to do it...

1. In the `bin` folder, create a file called `boxing.rs`.

2. Add the following code and run it with `cargo run --bin boxing`:

```
1    use std::fs::File;
2    use std::io::BufReader;
3    use std::result::Result;
4    use std::error::Error;
5    use std::io::Read;
6    use std::fmt::Debug;
7
8    #[derive(Debug)]
9    struct Node<T> {
10       data: T,
11       child_nodes: Option<(BoxedNode<T>, BoxedNode<T>)>,
12   }
13   type BoxedNode<T> = Box<Node<T>>;
14
```

```
15    impl<T> Node<T> {
16      fn new(data: T) -> Self {
17        Node {
18          data,
19          child_nodes: None,
20        }
21      }
22
23      fn is_leaf(&self) -> bool {
24        self.child_nodes.is_none()
25      }
26
27      fn add_child_nodes(&mut self, a: Node<T>, b: Node<T>) {
28        assert!(
29          self.is_leaf(),
30          "Tried to add child_nodes to a node that is not a leaf"
31        );
32        self.child_nodes = Some((Box::new(a), Box::new(b)));
33      }
34    }
35
36    // Boxes enable you to use traditional OOP polymorph
37    trait Animal: Debug {
38      fn sound(&self) -> &'static str;
39    }
40
41    #[derive(Debug)]
42    struct Dog;
43    impl Animal for Dog {
44      fn sound(&self) -> &'static str {
45        "Woof!"
46      }
47    }
48
49    #[derive(Debug)]
50    struct Cat;
51    impl Animal for Cat {
52      fn sound(&self) -> &'static str {
53        "Meow!"
54      }
55    }
56
57    fn main() {
58      let mut root = Node::new(12);
59      root.add_child_nodes(Node::new(3), Node::new(-24));
60      root.child_nodes
61        .as_mut()
62        .unwrap()
```

```
63        0
64          .add_child_nodes(Node::new(0), Node::new(1803));
65      println!("Our binary tree looks like this: {:?}", root);
66
67      // Polymorphism
68      let mut zoo: Vec<Box<Animal>> = Vec::new();
69      zoo.push(Box::new(Dog {}));
70      zoo.push(Box::new(Cat {}));
71      for animal in zoo {
72        println!("{:?} says {}", animal, animal.sound());
73      }
74
75      for word in caps_words_iter("do you feel lucky, punk?") {
76        println!("{}", word);
77      }
78
79      // Assuming a file called number.txt exists
80      let num = read_file_as_number("number.txt").expect("Failed
        read the file as a number");
81      println!("number.txt contains the number {}", num);
82
83      // Dynamically composing functions
84      let multiplier = create_multiplier(23);
85      let result = multiplier(3);
86      println!("23 * 3 = {}", result);
87    }
88
89    // Via trait objects we can return any iterator
90    fn caps_words_iter<'a>(text: &'a str) -> Box<Iterator<Item =
      String> + 'a> {
91      // Return an iterator over every word converted into
        ALL_CAPS
92      Box::new(text.trim().split(' ').map(|word|
        word.to_uppercase()))
93    }
94
95    // Same goes for errors
96    fn read_file_as_number(filename: &str) -> Result<i32,
      Box<Error>> {
97      let file = File::open(filename)?;
98      let mut buf_reader = BufReader::new(file);
99      let mut content = String::new();
100     buf_reader.read_to_string(&mut content)?;
101     let number: i32 = content.parse()?;
102     Ok(number)
103   }
104
105   fn create_multiplier(a: i32) -> Box<Fn(i32) -> i32> {
```

```
106     Box::new(move |b| a * b)
107  }
```

# How it works...

The first thing that we are going to explore are recursive types, that is, a type that contains itself. This cannot be done directly, as the compiler needs to know in advance how much space a type requires. Consider the following `struct`:

```
struct Foo {
    bar: i32
}
```

The compiler will ask itself, `How much space does it take to create a Foo?` and see that it needs just enough space to hold an `i32`. And how much does an `i32` need? Exactly 32 bits. Now, consider the following:

```
struct Foo {
    bar: i32,
    baz: Foo,
}
```

How much space does `Foo` need? Enough to hold an `i32` and a `Foo`. How much is an `i32`? 32 bits. And `Foo`? Enough to hold an `i32` and a `Foo`. And how much does that `Foo` take? Enough for a `Foo`, and so on, until the heat death of the universe. Clearly, we don't want to spend that long on compiling. Let's take a look at the solution to our problem:

```
struct Foo {
    bar: i32,
    baz: Box<Foo>,
}
```

One last time, how big is `Foo`? Enough to hold an `i32` and a `Foo`. How big is an `i32`? 32 bits. How big is a `Box<Foo>`? Just as big as a box of any other type, namely 64 bit. Every `Box` will always have the same size, as they are all the same thing, a pointer to some type in the heap. This way, we resolved our problem, as the compiler now knows the exact size of the type at compile time and is happy. And because it is happy, we are happy.

In our code example, we illustrate one possible use case for a recursive type, a naive binary tree implementation [9]. In case you didn't know, a binary tree consists of a clump of data, which is called a *node*, that can be connected to either zero or two other *child nodes*. A node that is connected to zero nodes is a *leaf*. In our example, we build such a tree that will look like this:

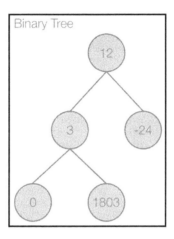

We implement it as a `struct Node` that contains any data and optionally a pair of `BoxedNode`, which is just an alias for `Box<Node>`.

A real binary tree implementation that is optimized for speed will be a little bit more complex than our example. While the concept of recursion fits very nicely into a binary tree, it is rather inefficient to store every node separately somewhere in the heap. Real implementations will instead just appear to be recursive for the user but internally store the nodes in a `Vec<Node>`. This way, the nodes profit from speed gains by simply being allocated in a continuous memory block, as this will optimize caching. Rust's `BTreeMap` and `BTreeSet` follow this concept as well.

A binary tree is an excellent kind of data structure for data traversal. You can read about some of its biggest use cases at the following StackOverflow answer by Danny Pflughoeft: `https://stackoverflow.com/questions/2130416/what-are-the-applications-of-binary-trees#2200588`.

The next thing that a `Box` enables us to do is classic polymorphism how you will recognize it from other languages. For this, we prepare a trait called `Animal` [37] that has a method to produce a `sound()`. Its implementor, `Dog` [42], will produce `"Woof!"` [45] and the `Cat` [50] implementor will produce `"Meow!"` [53]. Our goal is to store both a `Dog` and a `Cat` in a `Vec` of `Animal`. We can do this by creating a so-called *trait object*. It is created by a `Box` of a trait, like in our example in the following line:

```
let mut zoo: Vec<Box<Animal>> = Vec::new();
```

This way, we intentionally erase type information from the actual type in the `Box`. The compiler no longer knows which type is in the `Box`, only that it implements `Animal`, which is all that it needs to know. As you can see by running the code, the Rust runtime will still execute the correct functions and give the `Dog` and the `Cat` different sounds.

With the same mechanism, we can return a trait object of `Iterator` [90]:

```
fn caps_words_iter<'a>(text: &'a str) -> Box<Iterator<Item = String> +
'a> { ... }
```

This way, we can mix and match iterators inside `caps_words_iter()` without caring for the exact return type, so long as it implements `Iterator`, which they all do. Remember that we can't just return `Iterator` directly without any `Box` around it, as we cannot return a trait. A trait object, however, is completely fine.

On we go to `read_file_as_number()` [96]. This method reads a file and returns the content parsed as an `i32`. This file will not be generated for you, so you will have to either download it from our GitHub repo or manually create a file called `number.txt` that contains a number, say `777`. From the signature, you can gather that this time we are boxing the `Error`. This lets us mix the error type returned. Indeed, this method does return two different kinds of errors: `std::io::Error` and `std::num::ParseIntError`.

The last thing that we are going to look at is how to return closures with `create_multiplier()` [105]. As all closures implement either `Fn`, `FnOnce`, and/or `FnMut`, we can return a trait object for them. This way, we can create, compose, and change functions at runtime, just like with functional languages.

# There's more...

You might have noticed that returning a `Box<Iterator>` or a `Box<Error>` comes at a small cost in terms of efficiency, as it requires moving an object onto the heap without it having any reason to go there. There are currently two ways around this.

For `Box<Error>`, you should instead create an own `Error` type, combining all the possible errors that can be returned from your function. This is detailed in `Chapter 6`, *Handling Errors; Providing user-defined Error types*.

For `Box<Iterator>`, you can analyze the compiler's output in order to find out the exact true type that you're returning. This works for small iterators, but any complex iterator will take a long time to crack. Because this situation is not really desirable, the Rust team has approved the introduction of *abstract types*, which will be introduced in `Chapter 10`, *Using Experimental Nightly Features; Returning abstract types* because it has not yet hit stable Rust.

# See also

- *Providing user-defined error types* recipe in `Chapter 6`, *Handling Errors*
- *Returning abstract types* recipe in `Chapter 10`, *Using Experimental Nightly Features*

# Sharing ownership with smart pointers

Some ownership relationships are not as straightforward as *type A owns B*. Sometimes, an entire group of types owns another type. To handle this, we need another smart pointer that behaves mostly like `Box` but only deletes the underlying resource if no one needs it anymore, it is `Rc`, which stands for Reference Counted.

# How to do it...

1. In the `bin` folder, create a file called `shared.rs`

2. Add the following code and run it with `cargo run --bin shared`:

```
1    use std::rc::Rc;
2
3    // The ball will survive until all kids are done playing with
         it
4    struct Kid {
5      ball: Rc<Ball>,
6    }
7    struct Ball;
8
9    fn main() {
10     {
11       // rc is created and count is at 1
12       let foo = Rc::new("foo");
13       // foo goes out of scope; count decreases
14       // count is zero; the object gets destroyed
15     }
16
17     {
18       // rc is created and count is at 1
19       let bar = Rc::new("bar");
20       // rc is cloned; count increases to 2
21       let second_bar = Rc::clone(&bar);
22       // bar goes out of scode; count decreases to 1
23       // bar goes out of scode; count decreases to 0
24     }
25
26     {
27       // rc is created and count is at 1
28       let baz = Rc::new("baz");
29       {
30         // rc is cloned; count increases to 2
31         let second_baz = Rc::clone(&baz);
32         // second_baz goes out of scode; count decreases to 1
33       }
34       // baz goes out of scode; count decreases to 0
35     }
36     let kid_one = spawn_kid_with_new_ball();
37     let kid_two = Kid {
38       ball: Rc::clone(&kid_one.ball),
39     };
40     let kid_three = Kid {
41       ball: Rc::clone(&kid_one.ball),
42     };
43     // ball lives until here
44   }
```

```
45
46   fn spawn_kid_with_new_ball() -> Kid {
47     let ball = Rc::new(Ball);
48     Kid {
49       ball: Rc::clone(&ball),
50     }
51     // Although the ball goes out of scope here, the object
         behind it
52
53     // will survive as part of the kid
54   }
```

# How it works...

The heart and soul of an Rc is its internal counter of how many objects own it at the moment. Every time the Rc is cloned, it increases by one, and every time one of its clones go out of scope, it decreases by one. The moment this counter reaches zero, the objects behind the Rc are destroyed. The main method contains some annotated examples of values the counter reaches during its lifetime to help you understand how the mechanism works.

The effect of the simple rules presented is that a resource behind an Rc will only be deleted once it's no longer used, at the slim cost of a very small runtime performance loss because of the ongoing counting. This *delayed deletion* effect is ideal for resources that are shared between objects. Simply wrap them in an Rc and they will make sure that everything survives long enough. This is the equivalent of shared_ptr in C++.

# There's more...

In one edge case, reference counts can cause a *memory leak*, that is, accidentally preventing resources from ever being deleted. This happens when two objects exist that both contain an Rc pointing to each other. Because of this circular dependence, none of them will stop using the other and so the two objects will continue existing and pointing at each other long after your code has stopped using them. The solution here is to pick the weaker link in the hierarchy and replace its Rc for a Weak, which contains a *non-owning reference* instead. Because this situation is fairly rare, however, we are not going to look at it in detail. Instead, simply remember the possibility of a memory leak and come back to read this again when it arises.

Rc is inherently singlethreaded. If you need its functionality in a multithreaded environment (such as the one we are going to explore in Chapter 7, *Parallelism and Rayon; Sharing resources in multithreaded closures*), you can use Arc instead. It stands for Atomically Reference Counted and behaves the same way as Rc.

## See also

- *Sharing resources in multithreaded closures* recipe in Chapter 7, *Parallelism and Rayon*

# Working with interior mutability

Although Rust's borrow checker is one of its biggest selling points, alongside its clever error-handling concept and impressive tooling, it cannot read minds yet. Sometimes you might have to take things into your own hands and borrow objects manually. This is done with the concept of *interior mutability*, which states that certain types can wrap objects while being non-mutable and still operate on them mutably.

## How to do it...

1. In the bin folder, create a file called interior_mutability.rs.

2. Add the following code and run it with cargo test --bin interior_mutability:

```
1    trait EmailSender {
2        fn send_mail(&self, msg: &Email) -> Option<String>;
3    }
4
5    #[derive(Debug, Clone)]
6    struct Email {
7        from: String,
8        to: String,
9        msg: String,
10   }
11
12   #[derive(Debug)]
13   struct Customer {
```

```
14      address: String,
15      wants_news: bool,
16    }
17
18    // Send news to every customer that wants to receive them
19    fn publish_news(msg: &str, sender: &EmailSender, customers: &
      [Customer]) -> Option<i32> {
20      let mut count = 0;
21      let mut mail = Email {
22      from: "Rust Newsletter".to_string(),
23      to: "".to_string(),
24      msg: msg.to_string(),
25    };
26    for customer in customers {
27      if !customer.wants_news {
28        continue;
29      }
30      mail.to = customer.address.to_string();
31      if sender.send_mail(&mail).is_none() {
32        return None;
33      }
34      count += 1;
35    }
36    Some(count)
37  }
38
39    fn main() {
40    // No code running as we are concentrating on the tests
instead
41    }
42
43
44    #[cfg(test)]
45    mod tests {
46      use super::*;
47      use std::cell::RefCell;
48
49      struct MockEmailSender {
50        // sent_mails can be modified even if MockEmailSender is
            immutable
51        sent_mails: RefCell<Vec<Email>>,
52      }
53      impl MockEmailSender {
54        fn new() -> Self {
55          MockEmailSender {
56            sent_mails: RefCell::new(Vec::new()),
57          }
58        }
```

```
59      }
60
61      impl EmailSender for MockEmailSender {
62      fn send_mail(&self, msg: &Email) -> Option<String> {
63        // Borrow sent_mails mutably
64        self.sent_mails.borrow_mut().push(msg.clone());
65        Some("200 OK".to_string())
66      }
67    }
68
69    #[test]
70    fn sends_zero_to_zero_customers() {
71      let sent = publish_news("hello world!",
         &MockEmailSender::new(), &[]);
72      assert_eq!(Some(0), sent);
73    }
74
75    #[test]
76    fn sends_one_to_one_willing() {
77      let customer = Customer {
78        address: "herbert@herbert.com".to_string(),
79        wants_news: true,
80      };
81      let sent = publish_news("hello world!",
         &MockEmailSender::new(), &[customer]);
82      assert_eq!(Some(1), sent);
83    }
84
85  #[test]
86    fn sends_none_to_unwilling() {
87      let customer_one = Customer {
88        address: "herbert@herbert.com".to_string(),
89        wants_news: false,
90      };
91      let customer_two = Customer {
92        address: "michael@jackson.com".to_string(),
93        wants_news: false,
94      };
95      let sent = publish_news(
96        "hello world!",
97         &MockEmailSender::new(),
98         &[customer_one, customer_two],
99      );
100     assert_eq!(Some(0), sent);
101    }
102
103    #[test]
104    fn sends_correct_mail() {
```

```
105        let customer = Customer {
106           address: "herbert@herbert.com".to_string(),
107           wants_news: true,
108        };
109        let sender = MockEmailSender::new();
110        publish_news("hello world!", &sender, &
           [customer]).expect("Failed to send mail");
111
112        // Borrow sent_mails immutable
113        let mails = sender.sent_mails.borrow();
114        assert_eq!(1, mails.len());
115        assert_eq!("Rust Newsletter", mails[0].from);
116        assert_eq!("herbert@herbert.com", mails[0].to);
117        assert_eq!("hello world!", mails[0].msg);
118     }
119 }
```

# How it works...

The protagonist of this recipe is `RefCell`, a wrapper around any type that moves the borrow checker's rule enforcement from compile time to runtime. The basics are pretty easy, you borrow the underlying value immutably by calling `.borrow()` and borrow it mutably by calling `.borrow_mut()`. If you don't follow the golden rule of only having multiple readers or one single writer at the same time, the program goes into `panic!`. One application for this is making members of your structs mutable even though your struct itself is immutable. The best use case to show where this is useful is mocking, the art of faking infrastructure for testing purposes.

The idea of our example is as follows, we want to send a newsletter to every customer that is interested. For that, we have the `EmailSender` trait[1], which just specifies a method to send an `Email` and return a response[2]. It's good practice to try to define functionality through traits in order to mock them.

Our `publish_news` function [19] takes a message, an `EmailSender` and a slice of `Customer` (please don't imagine that literally), and sends the message to all customers who want to receive news. If it encounters an error, it returns `None`[32], otherwise, it returns the number of newsletters it sent [36].

You probably don't want to send an email to your customers every time you test your code, which is why we create `MockEmailSender`[49] inside the test configuration, which doesn't actually send anything but instead stores all mail in a `Vec` [64]. In order to do this, it needs to modify its member despite being immutable. That's exactly what `RefCell` is for! Thanks to this, we can efficiently test `publish_news()`, as we can access all messages it would have sent and compare them with what we expect.

## There's more...

There are many types that use interior mutability. Among them are `Cell`, which, instead of handing out references, simply copies the value it stores. This is nice when storing primitive types such as `i32` or `bool`, as they all implement copy anyway.

Others are `RwLock` and `Mutex`, which are important for parallelism, as we shall see in their recipes in `Chapter 7`, *Parallelism and Rayon; Access resources in parallel with RwLocks*.

## See also

- *Access resources in parallel with RwLocks* recipe in `Chapter 7`, *Parallelism and Rayon*

# 6
# Handling Errors

In this chapter, we will cover the following recipes:

- Providing user-defined error types
- Providing logging
- Creating a custom logger
- Implementing the Drop trait
- Understanding RAII

## Introduction

Mistakes happen, and that's okay. We are only human after all. The important thing in life and in programming is not which errors we make, but how we deal with them. Rust helps us with the programming aspect of this principle by providing us with an error handling concept that guarantees that we *have* to think about the consequences of failure when dealing with functions that can fail, as they don't return a value directly but wrapped in a `Result` that has to be opened somehow. The only thing left is designing our code in a way that integrates nicely with this concept.

## Providing user-defined error types

In the previous chapters, we learned about a few ways to handle functions that have to deal with different kinds of errors. So far, we have:

- Simply panicked when encountering them

- Returned only one kind of error and converted all others into it
- Returned different kinds of errors in a `Box`

Most of these have been used because we didn't reach this recipe yet. Now, we are going to learn about the preferred way of doing things, creating a custom kind of `Error` that contains multiple sub-errors.

# How to do it...

1. Create a Rust project to work on during this chapter with `cargo new chapter-six`.

2. Navigate to the newly created `chapter-six` folder. For the rest of this chapter, we will assume that your command line is currently in this directory.

3. Inside the folder `src`, create a new folder called `bin`.

4. Delete the generated `lib.rs` file, as we are not creating a library.

5. In the folder `src/bin`, create a file called `custom_error.rs`.

6. Add the following code and run it with `cargo run --bin custom_error`:

```
1   use std::{error, fmt, io, num, result};
2   use std::fs::File;
3   use std::io::{BufReader, Read};
4
5   #[derive(Debug)]
6   // This is going to be our custom Error type
7   enum AgeReaderError {
8     Io(io::Error),
9     Parse(num::ParseIntError),
10    NegativeAge(),
11  }
12
13  // It is common to alias Result in an Error module
14  type Result<T> = result::Result<T, AgeReaderError>;
15
16  impl error::Error for AgeReaderError {
17    fn description(&self) -> &str {
18      // Defer to the existing description if possible
19      match *self {
20      AgeReaderError::Io(ref err) => err.description(),
21      AgeReaderError::Parse(ref err) => err.description(),
22      // Descriptions should be as short as possible
23      AgeReaderError::NegativeAge() => "Age is negative",
24      }
```

```
25     }
26
27     fn cause(&self) -> Option<&error::Error> {
28       // Return the underlying error, if any
29       match *self {
30         AgeReaderError::Io(ref err) => Some(err),
31         AgeReaderError::Parse(ref err) => Some(err),
32         AgeReaderError::NegativeAge() => None,
33       }
34     }
35   }
36
37   impl fmt::Display for AgeReaderError {
38     fn fmt(&self, f: &mut fmt::Formatter) -> fmt::Result {
39       // Write a detailed description of the problem
40       match *self {
41         AgeReaderError::Io(ref err) => write!(f, "IO error: {}",
            err),
42         AgeReaderError::Parse(ref err) => write!(f, "Parse
            error: {}", err),
43         AgeReaderError::NegativeAge() => write!(f, "Logic error:
            Age cannot be negative"),
44       }
45     }
46   }
47
48   // Implement From<T> for every sub-error
49   impl From<io::Error> for AgeReaderError {
50     fn from(err: io::Error) -> AgeReaderError {
51     AgeReaderError::Io(err)
52     }
53   }
54
55   impl From<num::ParseIntError> for AgeReaderError {
56     fn from(err: num::ParseIntError) -> AgeReaderError {
57     AgeReaderError::Parse(err)
58     }
59   }
60
61   fn main() {
62     // Assuming a file called age.txt exists
63     const FILENAME: &str = "age.txt";
64     let result = read_age(FILENAME);
65     match result {
66       Ok(num) => println!("{} contains the age {}", FILENAME,
            num),
67       Err(AgeReaderError::Io(err)) => eprintln!("Failed to open
            the file {}: {}", FILENAME, err),
```

```
68        Err(AgeReaderError::Parse(err)) => eprintln!(
69          "Failed to read the contents of {} as a number: {}",
70           FILENAME, err
71           ),
72        Err(AgeReaderError::NegativeAge()) => eprintln!("The age in
          the file is negative"),
73        }
74    }
75
76  // Read an age out of a file
77  fn read_age(filename: &str) -> Result<i32> {
78    let file = File::open(filename)?;
79    let mut buf_reader = BufReader::new(file);
80    let mut content = String::new();
81    buf_reader.read_to_string(&mut content)?;
82    let age: i32 = content.trim().parse()?;
83    if age.is_positive() {
84      Ok(age)
85    } else {
86      Err(AgeReaderError::NegativeAge())
87    }
88  }
```

# How it works...

The purpose of our example is to read a file, `age.txt`, and return the number written in it, assuming that it represents some kind of age. We can encounter three errors during this process:

- Failure to read the file (maybe it doesn't exist)
- Failure to read its content as a number (it could contain text as well)
- The number could be negative

These possible error states are the possible variants of our `Error enum`: `AgeReaderError`[7]. It is usual to name the variants after the sub-errors they represent. Because a failure to read the file raises an `io::Error`, we name our corresponding variant `AgeReaderError::Io`[8]. A failure to parse a `&str` as an `i32` raises a `num::ParseIntError`, so we name our encompassing variant `AgeReaderError::Parse`[9].

These two `std` errors show the naming convention of errors neatly. If you have many different errors that can be returned by a module, export them via their full name, such as `num::ParseIntError`. If your module only returns one kind of `Error`, simply export it as `Error`, such as `io::Error`. We intentionally don't follow this convention in the recipe because the distinct name `AgeReaderError` makes it easier to talk about it. If this recipe was included, one for one, in a crate, we could achieve the conventional effect by exporting it as `pub type Error = AgeReaderError;`.

The next thing we create is an alias for our own `Result`[14]:

```
type Result<T> = result::Result<T, AgeReaderError>;
```

This is an extremely common pattern for your own errors, which makes working with them a charm, as we see in the return type of `read_age`[77]:

```
fn read_age(filename: &str) -> Result<i32> { ... }
```

Looks nice, doesn't it? In order to use our `enum` as an `Error` though, we need to implement it first [16]. The `Error` trait requires two things: a `description`[17], which is a short explanation of what went wrong, and a `cause`[27], which is simply a *redirection* to the underlying error, if any. You can (and should) provide a detailed description of the problem at hand by also implementing `Display` for your `Error`[37]. In all of these implementations, you should refer to the underlying error if possible, as with the following line [20]:

```
AgeReaderError::Io(ref err) => err.description()
```

The last thing you need to provide for a good own `Error` is a `From` implementation for every sub-error. In our case this would be `From<io::Error>`[49] and `From<num::ParseIntError>`[55]. This way, the `try` operator (?) will automatically convert the involved errors for us.

After implementing all necessary traits, you can return the custom `Error` from any function and unwrap values in it with the aforementioned operator. In this example, when checking the result of `read_age`, we didn't have to `match` the returned value. In a real `main` function, we would probably just call `.expect("...")` on it, but we matched the individual error variants anyway to show you how nicely you can react to different problems when using known error types [65 to 73]:

```
match result {
    Ok(num) => println!("{} contains the age {}", FILENAME, num),
    Err(AgeReaderError::Io(err)) => eprintln!("Failed to open the file
```

```
        {}: {}", FILENAME, err),
        Err(AgeReaderError::Parse(err)) => eprintln!(
            "Failed to read the contents of {} as a number: {}",
            FILENAME, err
        ),
        Err(AgeReaderError::NegativeAge()) => eprintln!("The age in the
    file is negative"),
    }
```

# There's more...

A crate's `Error` is usually put inside an own `error` module for organizational reasons and then exported directly for optimal usability. The relevant `lib.rs` entries would look like this:

```
mod error;
pub use error::Error;
```

# Providing logging

In a big application, things will sooner or later not go as planned. But that's okay, as long as you have provided a system for your users to know what went wrong and, if possible, why. One time-tested tool to accomplish this is detailed logs that let the user specify for themselves how much diagnosis they want to see.

# How to do it...

Follow these steps:

1. Open the `Cargo.toml` file that has been generated earlier for you.

2. Under `[dependencies]`, add the following line:

```
log = "0.4.1"
env_logger = "0.5.3"
```

3. If you want, you can go to log's (https://crates.io/crates/log) or env_logger's (https://crates.io/crates/env_log) crates.io pages to check for the newest version and use that one instead.

4. In the folder `bin`, create a file called `logging.rs`.

5. Add the following code and run it with `RUST_LOG=logging cargo run --bin logging` if you're on a Unix-based system. Otherwise, run `$env:RUST_LOG="logging"; cargo run --bin logging` on Windows:

```
1    extern crate env_logger;
2    #[macro_use]
3    extern crate log;
4    use log::Level;
5
6    fn main() {
7        // env_logger's priority levels are:
8        // error > warn > info > debug > trace
9        env_logger::init();
10       // All logging calls log! in the background
11       log!(Level::Debug, "env_logger has been initialized");
12
13       // There are convenience macros for every logging level
             however
14       info!("The program has started!");
15
16       // A log's target is its parent module per default
17       // ('logging' in our case, as we're in a binary)
18       // We can override this target however:
19       info!(target: "extra_info", "This is additional info that
             will only show if you \
20       activate info level logging for the extra_info target");
21
22       warn!("Something that requires your attention happened");
23
24       // Only execute code if logging level is active
25       if log_enabled!(Level::Debug) {
26       let data = expensive_operation();
27       debug!("The expensive operation returned: \"{}\"", data);
28       }
29
30       error!("Something terrible happened!");
31   }
32
33   fn expensive_operation() -> String {
34       trace!("Starting an expensive operation");
35       let data = "Imagine this is a very very expensive
             task".to_string();
36       trace!("Finished the expensive operation");
37       data
38   }
```

# How it works...

Rust's logging system is based on the `log` crate, which provides a common *facade* for all things logging. This means that it doesn't actually provide any functionality, just the interface. The implementation is left to other crates, `env_logger` in our case. This split into facade and implementation is pretty useful, as anyone can create a cool new way of logging stuff which is automatically compatible with any crate.

 The choice of logging implementation used should be up to the consumer of your code. If you write a crate, don't use any implementation but simply log all things via the `log` crate only. Your (or someone else's) executable that uses the crate can then simply initialize their logger of choice[9] in order to actually process the log calls.

The `log` crate provides the `log!` macro[11], which accepts a log `Level`, a message that can be formatted the same way as in `println!`, and an optional `target`. You could log stuff like this, but it's more readable to use the convenience macros for every logging level, `error!`, `warn!`, `info!`, `debug!`, and `trace!`, which all simply call `log!` in the background. A log's `target`[19] is an additional property that helps the logger implementation group the logs thematically. If you omit the `target`, it defaults to the current `module`. So, for example, if you logged something from the `foo` crate, its `target` would default to `foo`. If you logged something in its submodule `foo::bar`, its `target` would default to `bar`. If you then consumed the crate in a `main.rs` and logged something there, its `target` would default to `main`.

Another goodie that `log` provides is the `log_enabled!` macro, which returns whether or not the currently active logger is set to process a certain warning level. This is especially useful in combination with `Debug` logs that provide useful information at the cost of an expensive operation.

`env_logger` is a logger implementation provided by the Rust nursery. It prints its logs on `stderr` and uses pretty colors for different logging levels if supported by your Terminal. It relies on a `RUST_LOG` envvar to filter which logs should be displayed. If you don't define said variable, it will default to `error`, which means that it will print only the log level `error` from all targets. As you can guess, other possible values include `warn`, `info`, `debug`, and `trace`. These will, however, not only filter the specified level, but all levels *above* it as well, where the hierarchy is defined like this:

```
error > warn > info > debug > trace
```

This means that setting your RUST_LOG to warn will show all warn and all error logs. Setting it to debug will show error, warn, info, and debug.

Instead of error levels, you can set RUST_LOG to targets, which will show all logs of the selected targets regardless of their log levels. This is what we do in our example, we set RUST_LOG to logging in order to show all logs with a target called logging, which is the standard target for all logs in our binary. If you wanted, you could combine a level filter with a target filter like this: logging=warn, which would only show warn and error logs with a target of logging.

You can combine different filters with a comma. If you want all logs of this example to be displayed, you can set your variable to logging,extra_info, which filters for both the targets logging and extra_info.

Lastly, you can filter your logs by content with a slash (/), after which you can write down a regex that has to be matched. If you set RUST_LOG to logging=debug/expensive for instance, only logs with the logging level of debug and upwards with the target of logging that also contain the word expensive will be displayed.

Wow, that's a lot of configuration! I advise you to experiment a bit with the different filtering modes and run the example in order to get a feeling for how the parts fit together. If you need additional information, all possibilities for the value of RUST_LOG in the current version of env_logger are documented at https://docs.rs/env_logger/.

# There's more...

If you've never worked with a logger before, you might wonder what the difference between certain log levels is. Of course, you can use them for whatever purpose you want, but the following conventions are usual for loggers in many languages:

| Log level | Usage | Example |
| --- | --- | --- |
| Error | Some major problem occurred that might terminate the program soon. If the application is a service that should always run, a system administrator should immediately be notified. | The connection to the database has been broken. |
| Warn | An issue that's not severe or has an automatic workaround has happened. Someone should check this out at some point and fix it. | A user's configuration file contains unrecognized options that have been ignored. |

| | | |
|---|---|---|
| Info | Some information that might be useful to look at at a later point. This logs normal conditions. | The user has started or stopped a process. A default value has been used because no configuration has been provided. |
| Debug | Information that is helpful to programmers or sysadmins when trying to fix a problem. Contrary to many other languages, a debug log is *not* removed in release builds. | The parameters passed to a major function. The current state of the application at various points. |
| Trace | Very low-level signals of control flow that are only useful to a programmer trying to chase a bug. Allows the reconstruction of a stack trace. | The parameters of a minor helper function. The beginning and end of a function. |

Many languages also contain a `Fatal` log level. In Rust, a good old `panic!()` is used for that. If you want to log your panics in some special way as well, you can replace the usual reaction to a panic by simply printing it to `stderr` by calling `std::panic::set_hook()` with whatever functionality you want. An example of what this might look like is as follows:

```
std::panic::set_hook(Box::new(|e| {
    println!("Oh noes, something went wrong D:");
    println!("{:?}", e);
}));
panic!("A thing broke");
```

A good alternative to `env_logger` is the `slog` crate, which provides excellent extensible structured logging at the cost of a steepened learning curve. Plus, its output looks pretty. If that sounds interesting, be sure to check it out at `https://github.com/slog-rs/slog`.

# Creating a custom logger

Sometimes you or your users might have very specific logging needs. In this recipe, we are going to learn how to create a custom logger to work with the `log` crate.

# How to do it...

1. Open the `Cargo.toml` file that was generated earlier for you.

2. Under `[dependencies]`, if you didn't do so in the last recipe, add the following line:

```
log = "0.4.1"
```

If you want, you can go to log's crates.io page (`https://crates.io/crates/log`) to check for the newest version and use that one instead.

3. In the folder `bin`, create a file called `custom_logger.rs`.

4. Add the following code and run it with `RUST_LOG=custom_logger cargo run --bin custom_logger` if you're on a Unix-based system. Otherwise, run `$env:RUST_LOG="custom_logger"; cargo run --bin custom_logger` on Windows:

```
1    #[macro_use]
2    extern crate log;
3
4    use log::{Level, Metadata, Record};
5    use std::fs::{File, OpenOptions};
6    use std::io::{self, BufWriter, Write};
7    use std::{error, fmt, result};
8    use std::sync::RwLock;
9    use std::time::{SystemTime, UNIX_EPOCH};
10
11   // This logger will write logs into a file on disk
12   struct FileLogger {
13     level: Level,
14     writer: RwLock<BufWriter<File>>,
15   }
16
17   impl log::Log for FileLogger {
18     fn enabled(&self, metadata: &Metadata) -> bool {
19       // Check if the logger is enabled for a certain log level
20       // Here, you could also add own custom filtering based on
          targets or regex
21       metadata.level() <= self.level
22     }
23
24     fn log(&self, record: &Record) {
25       if self.enabled(record.metadata()) {
26         let mut writer = self.writer
```

```
27              .write()
28              .expect("Failed to unlock log file writer in write
                  mode");
29          let now = SystemTime::now();
30          let timestamp = now.duration_since(UNIX_EPOCH).expect(
31            "Failed to generate timestamp: This system is
              operating before the unix epoch",
32          );
33          // Write the log into the buffer
34          write!(
35            writer,
36            "{} {} at {}: {}\n",
37            record.level(),
38            timestamp.as_secs(),
39            record.target(),
40            record.args()
41          ).expect("Failed to log to file");
42        }
43      self.flush();
44    }
45
46    fn flush(&self) {
47      // Write the buffered logs to disk
48      self.writer
49        .write()
50        .expect("Failed to unlock log file writer in write
                mode")
51        .flush()
52        .expect("Failed to flush log file writer");
53    }
54  }
55
56  impl FileLogger {
57    // A convenience method to set everything up nicely
58    fn init(level: Level, file_name: &str) -> Result<()> {
59      let file = OpenOptions::new()
60        .create(true)
61        .append(true)
62        .open(file_name)?;
63      let writer = RwLock::new(BufWriter::new(file));
64      let logger = FileLogger { level, writer };
65      // set the global level filter that log uses to optimize
            ignored logs
66      log::set_max_level(level.to_level_filter());
67      // set this logger as the one used by the log macros
68      log::set_boxed_logger(Box::new(logger))?;
69      Ok(())
70    }
```

```
71  }
```

This is the custom error used in our logger:

```
73   // Our custom error for our FileLogger
74   #[derive(Debug)]
75   enum FileLoggerError {
76     Io(io::Error),
77     SetLogger(log::SetLoggerError),
78   }
79
80   type Result<T> = result::Result<T, FileLoggerError>;
81   impl error::Error for FileLoggerError {
82     fn description(&self) -> &str {
83       match *self {
84         FileLoggerError::Io(ref err) => err.description(),
85         FileLoggerError::SetLogger(ref err) =>
            err.description(),
86       }
87     }
88
89     fn cause(&self) -> Option<&error::Error> {
90       match *self {
91         FileLoggerError::Io(ref err) => Some(err),
92         FileLoggerError::SetLogger(ref err) => Some(err),
93       }
94     }
95   }
96
97   impl fmt::Display for FileLoggerError {
98     fn fmt(&self, f: &mut fmt::Formatter) -> fmt::Result {
99       match *self {
100        FileLoggerError::Io(ref err) => write!(f, "IO error: {}",
            err),
101        FileLoggerError::SetLogger(ref err) => write!(f, "Parse
             error: {}", err),
102      }
103    }
104  }
105
106  impl From<io::Error> for FileLoggerError {
107    fn from(err: io::Error) -> FileLoggerError {
108      FileLoggerError::Io(err)
109    }
110  }
111
112  impl From<log::SetLoggerError> for FileLoggerError {
113    fn from(err: log::SetLoggerError) -> FileLoggerError {
```

```
114       FileLoggerError::SetLogger(err)
115   }
116 }
```

Initializing and using the logger:

```
118 fn main() {
119   FileLogger::init(Level::Info, "log.txt").expect("Failed to
        init
        FileLogger");
120   trace!("Beginning the operation");
121   info!("A lightning strikes a body");
122   warn!("It's moving");
123   error!("It's alive!");
124   debug!("Dr. Frankenstein now knows how it feels to be god");
125   trace!("End of the operation");
126 }
```

# How it works...

Our `FileLogger` will, as the name suggests, log things to a file. It also accepts a maximum logging level on initialization.

You should not get used to directly logging things on a disk. As stated by *The Twelve-Factor App guidelines* (`https://12factor.net/logs`), logs should be treated as event streams, in the form of a raw dump to `stdout`. The production environment can then route all log streams to their final destination over `systemd` or a dedicated log router such as `Logplex` (`https://github.com/heroku/logplex`) or `Fluentd` (`https://github.com/fluent/fluentd`). These will then decide if the logs should be sent to a file, an analysis system like `Splunk` (`https://www.splunk.com/`), or a data warehouse like `Hive` (`http://hive.apache.org/`).

Every logger needs to implement the `log::Log` trait, which consists of the `enabled`, `log`, and `flush` methods. `enabled` should return if a certain log event is accepted by the logger. Here, you can go wild with whatever filtering logic you want [18]. This method is never called directly by `log`, so its only purpose is to serve you as a helper method inside of the `log` method, which we are going to discuss shortly. `flush` [46] is treated the same way. It should apply whatever changes you have buffered in your logging, but it is never called by `log`.

In fact, if your logger doesn't interact with the filesystem or the network, it will probably simply implement `flush` by doing nothing:

```
fn flush(&self) {}
```

The real bread and butter of the `Log` implementation is the `log` method[24], though, as it is called whenever a logging macro is invoked. The implementation typically starts with the following line, followed by the actual logging and a finishing call to `self.flush()`[25]:

```
if self.enabled(record.metadata()) {
```

Our actual logging then consists of simply writing a combination of the current logging level, Unix timestamp, target, and logging message to the file and flushing it afterward.

Technically speaking, our call to `self.flush()` should be inside the `if` block as well, but that would require additional scope around the mutably borrowed `writer` in order to not borrow it twice. Because this is not relevant to the underlying lesson here, as in, how to create a logger, we placed it outside the block in order to make the example more readable. By the way, the way we borrow `writer` from an `RwLock` is the subject of the *Accessing resources in parallel with RwLocks* in `Chapter 8`, *Parallelism and Rayon*. For now, it's enough to know that an `RwLock` is a `RefCell` that is safe to use in a parallel environment such as a logger.

After implementing `Log` for `FileLogger`, the user can use it as the logger called by `log`. To do that, the user has to do two things:

- Tell `log` which log `Level` is going to be the maximum accepted by our logger via `log::set_max_level()` [66]. This is needed because `log` optimizes `.log()` calls on our logger away during runtime if they use log levels over our maximum level. The function accepts a `LevelFilter` instead of a `Level`, which is why we have to convert our level with `to_level_filter()` first [66]. The reason for this type is explained in the *There's more...* section.
- Specify the logger with `log::set_boxed_logger()` [68]. `log` accepts a box because it treats its logger implementation as a trait object, which we discussed in the *Boxing data* section of `Chapter 5`, *Advanced Data Structures*. If you want a (very) minor performance gain, you can also use `log::set_logger()`, which accepts a `static` which you would have to create via the `lazy_static` crate first. See `Chapter 5`, *Advanced Data Structures*, and the recipe *Creating lazy static objects*, for more on that.

This is conventionally done in a provided `.init()` method on the logger, just like with `env_logger`, which we implement in line [58]:

```
fn init(level: Level, file_name: &str) -> Result<()> {
    let file = OpenOptions::new()
        .create(true)
        .append(true)
        .open(file_name)?;
    let writer = RwLock::new(BufWriter::new(file));
    let logger = FileLogger { level, writer };
    log::set_max_level(level.to_level_filter());
    log::set_boxed_logger(Box::new(logger))?;
    Ok(())
}
```

While we're on it, we can also open the file in the same method. Other possibilities include letting the user pass a `File` directly to `init` as a parameter or, for maximum flexibility, making the logger a generic one that accepts any stream implementing `Write`.

We then return a custom error created in the lines that follow [74 to 116].

An example initialization of our logger might look like this [119]:

```
FileLogger::init(Level::Info, "log.txt").expect("Failed to init
FileLogger");
```

# There's more...

For simplicity's sake, `FileLogger` doesn't discriminate against any targets. A more sophisticated logger, like `env_logger`, can set different logging levels on different targets. For this purpose, `log` provides us with the `LevelFilter` enum, which has an `Off` state that corresponds to *no logging enabled for this target*. If you need to create such a logger, be sure to remember said enum. You can get some inspiration about how to implement target-based filters by looking at the source code of `env_logger` at `https://github.com/sebasmagri/env_logger/blob/master/src/filter/mod.rs`.

 In a really user-friendly logger, you'll want to display the timestamp in the user's own local time. For all things related to time measurement, time zones, and dates, check out the `chrono` crate at `https://crates.io/crates/chrono`.

# See also

- *Boxing data* recipe in Chapter 5, *Advanced Data Structures*
- *Creating lazy static objects* recipe in Chapter 5, *Advanced Data Structures*
- *Accessing resources in parallel with RwLocks* recipe in Chapter 7, *Parallelism and Rayon*

# Implementing the Drop trait

Where traditional object-oriented languages have destructors, Rust has the Drop trait, which consists of a single drop function that is called whenever a variable's lifetime has ended. By implementing it, you can perform whatever cleanup or advanced logging is necessary. You can also automatically free resources via RAII, as we're going to see in the next recipe.

# How to do it...

1. In the folder bin, create a file called drop.rs.

2. Add the following code and run it with cargo run --bin drop:

```
1    use std::fmt::Debug;
2
3    struct CustomSmartPointer<D>
4    where
5    D: Debug,
6    {
7    data: D,
8    }
9
10   impl<D> CustomSmartPointer<D>
11   where
12   D: Debug,
13   {
14       fn new(data: D) -> Self {
15       CustomSmartPointer { data }
16       }
17   }
18
19   impl<D> Drop for CustomSmartPointer<D>
```

```
20   where
21   D: Debug,
22   {
23     // This will automatically be called when a variable is
          dropped
24     // It cannot be called manually
25     fn drop(&mut self) {
26     println!("Dropping CustomSmartPointer with data `{:?}`",
          self.data);
27     }
28   }
29
30   fn main() {
31     let a = CustomSmartPointer::new("A");
32     let b = CustomSmartPointer::new("B");
33     let c = CustomSmartPointer::new("C");
34     let d = CustomSmartPointer::new("D");
35
36     // The next line would cause a compiler error,
37     // as destructors cannot be explicitly called
38     // c.drop();
39
40     // The correct way to drop variables early is the following:
41     std::mem::drop(c);
42   }
```

# How it works...

This example, adapted with slight changes from the second edition of the Rust book (`https://doc.rust-lang.org/book/second-edition/`), shows you how to start the implementation of a custom smart pointer. In our case, all it does is print the `Debug` information of the data stored when its dropped [26]. We do this by implementing the `Drop` trait with its single `drop` function [25], which the compiler automatically calls whenever a variable is dropped. All smart pointers are implemented this way.

The moment of a variable drop will nearly always be when it leaves its scope. For this reason, we cannot call the `drop` function directly[38]. The compiler will still call it when it exits its scope, so the cleanup will happen twice, resulting in undefined behavior. If you need to drop a variable early, you can tell the compiler to do so for you by calling `std::mem:drop` on it [41].

Variables that exit their scope are dropped in a **LIFO** way: **Last In, First Out**. That means that the last variable to be declared will be the first one to be dropped. If we allocate the variables a, b, c, and d in exactly that order, they will be dropped in the order d, c, b, a. In our example, we drop c early[41], so our order becomes c, d, b, a instead.

# There's more...

Do you want to know how a sophisticated low-level function like `std::mem::drop` is implemented:

```
pub fn drop<T>(_x: T) { }
```

That's right, it does nothing! The reason this works is that it takes T by value, moving it into the function. The function does nothing and all its owned variables go out of scope. Hurray for Rust's borrow checker!

# See also

- *Boxing data* recipe in `Chapter 5`, *Advanced Data Structures*.
- *Sharing ownership with smart pointers* recipe in `Chapter 5`, *Advanced Data Structures*.

# Understanding RAII

We can go one step further than simple destructors. We can create structs that can give the user temporary access to some resource or functionality and automatically revoke it again when the user is done. This concept is called **RAII**, which stands for **Resource Acquisition Is Initialization**. Or, in other words, the validity of a resource is tied to the lifetime of a variable.

# How to do it...

Follow these steps:

1. Open the `Cargo.toml` file that was generated earlier for you.

2. In the folder `bin`, create a file called `raii.rs`.

3. Add the following code and run it with `cargo run --bin raii`:

```
1   use std::ops::Deref;
2
3   // This represents a low level, close to the metal OS feature that
4   // needs to be locked and unlocked in some way in order to be accessed
5   // and is usually unsafe to use directly
6   struct SomeOsSpecificFunctionalityHandle;
7
8   // This is a safe wrapper around the low level struct
9   struct SomeOsFunctionality<T> {
10    // The data variable represents whatever useful information
11    // the user might provide to the OS functionality
12    data: T,
13    // The underlying struct is usually not savely movable,
14    // so it's given a constant address in a box
15    inner: Box<SomeOsSpecificFunctionalityHandle>,
16  }
17
18  // Access to a locked SomeOsFunctionality is wrapped in a guard
19  // that automatically unlocks it when dropped
20  struct SomeOsFunctionalityGuard<'a, T: 'a> {
21    lock: &'a SomeOsFunctionality<T>,
22  }
23
24  impl SomeOsSpecificFunctionalityHandle {
25    unsafe fn lock(&self) {
26      // Here goes the unsafe low level code
27    }
28    unsafe fn unlock(&self) {
29      // Here goes the unsafe low level code
30    }
31  }
```

Now comes the implementations for the `struct`s:

```
33  impl<T> SomeOsFunctionality<T> {
34    fn new(data: T) -> Self {
35      let handle = SomeOsSpecificFunctionalityHandle;
36        SomeOsFunctionality {
37          data,
38          inner: Box::new(handle),
39        }
40    }
41
```

```
42    fn lock(&self) -> SomeOsFunctionalityGuard<T> {
43      // Lock the underlying resource.
44      unsafe {
45        self.inner.lock();
46      }
47
48      // Wrap a reference to our locked selves in a guard
49      SomeOsFunctionalityGuard { lock: self }
50    }
51  }
52
53  // Automatically unlock the underlying resource on drop
54  impl<'a, T> Drop for SomeOsFunctionalityGuard<'a, T> {
55    fn drop(&mut self) {
56      unsafe {
57        self.lock.inner.unlock();
58      }
59    }
60  }
61
62  // Implementing Deref means we can directly
63  // treat SomeOsFunctionalityGuard as if it was T
64  impl<'a, T> Deref for SomeOsFunctionalityGuard<'a, T> {
65    type Target = T;
66
67    fn deref(&self) -> &T {
68    &self.lock.data
69    }
70  }
```

And finally, the actual usage:

```
72  fn main() {
73    let foo = SomeOsFunctionality::new("Hello World");
74    {
75      // Locking foo returns an unlocked guard
76      let bar = foo.lock();
77      // Because of the Deref implementation on the guard,
78      // we can use it as if it was the underlying data
79      println!("The string behind foo is {} characters long",
       bar.len());
80
81      // foo is automatically unlocked when we exit this scope
82    }
83    // foo could now be unlocked again if needed
84  }
```

# How it works...

Well, that's a load of complicated code.

Let's start by introducing the structures that participate in this example:

- `SomeOsSpecificFunctionalityHandle` [6] stands for an unspecified feature of your operating system that operates on some data and is presumably unsafe to use directly. We assume this feature locks some resource of the operating system that needs to be unlocked again.
- `SomeOsFunctionality` [9] represents a safe wrapper around the feature, plus some data `T` that might be useful for it.
- `SomeOsFunctionalityGuard` [20] is an RAII guard created by using the `lock` function. When it is dropped, it will automatically unlock the underlying resource. Additionally, it can be directly used as if it was the data `T` itself.

These functions might look a bit abstract, as they don't do anything specific, but instead act on *some* unspecified OS feature. This is because most of the really useful candidates are already present in the standard library—see `File`, `RwLock`, `Mutex`, and so on. What's left are particularly domain-specific use cases when writing low-level libraries or dealing with some special, homemade resource that needs automatic unlocking. When you see yourself writing either, you will appreciate the elegance of RAII.

The implementation of the structs introduces some new concepts that might look a bit confusing if encountered for the first time. In the implementation of `SomeOsSpecificFunctionalityHandle`, we can spot some `unsafe` keywords [25, 28 and 44]:

```
impl SomeOsSpecificFunctionalityHandle {
    unsafe fn lock(&self) {
        // Here goes the unsafe low level code
    }
    unsafe fn unlock(&self) {
        // Here goes the unsafe low level code
    }
}
...
fn lock(&self) -> SomeOsFunctionalityGuard<T> {
    // Lock the underlying resource.
    unsafe {
        self.inner.lock();
    }
```

```
        // Wrap a reference to our locked selves in a guard
        SomeOsFunctionalityGuard { lock: self }
    }
```

Let's start with the unsafe block [44 to 46]:

```
    unsafe {
        self.inner.lock();
    }
```

The `unsafe` keyword tells the compiler to treat the previous block in a special way. It disables the borrow checker and lets you do all kinds of crazy stuff: dereference raw pointers like in C, modify a mutable static variable, and call unsafe functions. In return, the compiler doesn't give you any guarantees about it either. It might, for instance, access invalid memory, resulting in a **SEGFAULT**. If you want to read more about the `unsafe` keyword, check out its section in the second edition of the official Rust book at `https://doc.rust-lang.org/book/second-edition/ch19-01-unsafe-rust.html`.

Generally speaking, writing unsafe code should be avoided. It is, however, okay to do so when:

- You're writing some code that directly interfaces with the OS and you want to create a safe wrapper around the unsafe parts, which is what we are doing here
- You are absolutely 100% completely certain that what you're doing, in a very specific context, is actually not problematic, contrary to the compiler's opinion

If you're wondering why the `unsafe` block is empty, that's again because we are not using any actual OS resources in this recipe. If you wanted to use any, the code handling them would go in those two empty blocks.

The other use for the `unsafe` keyword is the following [25]:

```
    unsafe fn lock(&self) { ... }
```

This marks the function itself as unsafe, meaning that it can only be called inside `unsafe` blocks. Remember, calling `unsafe` code in a function doesn't make the function automatically unsafe because the function could be a safe wrapper around it.

Let's move on now from our hypothetical low-level implementation of `SomeOsSpecificFunctionalityHandle` to our realistic implementation of its safe wrapper, `SomeOsFunctionality`[33]. Its constructor comes with no surprises (see `Chapter 1`, *Learning the Basics* and the *Using the constructor pattern* recipe if you need a refresher on that):

```
fn new(data: T) -> Self {
    let handle = SomeOsSpecificFunctionalityHandle;
    SomeOsFunctionality {
        data,
        inner: Box::new(handle),
    }
}
```

We simply prepare the underlying OS functionality and store it with the user-provided data in our `struct`. We `Box` the handle because, as explained in a comment in the code earlier at lines [13 and 14], the low-level struct interfacing with the OS is often not safe to move. Because we don't want to restrict our user from moving our safe wrapper, however, we make the handle movable by putting in on the heap via a `Box`, which gives it a permanent address. What is then moved is simply the smart pointer pointing to the address. For more about that, read `Chapter 5`, *Advanced Data Structures* and the *Boxing data* recipe.

The actual wrapping takes place in the `lock` method:

```
fn lock(&self) -> SomeOsFunctionalityGuard<T> {
    // Lock the underlying resource.
    unsafe {
        self.inner.lock();
    }

    // Wrap a reference to our locked selves in a guard
    SomeOsFunctionalityGuard { lock: self }
}
```

When working with an actual OS feature or custom resource, you'll want to guarantee that `self.inner.lock()` is safe to call in this context before doing so, otherwise, the wrapper won't be safe. This is also where you can do interesting things with `self.data`, which you can potentially use in combination with the resource mentioned.

After locking our stuff up, we return a RAII guard with a reference to our structure [49] that will unlock our resource when it is dropped. Looking at the implementation of SomeOsFunctionalityGuard, you can see that we don't need to implement any kind of new function for it. We just need to implement two traits. We begin with Drop[54], which you have met in the previous recipe. Implementing it means that we can unlock the resource when the guard is dropped by accessing it through our reference to SomeOsFunctionality. Again, make sure to arrange the environment in a way that guarantees that self.lock.inner.unlock() is actually safe before calling it.

Since we are basically creating a kind of smart pointer to data, we can use the Deref trait [64]. Implementing Deref for B with a Target of A allows a reference to B to be dereferenced into A. Or in other, slightly less accurate words, it lets B act as if it was A. In our case, implementing Deref for SomeOsFunctionalityGuard with a Target of T means that we can use our guard as if it was the underlying data. Because this can cause great confusion to the user if implemented poorly, Rust advises you to only implement it on smart pointers and nothing else.

Implementing Deref is of course not mandatory for the RAII pattern, but can prove pretty useful, as we're going to see in a moment.

Let's look at how we can now use all of our fancy functions:

```
fn main() {
    let foo = SomeOsFunctionality::new("Hello World");
    {
        let bar = foo.lock();
        println!("The string behind foo is {} characters long",
        bar.len());
    }
}
```

The user should never have to use SomeOsSpecificFunctionalityHandle directly, as it's unsafe. Instead, he can construct an instance of SomeOsFunctionality, which he can pass around and store however he wants [73]. Whenever he needs to use the cool feature behind it, he can call lock in whatever scope he is in right now, and he will receive a guard that will clean up after him after the work is done [81]. Because he implemented Deref, he can use the guard directly as if it was the underlying data. In our example, data is a &str, so we can use the methods of str directly on our guard like we do in line [79] by calling .len() on it.

After this little scope ends, our guard calls `unlock` on the resource and, because `foo` independently still lives on, we can continue locking it again however much we want.

# There's more...

This example is tailored to be in line with the implementations of `RwLock` and `Mutex`. The only thing missing is an extra layer of indirection that has been omitted to not make this recipe even more complex. `SomeOsSpecificFunctionalityHandle` shouldn't contain actual implementations of `lock` and `unlock`, but instead, pass the calls onto a stored implementation that is specific to whatever OS you're using. For example, say you have a struct, `windows::SomeOsSpecificFunctionalityHandle`, for a Windows-based implementation and a struct, `unix::SomeOsSpecificFunctionalityHandle`, for a Unix-based implementation. `SomeOsSpecificFunctionalityHandle` should then, conditionally, depending on the operating system that is being run, pass its `lock` and `unlock` calls onto the correct implementations. These may have many more features. The Windows one could maybe have a `awesome_windows_thing()` function that might be useful to the unlucky Windows developer that needs it. The Unix implementation could have a `confusing_posix_thing()` function that does some very weird things that only Unix hackers would understand. The important thing is that our `SomeOsSpecificFunctionalityHandle` should represent a common interface of the implementations. In our case, that means that every supported OS has the ability to `lock` and `unlock` the resource in question.

# See also

- *Using the constructor pattern* recipe in `Chapter 1`, *Learning the Basics*
- *Boxing data* recipe in `Chapter 5`, *Advanced Data Structures*
- *Accessing resources in parallel with RwLocks* recipe in `Chapter 7`, *Parallelism and Rayon*

# 7
# Parallelism and Rayon

In this chapter, we will cover the following recipes:

- Parallelizing iterators
- Running two operations together
- Sending data across threads
- Sharing resources in multithreaded closures
- Accessing resources in parallel with RwLocks
- Atomically accessing primitives
- Putting it all together in a connection handler

## Introduction

There used to be a time when your code got faster every year automatically, as processors got better and better. But nowadays, as Herb Sutter famously stated, *The Free Lunch Is Over* (http://www.gotw.ca/publications/concurrency-ddj.htm). The age of not better, but more numerous processor cores arrived a long time ago. Not all programming languages are well suited for this radical change towards omnipresent concurrency.

Rust was designed with exactly this problem in mind. Its borrow checker makes sure that most concurrent algorithms work fine. It goes even further: your code won't even compile if it's not parallelizable, even if you don't yet use more than one thread. Because of these unique guarantees, one of Rust's main selling points has been dubbed *fearless concurrency*.

And we are about to find out why.

# Parallelizing iterators

Wouldn't it be cool to have a magic button that allowed you to just make any algorithm parallel, without you doing anything? Well, as long as your algorithm uses iterators, rayon is exactly that!

# How to do it...

1. Create a Rust project to work on during this chapter with cargo new chapter-seven.
2. Navigate into the newly-created chapter-seven folder. For the rest of this chapter, we will assume that your command line is currently in this directory.
3. Open the Cargo.toml file that has been generated for you.
4. Under [dependencies], add the following line:

   ```
   rayon = "1.0.0"
   ```

   If you want, you can go to rayon's crates.io page (https://crates.io/crates/rayon) to check for the newest version and use that one instead.

5. Inside the src folder, create a new folder called bin.
6. Delete the generated lib.rs file, as we are not creating a library.
7. In the src/bin folder, create a file called par_iter.rs.
8. Add the following code and run it with cargo run --bin par_iter:

   ```
   1   extern crate rayon;
   2   use rayon::prelude::*;
   3
   4   fn main() {
   5       let legend = "Did you ever hear the tragedy of Darth Plagueis
           The Wise?";
   6       let words: Vec<_> = legend.split_whitespace().collect();
   7
   8       // The following will execute in parallel,
   9       // so the exact order of execution is not foreseeable
   10  words.par_iter().for_each(|val| println!("{}", val));
   11
   12      // par_iter can do everything that a normal iterator does, but
   13      // in parallel. This way you can easily parallelize any
           algorithm
   14      let words_with_a: Vec<_> = words
   15          .par_iter()
   ```

```
16          .filter(|val| val.find('a').is_some())
17          .collect();
18
19      println!(
20          "The following words contain the letter 'a': {:?}",
21          words_with_a
22      );
23  }
```

# How it works...

rayon implements the trait ParallelIterator for every type that implements its standard library equivalent Iterator, which we got to know in Chapter 2, *Working with Collections; Access Collections as iterators*. In fact, you can use all the knowledge from said recipe again here. The methods provided by the ParallelIterator trait are nearly the same as the ones provided by Iterator, so in virtually all cases where you notice an iterator operation taking too long and bottlenecking you, you can simply replace .iter() with .par_iter() [10]. Similarly, for moving iterators, you can use .into_par_iter() instead of .into_iter().

rayon handles all the tedious work for you, as it automatically distributes the work evenly between all of your available cores. Just keep in mind that despite this magic, you're still dealing with parallelism here, so you have no guarantees about the order in which the items in your iterator are going to be handled, as evidenced by line [10], which will print in a different order each time you execute the program:

```
words.par_iter().for_each(|val| println!("{}", val));
```

# See also

- *Access collections as iterators* recipe in Chapter 2, *Working with Collections*

# Running two operations together

The parallel iterators from the last recipe are internally built upon a more fundamental function, `rayon::join`, which takes two closures and *potentially* runs them in parallel. This way, even the balance of performance gain versus the overhead of spawning a thread has been done for you.

If you have an algorithm that doesn't use iterators but still consists of some clearly separated parts that could benefit from running concurrently, consider using `rayon::join` for that.

# How to do it...

1. Open the `Cargo.toml` file that was generated earlier for you.

2. If you didn't do so in the last recipe, under `[dependencies]`, add the following line:

   ```
   rayon = "1.0.0"
   ```

3. If you want, you can go to `rayon`'s crates.io page (`https://crates.io/crates/rayon`) to check for the newest version and use that one instead.

4. In the folder `bin`, create a file called `join.rs`.

5. Add the following code and run it with `cargo run --bin join`:

```
1 extern crate rayon;
2
3  #[derive(Debug)]
4  struct Rectangle {
5    height: u32,
6    width: u32,
7  }
8
9  impl Rectangle {
10    fn area(&self) -> u32 {
11      self.height * self.width
12    }
13    fn perimeter(&self) -> u32 {
14      2 * (self.height + self.width)
15    }
16  }
```

```
17
18   fn main() {
19     let rect = Rectangle {
20         height: 30,
21         width: 20,
22     };
23     // rayon::join makes closures run potentially in parallel and
24     // returns their returned values in a tuple
25     let (area, perimeter) = rayon::join(|| rect.area(), ||
       rect.perimeter());
26     println!("{:?}", rect);
27     println!("area: {}", area);
28     println!("perimeter: {}", perimeter);
29
30     let fib = fibonacci(6);
31     println!("The sixth number in the fibonacci sequence is {}",
       fib);
32   }
33
34   fn fibonacci(n: u32) -> u32 {
35     if n == 0 || n == 1 {
36       n
37     } else {
38       // rayon::join can really shine in recursive functions
39       let (a, b) = rayon::join(|| fibonacci(n - 1), ||
fibonacci(n
            - 2));
40         a + b
41     }
42   }
```

# How it works...

rayon::join is pretty simple. It takes two closures, potentially runs them in parallel, and returns their returned values in a tuple [25]. Wait a second, did we just say *potentially*? Isn't it always better to run things in parallel?

Nope, at least not always. Sure, if you really care about things running together at all times without blocking, say a GUI and its underlying I/O where you definitely don't want the mouse cursor to freeze when opening a file, you always need to have all processes running in their own thread. But most applications for concurrency don't have this requirement. A big part of what makes concurrency so important is its ability to run code that would normally run sequentially (that is, one line after another) in parallel if required. Notice the choice of words here—*code that would normally run sequentially*. These kinds of algorithms do not inherently need concurrency, but they might get a boost out of it. Now comes the *potential* part—firing up a thread might not be worth it.

To understand why, let's look at the hardware side of things. We are not going to dive too deep into this territory because:

a) the fact that you're reading this book makes me think you're more of a software person and b) the exact mechanisms of CPUs tend to change very rapidly nowadays and we don't want the information provided here to be outdated in a year.

Your CPU divides its work among its *cores*. A core is the basic computation unit of the CPU. If the device you're reading this on is not made out of paper and younger than two decades, it most probably contains multiple cores. These kinds of cores are called *physical* and can work on different things at the same time. A physical core itself also has ways to perform multiple jobs. Some can divide themselves into multiple *logical* cores, splitting work further. For example, an Intel CPU can use *hyper-threading*, which means that if a program only uses the integer addition unit of a physical core, a virtual core might start working on the floating points addition unit for another program until the first one is done.

If you don't care about the available amount of cores and simply start new threads without limit, the operating system will start creating threads that don't actually run concurrently, because it ran out of cores. In this case, it will perform *context switching*, which means that it stores the current state of the thread, pauses it, works on another thread for a split second, and then resumes the thread again. As you can imagine, this costs quite some resources.

This is why if it's not vital to run two things in parallel, you should first check if there are any cores *idle* (that is, available) in the first place. Because `rayon::join` does this check for you; among other things, it will only run the two closures in parallel if it's actually worth it to do so. If you need to do this work yourself, check out the `num_cpus` crate (`https://crates.io/crates/num_cpus`).

By the way, the parallel iterators from the last recipe go even further: If the amount of elements and work in them is so small that it would cost more to initiate a new thread for them than to run it sequentially, they will automatically forego concurrency for you.

# There's more...

The underlying mechanism of `rayon` is *work stealing*. This means that when we call the following function, the current thread will immediately start working on a and place b in a queue:

```
rayon::join(a, b);
```

Meanwhile, whenever a core is idle, `rayon` will let it work on the next task in the queue. The new thread then *steals* the task from the others. In our case, that would be b. If a happens to finish before b, the main thread will look into the queue and try to steal work as well. The queue can contain more than two items if `rayon::join` is called multiple times in a recursive function.

The author of `rayon`, Niko Matsakis, wrote down the following pseudo Rust code to illustrate this principle in his introductory blog post at `http://smallcultfollowing.com/babysteps/blog/2015/12/18/rayon-data-parallelism-in-rust/`:

```
fn join<A,B>(oper_a: A, oper_b: B)
    where A: FnOnce() + Send,
          B: FnOnce() + Send,
{
    // Advertise `oper_b` to other threads as something
    // they might steal:
    let job = push onto_local_queue(oper_b);
    // Execute `oper_a` ourselves:
    oper_a();
    // Check whether anybody stole `oper_b`:
    if pop_from_local_queue(oper_b) {
        // Not stolen, do it ourselves.
        oper_b();
    } else {
        // Stolen, wait for them to finish. In the
        // meantime, try to steal from others:
        while not_yet_complete(job) {
            steal_from_others();
        }
        result_b = job.result();
    }
}
```

By the way, the recursive Fibonacci implementation provided in this example [34] is easy to look at and illustrates the point of using `rayon::join`, but is also really, really inefficient. To learn why, and how to improve on it, check out the `Chapter 10`, *Using Experimental Nightly Features; Benchmarking your code.*

## See also

- *Benchmarking your code* recipe in Chapter 10, *Using Experimental Nightly Features*

# Sharing resources in multithreaded closures

It's time to look at parallelism at a lower level, without any crates to help us. We will now check out how to share a resource across threads so that they all can work with the same object. This recipe will also serve as a refresher on manually creating threads, in case it's been a while since you learned about it.

## How to do it...

1. In the folder `bin`, create a file called `sharing_in_closures.rs`.

2. Add the following code and run it with `cargo run --bin sharing_in_closures`:

```
1   use std::thread;
2   use std::sync::Arc;
3
4   fn main() {
5     // An Arc ("Atomically Reference Counted") is used the exact
6     // same way as an Rc, but also works in a parallel context
7     let some_resource = Arc::new("Hello World".to_string());
8
9     // We use it to give a new thread ownership of a clone of the
          Arc
10    let thread_a = {
11      // It is very common to give the clone the same name as the
            original
12      let some_resource = some_resource.clone();
13      // The clone is then moved into the closure:
14      thread::spawn(move || {
15        println!("Thread A says: {}", some_resource);
16      })
17    };
18    let thread_b = {
19        let some_resource = some_resource.clone();
20        thread::spawn(move || {
21          println!("Thread B says: {}", some_resource);
```

```
22            })
23     };
24
25     // .join() blocks the main thread until the other thread is
done
26     thread_a.join().expect("Thread A panicked");
27     thread_b.join().expect("Thread B panicked");
28     }
```

# How it works...

A fundamental building block of parallelism in Rust is the Arc, which stands for **Atomically Reference Counted**. Functionally, it works the same way as an Rc, which we have looked at in Chapter 5, *Advanced Data Structures; Sharing ownership with smart pointers*. The only difference is that the reference counting is done using *atomic primitives*, which are versions of primitive data types like usize that have well-defined parallel interactions. This has two consequences:

- An Arc is slightly slower than an Rc, as the reference counting involves a bit more work
- An Arc can be used safely across threads

The constructor of Arc looks the same as Rc[7]:

```
let some_resource = Arc::new("Hello World".to_string());
```

This creates an Arc over a String. A String is a struct that is not inherently saved to be manipulated across threads. In Rust terms, we say that String is not Sync (more about that later in the recipe *Atomically access primitives*).

Now let's look at how a thread is initialized. thread::spawn() takes a closure and executes it in a new thread. Because this is done in parallel, the main thread doesn't wait until the thread is done; it continues working right after its creation.

The following creates a thread that prints out the content of `some_resource` and gives us a handle to that thread called `thread_a`[10]:

```
let thread_a = {
    let some_resource = some_resource.clone();
    thread::spawn(move || {
        println!("Thread A says: {}", some_resource);
    })
};
```

Afterward (or at the same time), we do the exact same thing in a second thread called `thread_b`.

To understand why we need an `Arc` and can't just pass the resource directly to the closure, let's take a closer look at how closures work.

Closures in Rust can only operate on three kinds of variables:

- Arguments passed to them
- `static` variables (variables with the `'static` lifetime; see Chapter 5, *Advanced Data Structures; Creating lazy static objects*)
- Variables it owns, either by creating them or by moving them into the closure

With this in mind, let's look at the most simplistic approach an inexperienced Rust programmer might take:

```
let thread_a = thread::spawn(|| {
    println!("Thread A says: {}", some_resource);
});
```

If we try to run this, the compiler tells us the following:

```
error[E03731]: closure may outlive the current function, but it borrows `some_resource`, which is owned by the current function
  --> src/main.rs:7:34
   |
7  |     let thread_a = thread::spawn(|| {
   |                                  ^^ may outlive borrowed value `some_resource`
8  |         println!("Thread A says: {}", some_resource);
   |                                       ------------- `some_resource` is borrowed here
help: to force the closure to take ownership of `some_resource` (and any other referenced variables), use the `move` keyword
   |
7  |     let thread_a = thread::spawn(move || {
   |                                  ^^^^^^^
```

Seems like it doesn't like our usage of `some_resource`. Look at the rules for variable usage in closures again:

- `some_resource` has not been passed as an argument
- It is not `static`
- It was neither created in the closure nor moved into it

But what does *closure may outlive the current function* mean? Well, because closures can be stored in a normal variable, they can be returned from a function. Imagine now if we programmed a function that created a variable called `some_resource`, used it inside a closure, and returned it. Since the function owns `some_resource`, it would be dropped while returning the closure, making any reference to it invalid. We don't want any invalid variables, so the compiler stops us from potentially enabling them. Instead, it suggests moving the ownership of `some_resource` into the closure by using the `move` keyword. Let's try that:

```
let thread_a = thread::spawn(move || {
    println!("Thread A says: {}", some_resource);
});
```

The compiler responds with this:

```
error[E0382]: use of moved value: `some_resource`
  --> src/main.rs:11:29
   |
7  |       let thread_a = thread::spawn(move || {
   |                                    ------- value moved (into closure) here
...
11 |           let some_resource = some_resource.clone();
   |                               ^^^^^^^^^^^^^ value used here after move
   |
   = note: move occurs because `some_resource` has type `std::sync::Arc<std::string::String>`, which does not implement the `Copy` trait
```

Because we moved `some_resource` into the closure inside of `thread_a`, `thread_b` can no longer use it! The solution is to create a clone of the reference to `some_resource` and only move the clone into the closure:

```
let some_resource_clone = some_resource.clone();
let thread_a = thread::spawn(move || {
    println!("Thread A says: {}", some_resource_clone);
});
```

This now runs perfectly fine, but it looks a bit weird, as we are now carrying the mental baggage of the knowledge that the resource we're dealing with is, in fact, a `clone`. This can be solved in a more elegant way by putting the clone into a new scope, where it can have the same name as the original, leaving us with the final version of our code:

```
let thread_a = {
    let some_resource = some_resource.clone();
    thread::spawn(move || {
        println!("Thread A says: {}", some_resource);
    })
};
```

Looks way clearer, doesn't it? This way of passing `Rc` and `Arc` variables to a closure is a well-known Rust idiom that we are going to use in all other recipes of the chapter from here on out.

The last thing we are going to do in this recipe is join the two threads by calling `.join()` on them [26 and 27]. Joining a thread means blocking the current thread until the joined thread is done with its work. It's called like that because we *join the two threads of our program back into a single one*. It helps to visually imagine actual sewing threads when thinking about this concept.

We join them before the end of the program, as otherwise, we would have no guarantee that they would actually run all the way through before our program quits. Generally speaking, you should `join` your threads when you need their results and can't wait for them any longer, or they're about to be dropped otherwise.

## See also

- *Sharing ownership with smart pointers* and *Creating lazy static objects* recipes in `Chapter 5`, *Advanced Data Structures*

# Sending data across threads

So far, we've looked at threads that work independently. Now, let's take a look at intertwined threads that need to share data. This situation is common when setting up servers, as the thread receiving client messages is usually not the same as the one that actually handles and responds to the client input. Rust gives us the concept of *channels* as a solution. A channel is split into a *sender* and a *receiver* which can share data across threads.

# How to do it...

1. Open the `Cargo.toml` file that was generated earlier for you.

2. Under `[dependencies]`, add the following line:

   ```
   rand = "0.4.2"
   ```

3. If you want, you can go to rand's crates.io page (`https://crates.io/crates/rand`) to check for the newest version and use that one instead.

4. In the folder `bin`, create a file called `channels.rs`.

5. Add the following code and run it with `cargo run --bin channels`:

```rust
1   extern crate rand;
2
3   use rand::Rng;
4   use std::thread;
5   // mpsc stands for "Multi-producer, single-consumer"
6   use std::sync::mpsc::channel;
7
8   fn main() {
9       // channel() creates a connected pair of a sender and a
            receiver.
10      // They are usually called tx and rx, which stand for
11      // "transmission" and "reception"
12      let (tx, rx) = channel();
13      for i in 0..10 {
14          // Because an mpsc channel is "Multi-producer",
15          // the sender can be cloned infinitely
16          let tx = tx.clone();
17          thread::spawn(move || {
18              println!("sending: {}", i);
19              // send() pushes arbitrary data to the connected
                    receiver
20              tx.send(i).expect("Disconnected from receiver");
21          });
22      }
23      for _ in 0..10 {
24          // recv() blocks the current thread
25          // until a message was received
26          let msg = rx.recv().expect("Disconnected from sender");
27          println!("received: {}", msg);
28      }
29
```

```
30     let (tx, rx) = channel();
31     const DISCONNECT: &str = "Goodbye!";
32     // The following thread will send random messages
33     // until a goodbye message was sent
34     thread::spawn(move || {
35         let mut rng = rand::thread_rng();
36         loop {
37           let msg = match rng.gen_range(0, 5) {
38               0 => "Hi",
39               1 => DISCONNECT,
40               2 => "Howdy there, cowboy",
41               3 => "How are you?",
42               4 => "I'm good, thanks",
43               _ => unreachable!(),
44           };
45           println!("sending: {}", msg);
46           tx.send(msg).expect("Disconnected from receiver");
47           if msg == DISCONNECT {
48              break;
49           }
50        }
51   });
52
53   // An iterator over messages in a receiver is infinite.
54   // It will block the current thread until a message is
     available
55   for msg in rx {
56       println!("received: {}", msg);
57    }
58  }
```

# How it works...

As explained in the comments of the code, calling `std::sync::mpsc::channel()`
generates a tuple consisting of a `Sender` and a `Receiver`, which are conventionally called
`tx` for *transmission* and `rx` for *reception* [12].

This naming convention doesn't come from Rust, but has been a standard
in the telecommunications industry since at least 1960 when the RS-232
(**Recommended Standard 232**) was introduced, detailing how computers
and modems should communicate with each other.

These two halves of the same channel can communicate with each other independently of the current thread they're in. The module's name, `mspc`, tells us that this channel is a `Multi-producer, single-consumer` channel, which means that we can `clone` our sender as many times as we want. We can use this fact to our advantage when dealing with closures [16 to 21]:

```
for i in 0..10 {
    let tx = tx.clone();
    thread::spawn(move || {
        println!("sending: {}", i);
        tx.send(i).expect("Disconnected from receiver");
    });
}
```

We do not need to wrap our sender in an `Arc`, because it natively supports arbitrary cloning! Inside of the closure you can see the sender's main functionality. The `send()` method sends data across threads to the receiver. It will return an error if the receiver is not available anymore, as in when it is dropped too early. In this thread here, we will simply send the numbers 0 to 9 concurrently to the receiver. One thing to note is that because a channel's halves are statically typed, they are only going to be able to send one specific data type around. If the first thing you send is an `i32`, your channel will only work with `i32`. If you send a `String`, it will be a `String` channel.

On to the receiver we go [23 to 28]:

```
for _ in 0..10 {
    let msg = rx.recv().expect("Disconnected from sender");
    println!("received: {}", msg);
}
```

The `recv()` method, which stands for *receive*, blocks the current thread until a message has arrived. Similar to its counterpart, it returns an error if the sender is unavailable. Because we know that we only sent 10 messages, we only call it 10 times. There is no need to explicitly `join` the threads we created for the sender, because `recv()` blocked the main thread until no more messages were left, which means that the sender finished sending all they had to send, that is, all the threads already finished their job. This way, we already joined them.

But in real life, you do not have a guarantee about the amount of times a client will send information to you. For a more realistic demonstration, we will now create a thread that sends random messages [37] to the receiver until it finally has enough and quits by sending `"Goodbye!"` [48]. Note how we created a new channel pair, as the old one was set to the type `i32` because integer literals such as 1 or 2 are treated as `i32` by default.

While the sending code looks almost identical to the one before, the receiving end looks a bit different [55 to 57]:

```
for msg in rx {
    println!("received: {}", msg);
}
```

As you can see, a receiver can be iterated over. It behaves like an infinite iterator over all messages that will ever come, blocking when waiting for a new one, similar to calling `recv()` in a loop. The difference is that the iteration will automatically stop when the sender is unavailable. Because we terminate the sending thread when it sends `"Goodbye!"` [48], this iteration over the receiver will also stop when receiving it, as the sender will have been dropped at that point. Because this means that we have a guarantee about the sending thread being finished, we do not need to join it.

# There's more...

A channel is not `Sync` and, as such, can only be moved across channels but not shared between them. If you need the channel to be `Sync` you can use `std::sync::mpsc::sync_channel`, which blocks when a buffer of unanswered messages is full. An example for when this might be necessary is when a web framework offers to manage your types but only works with `Sync` structs. You can read more on `Sync` in the recipe *Atomically access primitives*.

The `mpsc` channels, as their name suggests, allow many senders but only one receiver. Most of the time, this will be good enough, but if you find yourself needing the exact opposite, as in one sender and multiple receivers, check out Sean McArthur's `spmc` crate at `https://crates.io/crates/spmc`, which provides you with `Single-producer, multi-consumer` channels.

# See also

- *Access collections as Iterator* recipe in `Chapter 2`, *Working with Collections*

# Accessing resources in parallel with RwLocks

When we shared resources with an `Arc`, we only did so immutably. The moment we want our threads to mutate our resources, we need to use some kind of locking mechanism to secure the golden rule of parallelism: multiple readers or one writer. `RwLock` enforces just that rule across threads and blocks them if they violate the rule.

## How to do it...

1. In the folder `bin`, create a file called `rw_lock.rs`.

2. Add the following code and run it with `cargo run --bin rwlock`:

```
1 use std::sync::{Arc, RwLock};
2 use std::thread;
3
4 fn main() {
5 // An RwLock works like the RefCell, but blocks the current
6 // thread if the resource is unavailable
7 let resource = Arc::new(RwLock::new("Hello
    World!".to_string()));
8
9 // The reader_a thread will print the current content of
10 // our resource fourty times
11 let reader_a = {
12 let resource = resource.clone();
13 thread::spawn(move || {
14 for _ in 0..40 {
15 // Lock resource for reading access
16 let resource = resource
17 .read()
18 .expect("Failed to lock resource for reading");
19 println!("Reader A says: {}", resource);
20 }
21 })
22 };
23
24 // The reader_b thread will print the current content of
25 // our resource fourty times as well. Because RwLock allows
26 // multiple readers, it will execute at the same time as
        reader_a
```

```
27 let reader_b = {
28 let resource = resource.clone();
29 thread::spawn(move || {
30 for _ in 0..40 {
31 // Lock resource for reading access
32 let resource = resource
33 .read()
34 .expect("Failed to lock resource for reading");
35 println!("Reader B says: {}", resource);
36 }
37 })
38 };
39
40 // The writer thread will modify the resource ten times.
41 // Because RwLock enforces Rust's access rules
42 // (multiple readers xor one writer), this thread will wait
           until
43 // thread_a and thread_b are not using the resource and then
           block
44 // them both until its done.
45 let writer = {
46 let resource = resource.clone();
47 thread::spawn(move || {
48 for _ in 0..10 {
49 // Lock resource for writing access
50 let mut resource = resource
51 .write()
52 .expect("Failed to lock resource for writing");
53
54 resource.push('!');
55 }
56 })
57 };
58
59 reader_a.join().expect("Reader A panicked");
60 reader_b.join().expect("Reader B panicked");
61 writer.join().expect("Writer panicked");
62 }
```

# How it works...

The RwLock is the parallel equivalent of the RefCell we worked with in Chapter 5,
*Advanced Data Structures; Working with interior mutability*. The big difference is that, while
RefCell panics on a violation of Rust's ownership concept, RwLock simply blocks the
current thread until the violation is over.

The analog of the `borrow()` method of `RefCell` is `read()` [17], which locks the resource for immutable access. The analog of `borrow_mut()` is `write()` [51], which locks the resource for mutable access. Makes sense, doesn't it?

These methods return a `Result`, which tells us whether the thread is *poisoned*. The meaning of poisoning is different for every lock. In an `RwLock`, it means that the thread that locked the resource for `write` access panicked. This way, you can react to panics in other threads and treat them in some way. One example where this can be useful is sending some logs to a server before a crash happens in order to diagnose the problem. In most cases, though, it will be okay if you simply `panic` along, as a `panic` usually stands for a critical failure that cannot be mended.

In our example, we demonstrate the concept by setting up two threads that request `read` access: `reader_a` [11] and `reader_b` [27]. Because an `RwLock` allows multiple readers, they will concurrently print out the value of our resource [19 and 35]. In the meantime, `writer` [45] tries to lock the resource for `write` access. It will have to wait until both `reader_a` and `reader_b` are currently not using the resource. By the same rules, when the `writer` gets their turn and mutates the resource [54], both `reader_a` and `reader_b` have to wait until it's done.

Because all of this happens roughly at the same time, every execution of this example is going to give you slightly different results. I encourage you to run the program multiple times and compare the output.

# There's more...

Despite its nice usability, `RwLock` is still no silver bullet for all concurrent problems. There is a concept in concurrent programming called *deadlock*. It arises when two processes wait for the unlocking of resources that the other holds. This will lead to them waiting forever, as no one is ready to take the first step. Kind of like teenagers in love. An example of this would be a `writer_a` requesting access to a file that `writer_b` holds. `writer_b`, in the meantime, needs some kind of user information from `writer_a` before he can give up the file lock. The best way to avoid this problem is to keep it in the back of your mind and remember it when you're about to create processes that depend on each other.

Another lock that is fairly popular in other languages is the `Mutex`, which Rust also provides under `std::sync::Mutex`. When it locks resources, it treats every process like a writer, so no two threads will *ever* be able to work at the same time with a `Mutex`, even if they don't mutate the data. We are going to create a very simple implementation of it ourselves in the next recipe.

## See also

- *Working with interior mutability* recipe in `Chapter 5`, *Advanced Data Structures*

# Atomically accessing primitives

When reading about all of these parallel structures, you might have wondered how they are implemented. In this recipe, we are going to take a look under the hood and learn about the most basic parallel data types, which are called *atomics*. We are going to do this by implementing our very own `Mutex`.

## How to do it...

1. In the folder `bin`, create a file called `atomic.rs`.

2. Add the following code and run it with `cargo run --bin atomic`:

```
1 use std::sync::Arc;
2 use std::sync::atomic::{AtomicBool, AtomicUsize, Ordering,
ATOMIC_BOOL_INIT, ATOMIC_USIZE_INIT};
3 use std::thread;
4 use std::ops::{Deref, DerefMut};
5 use std::cell::UnsafeCell;
6
7 fn main() {
8 // Atomics are primitive types suited for
9 // well defined concurrent behaviour
10 let some_number = AtomicUsize::new(0);
11 // They are usually initialized by copying them from
12 // their global constants, so the following line does the same:
13 let some_number = ATOMIC_USIZE_INIT;
14
15 // load() gets the current value of the atomic
```

```
16 // Ordering tells the compiler how exactly to handle the
          interactions
17 // with other threads. SeqCst ("Sequentially Consistent") can
          always be used
18 // as it results in the same thing as if no parallelism was
          involved
19 let curr_val = some_number.load(Ordering::SeqCst);
20 println!("The current value of some_number is {}", curr_val);
21
22 // store() sets the variable
23 some_number.store(123, Ordering::SeqCst);
24 let curr_val = some_number.load(Ordering::SeqCst);
25 println!("The current value of some_number is {}", curr_val);
26
27 // swap() sets the variable and returns the old value
28 let old_val = some_number.swap(12_345, Ordering::SeqCst);
29 let curr_val = some_number.load(Ordering::SeqCst);
30 println!("The old value of some_number was {}", old_val);
31 println!("The current value of some_number is {}", curr_val);
32
33 // compare_and_swap only swaps the variable if it
34 // is currently equal to the first argument.
35 // It will always return the old variable
36 let comparison = 12_345;
37 let new_val = 6_789;
38 let old_val = some_number.compare_and_swap(comparison, new_val,
      Ordering::SeqCst);
39 if old_val == comparison {
40 println!("The value has been updated");
41 }
42
43 // The previous atomic code is equivalent to
44 // the following sequential code
45 let mut some_normal_number = 12_345;
46 let old_val = some_normal_number;
47 if old_val == comparison {
48 some_normal_number = new_val;
49 println!("The value has been updated sequentially");
50 }
51
52 // fetch_add() and fetch_sub() add/subtract a number from the
          value,
53 // returning the old value
54 let old_val_one = some_number.fetch_add(12, Ordering::SeqCst);
55 let old_val_two = some_number.fetch_sub(24, Ordering::SeqCst);
56 let curr_val = some_number.load(Ordering::SeqCst);
57 println!(
58 "some_number was first {}, then {} and is now {}",
```

```
59 old_val_one, old_val_two, curr_val
60 );
61
62 // fetch_or() performs an "or" ("||") operation on the variable
        and
63 // an argument and sets the variable to the result. It then
        returns the old value.
64 // For the other logical operations, fetch_and(), fetch_nand()
        and fetch_xor also exist
65 let some_bool = ATOMIC_BOOL_INIT;
66 let old_val = some_bool.fetch_or(true, Ordering::SeqCst);
67 let curr_val = some_bool.load(Ordering::SeqCst);
68 println!("({} || true) is {}", old_val, curr_val);
69
70 // The following is a demonstration of our own Mutex
        implementation,
71 // based on an AtomicBool that checks if it's locked or not
72 let naive_mutex = Arc::new(NaiveMutex::new(1));
73
74 // The updater thread will set the value in the mutex to 2
75 let updater = {
76 let naive_mutex = naive_mutex.clone();
77 thread::spawn(move || {
78 let mut val = naive_mutex.lock();
79 *val = 2;
80 })
81 };
82
83 // The updater thread will print the value in the mutex
84 let printer = {
85 let naive_mutex = naive_mutex.clone();
86 thread::spawn(move || {
87 let val = naive_mutex.lock();
88 println!("The value in the naive mutex is: {}", *val);
89 })
90 };
91
92 // The exact order of execution is unpredictable,
93 // but our mutex guarantees that the two threads will
94 // never access the data at the same time
95 updater.join().expect("The updater thread panicked");
96 printer.join().expect("The printer thread panicked");
97 }
```

3. Now comes the implementation of our very own homemade mutex:

```
 99 // NaiveMutex is an easy, albeit very suboptimal,
100 // implementation of a Mutex, similar to std::sync::Mutex
101 // A mutex is a lock that only allows one thread to access a
    ressource at all times
102 pub struct NaiveMutex<T> {
103 locked: AtomicBool,
104 // UnsafeCell is the underlying struct of every
105 // internally mutable container such as ours
106 data: UnsafeCell<T>,
107 }
108
109 // This is a RAII guard, identical to the one from the last
    chapter
110 pub struct NaiveMutexGuard<'a, T: 'a> {
111 naive_mutex: &'a NaiveMutex<T>,
112 }
113
114 impl<T> NaiveMutex<T> {
115 pub fn new(data: T) -> Self {
116 NaiveMutex {
117 locked: ATOMIC_BOOL_INIT,
118 data: UnsafeCell::new(data),
119 }
120 }
121
122 pub fn lock(&self) -> NaiveMutexGuard<T> {
123 // The following algorithm is called a "spinlock", because it
            keeps
124 // the current thread blocked by doing nothing (it keeps it
            "spinning")
125 while self.locked.compare_and_swap(false, true,
        Ordering::SeqCst) {}
126 NaiveMutexGuard { naive_mutex: self }
127 }
128 }
129
130 // Every type that is safe to send between threads is
automatically
131 // safe to share between threads if wrapped in our mutex, as it
132 // guarantees that no threads will access it ressource at the
same time
133 unsafe impl<T: Send> Sync for NaiveMutex<T> {}
134
135 // Automatically unlock the mutex on drop
136 impl<'a, T> Drop for NaiveMutexGuard<'a, T> {
137 fn drop(&mut self) {
```

```
138 self.naive_mutex.locked.store(false, Ordering::SeqCst);
139 }
140 }
141
142 // Automatically dereference to the underlying data
143 impl<'a, T> Deref for NaiveMutexGuard<'a, T> {
144 type Target = T;
145 fn deref(&self) -> &T {
146 unsafe { &*self.naive_mutex.data.get() }
147 }
148 }
149
150 impl<'a, T> DerefMut for NaiveMutexGuard<'a, T> {
151 fn deref_mut(&mut self) -> &mut T {
152 unsafe { &mut *self.naive_mutex.data.get() }
153 }
154 }
```

# How it works...

As of the time of writing, there are four `atomic` types in the standard library under the `std::sync::atomic` module: `AtomicBool`, `AtomicIsize`, `AtomicUsize`, and `AtomicPtr`. Each one of them represents a primitive type, namely `bool`, `isize`, `usize`, and `*mut`. We are not going to look at the last, which, being a pointer, you will probably only have to deal with when interfacing with programs written in other languages anyways.

In case you haven't encountered `isize` and `usize` before, they are representations of the smallest amount of bytes needed to address any part of the memory of your machine. On 32-bit targets this is 4 bytes, while 64-bit systems will need 8 bytes. `isize` uses those bytes to represent a *signed* number, as in an integer that can be negative. `usize` instead represents an *unsigned* number, which can only be positive but has a lot more capacity for huge numbers in that direction. They are usually used when dealing with collections capacities. For example, `Vec` returns a `usize` when calling its `.len()` method. Additionally, on the nightly toolchain, there are atomic variants of all other concrete integer types like `u8` or `i32`.

The `atomic` versions of our primitives work the same way as their cousins, with one important distinction: they have well-defined behavior when used in parallel environments. All their methods take a parameter of the type `atomic::Ordering`, which stands for which low-level concurrent strategy to use. In this example, we are only going to use `Ordering::SeqCst`, which stands for *sequentially consistent*. This, in turn, means that the behavior is quite intuitive. If some data is stored or modified using this ordering, another thread can see its content after the write as if the two threads ran one after another. Or, in other words, the behavior is *consistent* with that of a *sequential* series of events. This strategy will always work with all parallel algorithms. All other orderings merely relax the constraints on the data involved in order to get some kind of performance benefit.

With this knowledge in hand, you should be able to understand most things done in `main` up to the usage of `NaiveMutex`[72]. Note how some of the `atomic` methods are just different ways of doing the same as with our normal primitives, with the added twist of specifying an ordering and most of them returning the old value. For instance, `some_number.fetch_add(12, Ordering::SeqCst)`, apart from returning the old value of `some_number`, is essentially nothing but `some_number += 12`.

A real use case for atomics comes up in the second part of the example code, where we implement our very own `Mutex`. A mutex, prominently featured in all modern programming languages, is a kind of lock that does not allow *any* two threads to access a resource at the same time. After reading the last recipe, you know that you can imagine a `Mutex` as a kind of `RwLock` that always locks everything in `write` mode.

Let's jump a few lines forward in our code to [102].

```
pub struct NaiveMutex<T> {
    locked: AtomicBool,
    data: UnsafeCell<T>,
}
```

As you can see, we are going to base our `NaiveMutex` on a simple atomic flag, `locked`, which is going to track whether our mutex is available or not. The other member, `data`, holds the underlying resource we are interested in locking. Its type, `UnsafeCell`, is the underlying type of every struct that implements some kind of interior mutability (see `Chapter 5`, *Advanced Data Structures*; *Working with interior mutability*).

The next struct is going to look familiar to you if you've read `Chapter 6`, *Handling Errors*; *Understanding RAII*, as it's an RAII guard with a reference to its parent [110]:

```
pub struct NaiveMutexGuard<'a, T: 'a> {
    naive_mutex: &'a NaiveMutex<T>,
}
```

Let's take a look at how we lock a thread:

```
pub fn lock(&self) -> NaiveMutexGuard<T> {
    while self.locked.compare_and_swap(false, true, Ordering::SeqCst) {}
    NaiveMutexGuard { naive_mutex: self }
}
```

Looks a bit weird at first glance, doesn't it? `compare_and_swap` is one of the more complex `atomic` operations. It works as follows:

1. It compares the value of the atomic with the first parameter
2. If they are the same, it stores the second parameter in the atomic
3. Lastly, it returns the value of the atomic from before the function call

Let's apply that to our call:

- `compare_and_swap` checks if `self.locked` contains `false`
- If so, it sets `self.locked` to `true`
- In any case, it will return the old value

If the returned value is `true`, it means our mutex is currently locked. What should our thread do then? Absolutely nothing: `{ }`. Because we call this in a `while` loop, we will continue doing nothing (this is called *spinning*) until the situation changes. This algorithm is called **spinlock**.

When our mutex is finally available, we set its `locked` flag to `true` and return an RAII guard with a reference to our `NaiveMutex`.

This is not how the real `std::sync::Mutex` is implemented. Because exclusively locking a resource is a very basic concurrent task, operating systems natively support it. The `Mutex` implemented in the Rust standard library is still built by the RAII pattern as well, but uses the OS's mutex handles instead of our custom logic. Fun fact—the Windows implementation uses SRWLocks (https://msdn.microsoft.com/en-us/library/windows/desktop/aa904937(v=vs.85).aspx), which are Windows's native version of `RwLock`, as they proved to be faster than a native `Mutex`. So, on Windows at least, the two types really are very similar.

The implementation of `NaiveMutexGuard` provides the counterpart of `lock` during its dropping [138]:

```
fn drop(&mut self) {
    self.naive_mutex.locked.store(false, Ordering::SeqCst);
}
```

We simply `store` the value `false` in `self.locked` whenever our guard goes out of scope (see `Chapter 6`, *Handling Errors; Implementing the Drop trait*). The next two trait `NaiveMutexGuard` implements are `Deref` and `DerefMut`, which let us call methods of type `T` directly on `NaiveMutexGuard<T>`. They both share nearly the same implementation [146]:

```
unsafe { &*self.naive_mutex.data.get() }
```

Remember when we said that you'll have to deal with pointers on rare occasions? Well, this is one of those times.

`UnsafeCell` doesn't guarantee any borrowing safety, hence the name and the `unsafe` block. It relies on you to make sure all calls to it are actually safe. Because of this, it gives you a raw mutable pointer, which you can manipulate in any way you want. What we do here is dereference it with `*`, so `*mut T` becomes only `T`. Then we return a normal reference to that with `&` [146]. The only thing different in the implementation of `deref_mut` is that we instead return a mutable reference with `&mut` [152]. All of our `unsafe` calls are guaranteed to follow Rust's ownership principles, as we only allow one scope to borrow our resource anyway.

The last thing required for our `Mutex` implementation is the following line, which we skipped before:

```
unsafe impl<T: Send> Sync for NaiveMutex<T> {}
```

The `Sync` trait has a pretty small implementation, right? That's because it is a *marker*. It belongs to a family of traits that don't actually do anything themselves but only exist to tell the compiler something about the types that implement them. Another trait in the `std::marker` module is `Send`, which we also use here.

If a type `T` implements `Send`, it tells the world that it is safe to be moved (*sent*) between threads by passing it around as a value instead of a reference. Nearly all types of Rust implement `Send`.

If `T` is `Sync`, it tells the compiler that it is safe to be shared between threads (it behaves in a *synchronized* way) by passing it around per reference, `&T`. This is harder to accomplish than `Send`, but our `NaiveMutex` guarantees that types in it can be shared around, as we only allow one access to its inner type at a time. This is why we implement the `Sync` trait for every `Send` in our mutex. If it's safe to pass it around, it's automatically also safe to share it within `NaiveMutex`.

Back in `main` you can now find some usage examples of our `Mutex`[75 and 84], similar to the examples in the previous recipe.

# There's more...

Because `SeqCst` is good enough for most applications and the complexity involved in all other orderings, we are not going to look at any others. Don't be disappointed, however—Rust uses nearly the same `atomic` layout and functionality as C++, so there are plenty of sources to tell you how complex the issue really is. Anthony Williams, author of the well-known book *C++: Concurrency In Action* (http://www. cplusplusconcurrencyinaction.com/), uses an entire 45 pages (!) to simply describe all the atomic orderings and how to use them. An additional 44 pages go into showing examples of all of these orderings. Does an average program benefit from this level of dedication? Let's look at the man's own words, with the background knowledge that `std::memory_order_seq_cst` is how C++ calls `SeqCst`:

> *The basic premise is: do not use anything other than* `std::memory_order_seq_cst` *(the default) unless (a) you really **really** know what you are doing, and can **prove** that the relaxed usage is safe in all cases, and (b) your profiler demonstrates that the data structure and operations you are intending to use the relaxed orderings with are a bottleneck.*

Source: https://stackoverflow.com/a/9564877/5903309

In short, you should wait to learn about the different kinds of orderings until you have a very good reason to use them. This is, by the way, also the approach of Java, which makes all variables marked as `volatile` behave in a sequentially consistent way.

# See also

- *Working with interior mutability* recipe in Chapter 5, *Advanced Data Structures*
- *Implementing the Drop trait* and *Understanding RAII* recipe in Chapter 6, *Handling Errors*

# Putting it all together in a connection handler

We have looked at a lot of different practices in isolation now. The true strength of these building blocks, however, comes from combining them. This recipe is going to show you how to combine some of them into a realistic starting point for the connection handling part of a server.

# How to do it...

1. In the folder bin, create a file called connection_handler.rs.

2. Add the following code and run it with cargo run --bin connection_handler:

```rust
1 use std::sync::{Arc, RwLock};
2 use std::net::Ipv6Addr;
3 use std::collections::HashMap;
4 use std::{thread, time};
5 use std::sync::atomic::{AtomicUsize, Ordering,
ATOMIC_USIZE_INIT};
6
7 // Client holds whatever state your client might have
8 struct Client {
9 ip: Ipv6Addr,
10 }
11
12 // ConnectionHandler manages a list of connections
13 // in a parallelly safe way
14 struct ConnectionHandler {
15 // The clients are identified by a unique key
16 clients: RwLock<HashMap<usize, Client>>,
17 next_id: AtomicUsize,
```

```
18 }
19
20 impl Client {
21 fn new(ip: Ipv6Addr) -> Self {
22 Client { ip }
23 }
24 }
25
26 impl ConnectionHandler {
27 fn new() -> Self {
28 ConnectionHandler {
29 clients: RwLock::new(HashMap::new()),
30 next_id: ATOMIC_USIZE_INIT,
31 }
32 }
33
34 fn client_count(&self) -> usize {
35 self.clients
36 .read()
37 .expect("Failed to lock clients for reading")
38 .len()
39 }
40
41 fn add_connection(&self, ip: Ipv6Addr) -> usize {
42 let last = self.next_id.fetch_add(1, Ordering::SeqCst);
43 self.clients
44 .write()
45 .expect("Failed to lock clients for writing")
46 .insert(last, Client::new(ip));
47 last
48 }
49
50 fn remove_connection(&self, id: usize) -> Option<()> {
51 self.clients
52 .write()
53 .expect("Failed to lock clients for writing")
54 .remove(&id)
55 .and(Some(()))
56 }
57 }
```

Using our connection handler by simulating connecting and disconnecting clients:

```
59 fn main() {
60 let connections = Arc::new(ConnectionHandler::new());
61
62 // the connector thread will add a new connection every now and
         then
63 let connector = {
64 let connections = connections.clone();
65 let dummy_ip = Ipv6Addr::new(0, 0, 0, 0, 0, 0xffff, 0xc00a,
         0x2ff);
66 let ten_millis = time::Duration::from_millis(10);
67 thread::spawn(move || {
68 for _ in 0..20 {
69 connections.add_connection(dummy_ip);
70 thread::sleep(ten_millis);
71 }
72 })
73 };
74
75 // the disconnector thread will remove the third connection at
         some point
76 let disconnector = {
77 let connections = connections.clone();
78 let fifty_millis = time::Duration::from_millis(50);
79 thread::spawn(move || {
80 thread::sleep(fifty_millis);
81 connections.remove_connection(2);
82 })
83 };
84
85 // The main thread will print the active connections in a short
         interval
86 let five_millis = time::Duration::from_millis(5);
87 for _ in 0..40 {
88 let count = connections.client_count();
89 println!("Active connections: {}", count);
90 thread::sleep(five_millis);
91 }
92
93 connector.join().expect("The connector thread panicked");
94 disconnector
95 .join()
96 .expect("The disconnector thread panicked");
97 }
```

# How it works...

This recipe doesn't introduce any new modules or concepts. It's here to provide you with a general idea of how to combine all the things you've learned in this recipe in a somewhat realistic context. Specifically, our context consists of code that manages clients that connect with us in some way.

Client [8] holds all information relevant to a connection. As a basic example, it currently contains the client's IP address. Other possibilities would be the client's username, location, device, ping, and so on.

The ConnectionHandler [14] itself holds a list, more specifically a HashMap, of the active connections, indexed by a unique ID. Analogous to that, it also stores the ID for the next connection.

We are using unique IDs instead of a Vec<Client> because clients might be able to connect, multiple times, to whatever service we are providing on the same device. The easiest example for this is multiple tabs open in a browser, all accessing the same website. Generally speaking, it is good practice to always hold your data behind unique keys to save yourself from trouble down the road.

The implementations of the structs should be straightforward. Methods that need to modify the clients member lock it with .write(), all others with .read().

The code used to get a new ID at add_connection adds one to next_id and returns its last value, as usual for an atomic[42]:

```
let last = self.next_id.fetch_add(1, Ordering::SeqCst);
```

After adding the connection to the clients, we return the newly-acquired ID to the caller, so that they can store the ID however they want and reuse it when it's time to kick the client with remove_connection [50], which in turn returns an Option telling the caller if the removed ID was in the client list in the first place. We do not return the removed Client directly because that would reveal unnecessary implementation details to the user of ConnectionHandler.

The code in main simulates parallel access to the hypothetical service. A bunch of clients connect to our ConnectionHandler and some leave again. thread::sleep [70, 80 and 90] blocks the current thread for a specified time and is used here to simulate the effect of various events happening at irregular intervals, represented by the different waiting times for each task.

As with the `RwLock` example, this program will have very different output every time you run it, so try it out multiple times.

## There's more...

If you need to react to the messages from your clients in a different thread, you can use `channel`, which we looked at earlier in the chapter. One use case for this would be programming an online video game. You'll want to aggregate all input from your players, react to it by simulating your world, and then broadcast local changes to the players, with each of these tasks happening concurrently in a single thread.

# Working with Futures

**8**

In this chapter, we will cover the following recipes:

- Providing futures with a CPU pool and waiting for them
- Implementing error handling for futures
- Combining futures
- Using Streams
- Using Sinks
- Using the oneshot channel
- Returning futures
- Locking resources with BiLocks

## Introduction

Futures provide the building blocks for asynchronous computations with zero-cost abstraction. Asynchronous communication is useful for handling timeouts, computing across thread pools, network responses, and any function that does not immediately return a value.

In a synchronous block, the computer would execute each command sequentially after waiting for each command to return a value. If you were to apply the synchronous model when sending an email, you would send the message, stare at your inbox, and wait until you have received a response from your recipient.

Fortunately, life does not work synchronously. After we send an email, we could switch to another application or get off our chair. We can start performing other tasks such as getting the groceries, cooking dinner, or reading a book. Our attention can focus on, and perform, other tasks simultaneously. Periodically, we will check our inbox for a response from our recipient. The process of periodically checking for the new message illustrates the asynchronous model. Unlike humans, computers can check for a new message in our inbox and perform other tasks at the same time.

Rust's futures work by implementing the polling model, which utilizes a central component (for example, a piece of software, hardware devices, and network hosts) to handle status reports from other components. The central, or master, component sends signals to other components repetitively until the master component receives an update, an interruption signal, or the polling event has timed out.

To get a better understanding on how concurrency works within Rust's model, you can view Alex Crichton's concurrency presentations at `https://github.com/alexcrichton/talks`. Throughout our recipes, we will be using the `futures::executor::block_on` function within our main thread to return values. This is intentionally done for demonstrative purposes only. In a real application, you would use `block_on` within another a separate thread and your functions would return some sort of `futures::Future` implementation such as `futures::future::FutureResult`.

At the time of writing, futures is performing a lot of developmental changes throughout its code base. You can view futures' RFCs (Request For Comments) on their official repository at `https://github.com/rust-lang-nursery/futures-rfcs`

# Providing futures with a CPU pool and waiting for them

Futures are usually assigned to a `Task`, which gets assigned to an `Executor`. When a task is *awake*, the executor will place the task into a queue, and will call `poll()` on the task until the process has been completed. Futures offer us a few convenient ways to execute tasks:

- Spawn a future task manually with `futures::executor::block_on()`.

- Using `futures::executor::LocalPool`, which is useful for performing many small tasks on a single thread. In our future returns, we would not be required to implement `Send` since we are only involving the task on a single thread. However, you are required to use `futures::executor::spawn_local()` on the `Executor` if you omit the `Send` trait.
- Using `futures::executor::ThreadPool`, which allows us to offload tasks to other threads.

# How to do it...

1. Create a Rust project to work on during this chapter with `cargo new futures`.
2. Navigate into the newly-created `futures` folder. For the rest of this chapter, we will assume that your command line is within this directory.
3. Inside the `src` folder, create a new folder called `bin`.
4. Delete the generated `lib.rs` file, as we are not creating a library.
5. Open the `Cargo.toml` file that has been generated.
6. Under `[dependencies]`, add the following lines:

```
futures = "0.2.0-beta"
futures-util = "0.2.0-beta"
```

7. In the `src/bin` folder, create a file called `pool.rs`.
8. Add the following code and run it with `cargo run --bin pool`:

```
1    extern crate futures;
2
3    use futures::prelude::*;
4    use futures::task::Context;
5    use futures::channel::oneshot;
6    use futures::future::{FutureResult, lazy, ok};
7    use futures::executor::{block_on, Executor, LocalPool,
         ThreadPoolBuilder};
8
9    use std::cell::Cell;
10   use std::rc::Rc;
11   use std::sync::mpsc;
12   use std::thread;
13   use std::time::Duration;
```

Let's add our constants, enums, structures, and trait implementations:

```
15  #[derive(Clone, Copy, Debug)]
16  enum Status {
17    Loading,
18    FetchingData,
19    Loaded,
20  }
21
22  #[derive(Clone, Copy, Debug)]
23  struct Container {
24    name: &'static str,
25    status: Status,
26    ticks: u64,
27  }
28
29  impl Container {
30    fn new(name: &'static str) -> Self {
31      Container {
32        name: name,
33        status: Status::Loading,
34        ticks: 3,
35      }
36    }
37
38    // simulate ourselves retreiving a score from a remote
        database
39    fn pull_score(&mut self) -> FutureResult<u32, Never> {
40      self.status = Status::Loaded;
41      thread::sleep(Duration::from_secs(self.ticks));
42      ok(100)
43    }
44  }
45
46  impl Future for Container {
47    type Item = ();
48    type Error = Never;
49
50    fn poll(&mut self, _cx: &mut Context) -> Poll<Self::Item,
        Self::Error> {
51      Ok(Async::Ready(()))
52    }
53  }
55  const FINISHED: Result<(), Never> = Ok(());
56
57  fn new_status(unit: &'static str, status: Status) {
58    println!("{}: new status: {:?}", unit, status);
59  }
```

Let's add our first local threaded function:

```
61  fn local_until() {
62      let mut container = Container::new("acme");
63
64      // setup our green thread pool
65      let mut pool = LocalPool::new();
66      let mut exec = pool.executor();
67
68      // lazy will only execute the closure once the future has
        been polled
69      // we will simulate the poll by returning using the
        future::ok method
70
71      // typically, we perform some heavy computational process
        within this closure
72      // such as loading graphic assets, sound, other parts of our
        framework/library/etc.
73      let f = lazy(move |_| -> FutureResult<Container, Never> {
74          container.status = Status::FetchingData;
75          ok(container)
76      });
77
78      println!("container's current status: {:?}",
        container.status);
79
80      container = pool.run_until(f, &mut exec).unwrap();
81      new_status("local_until", container.status);
82
83      // just to demonstrate a simulation of "fetching data over a
        network"
84      println!("Fetching our container's score...");
85      let score = block_on(container.pull_score()).unwrap();
86      println!("Our container's score is: {:?}", score);
87
88      // see if our status has changed since we fetched our score
89      new_status("local_until", container.status);
90  }
```

And now for our locally-spawned threading examples:

```
92  fn local_spawns_completed() {
93      let (tx, rx) = oneshot::channel();
94      let mut container = Container::new("acme");
95
96      let mut pool = LocalPool::new();
97      let mut exec = pool.executor();
98
```

```
99    // change our container's status and then send it to our
      oneshot channel
100   exec.spawn_local(lazy(move |_| {
101       container.status = Status::Loaded;
102       tx.send(container).unwrap();
103       FINISHED
104     }))
105     .unwrap();
106
107   container = pool.run_until(rx, &mut exec).unwrap();
108   new_status("local_spanws_completed", container.status);
109 }
110
111 fn local_nested() {
112   let mut container = Container::new("acme");
114   // we will need Rc (reference counts) since
      we are referencing multiple owners
115   // and we are not using Arc (atomic reference counts)
      since we are only using
116   // a local pool which is on the same thread technically
117   let cnt = Rc::new(Cell::new(container));
118   let cnt_2 = cnt.clone();
119
120   let mut pool = LocalPool::new();
121   let mut exec = pool.executor();
122   let mut exec_2 = pool.executor();
123
124   let _ = exec.spawn_local(lazy(move |_| {
125     exec_2.spawn_local(lazy(move |_| {
126         let mut container = cnt_2.get();
127         container.status = Status::Loaded;
128
129         cnt_2.set(container);
130         FINISHED
131       }))
132       .unwrap();
133     FINISHED
134 }));
135
136   let _ = pool.run(&mut exec);
137
138   container = cnt.get();
139   new_status("local_nested", container.status);
140 }
```

And now for our thread pool example:

```
142 fn thread_pool() {
143    let (tx, rx) = mpsc::sync_channel(2);
144    let tx_2 = tx.clone();
145
146    // there are various thread builder options which are
       referenced at
147    // https://docs.rs/futures/0.2.0-
       beta/futures/executor/struct.ThreadPoolBuilder.html
148    let mut cpu_pool = ThreadPoolBuilder::new()
149      .pool_size(2) // default is the number of cpus
150      .create();
151
152    // We need to box this part since we need the Send +'static
trait
153    // in order to safely send information across threads
154    let _ = cpu_pool.spawn(Box::new(lazy(move |_| {
155      tx.send(1).unwrap();
156      FINISHED
157    })));
158
159    let f = lazy(move |_| {
160      tx_2.send(1).unwrap();
161      FINISHED
162    });
163
164    let _ = cpu_pool.run(f);
165
166    let cnt = rx.into_iter().count();
167    println!("Count should be 2: {:?}", cnt);
168 }
```

And lastly, our `main` function:

```
170 fn main() {
171    println!("local_until():");
172    local_until();
173
174    println!("\nlocal_spawns_completed():");
175    local_spawns_completed();
176
177    println!("\nlocal_nested():");
178    local_nested();
179
180    println!("\nthread_pool():");
181    thread_pool();
182 }
```

# How it works...

Let's start by introducing the `Future` trait:

- Implementing the `Future` trait requires only three constraints: an `Item` type, an `Error` type, and a `poll()` function. The actual trait looks as follows:

```
pub trait Future {
    type Item;
    type Error;
    fn poll(
        &mut self,
        cx: &mut Context
    ) -> Result<Async<Self::Item>, Self::Error>;
}
```

- The `Poll<Self::Item, Self::Error>` is a type that translates into `Result<Async<T>, E>`, where `T = Item` and `E = Error`. This is what our example is using on line 50.
- `poll()` is called upon whenever a `futures::task::Waker` (can also be known as a *Task*) is executed with one of our executors located at `futures::executor`, or manually woken up by building a `futures::task::Context` and running with a future wrapper such as `futures::future::poll_fn`.

Now, onto our `local_until()` function:

- `LocalPool` offers us the ability to run tasks concurrently using a single thread. This is useful for functions with minimal complexity, such as traditional I/O bound functions. `LocalPools` can have multiple `LocalExecutors` (as we have created one on line 65), which can spawn our task. Since our task is single-threaded, we do not need to `Box` or add the `Send` trait to our future.
- The `futures::future::lazy` function will create a new future, from a `FnOnce` closure, which becomes the same future as the one that the closure returns (any `futures::future::IntoFuture` trait), which in our case that future is `FutureResult<Container, Never>`.
- Executing the `run_until(F: Future)` function from the `LocalPool` will perform all of the future tasks until the `Future` (indicated as `F`) has been marked as completed. This function will return `Result<<F as Future>::Item, <F as Future>::Error>` upon completion. In the example, we are returning `futures::future::ok(Container)`, on line 75, so our `F::Item` will be our `Container`.

For our `local_spawns_completed()` function:

- First, we set up our `futures::channel::oneshot` channel (which is explained later, in the *Using the oneshot channel* section).
- We will use the `oneshot` channel's `futures::channel::oneshot::Receiver` as the future to run until completion within the `run_until()` function. This allows us to demonstrate how polling would work until a signal has been received from another thread or task (in our example, this happens on line 102 with the `tx.send(...)` command).
- The `LocalExecutor`'s `spawn_local()` is a special `spawn` function that gives us the capability of executing future functions without implementing the `Send` trait.

Next, our `local_nested()` function:

- We set up our usual `Container` and then declare a reference counter that will allow us to keep a value (this would be our `Container`) across multiple executors or threads. We do not need to use an atomic reference counter, since we are using `spawn_local()`, which performs the future on a green thread (a thread that is scheduled by a virtual machine or a runtime library).
- The `LocalPool`'s `run(exec: &mut Executor)` function will run any futures spawned within the pool until all of the futures have been completed. This also includes any executors that may `spawn` additional tasks within other tasks, as our example shows.

Onto our `thread_pool()` function:

- An `std::sync::mspc::sync_channel` is created with the intention of blocking the thread for demonstration purposes.
- Next, we created a `ThreadPool` with default settings and called its `spawn(F: Box<Future<Item = (), Error = Never> + 'static + Send>)` function, which will poll the task until completion whenever we decide to execute the pool.
- After setting up our tasks, we execute the `ThreadPool`'s `run(F: Future)` function, which will block the thread in which is invoking `run()` until the `F: Future` has been completed. The function will return a value upon the future's completion even if there are other tasks spawned, and running, within the pool. Using the `mspc::sync_channel` earlier helps mitigate this issue, but will block the thread upon being invoked.

- With the `ThreadPoolBuilder`, you can:
  - Set the number of worker threads
  - Adjust the stack size
  - Set a prefixed name for the pools
  - Run a function (with the signature as `Fn(usize) + Send + Sync + 'static`) after each worker thread has started, right before the worker thread runs any tasks
  - Execute a function (with the signature as `Fn(usize) + Send + Sync + 'static`) before each worker thread shuts down

# Handling errors in futures

In a real application, we would not be returning a value instantly from an asynchronous function that directly returns `Async::Ready<T>` or `FutureResult<T, E>`. Network requests time out, buffers become full, services become unavailable due to bugs or outages, and many more issues pop up on a daily basis. As much as we like to build order from chaos, usually chaos wins due to naturally-occurring entropy (programmers may know this as *scope creep*) and decay (software updates, new computer science paradigms, and so on). Luckily for us, the futures library offers us a simple way to implement error handling.

## How to do it...

1. Inside the `bin` folder, create a new file called `errors.rs`.
2. Add the following code and run it with `cargo run --bin errors`:

```
1    extern crate futures;
2
3    use futures::prelude::*;
4    use futures::executor::block_on;
5    use futures::stream;
6    use futures::task::Context;
7    use futures::future::{FutureResult, err};
```

3. After that, let's add our structures and implementations:

```
9     struct MyFuture {}
10    impl MyFuture {
11      fn new() -> Self {
12        MyFuture {}
13      }
```

```
14  }
15
16  fn map_error_example() -> FutureResult<(), &'static str> {
17    err::<(), &'static str>("map_error has occurred")
18  }
19
20  fn err_into_example() -> FutureResult<(), u8> {
21    err::<(), u8>(1)
22  }
23
24  fn or_else_example() -> FutureResult<(), &'static str> {
25    err::<(), &'static str>("or_else error has occurred")
26  }
27
28  impl Future for MyFuture {
29    type Item = ();
30    type Error = &'static str;
31
32    fn poll(&mut self, _cx: &mut Context) -> Poll<Self::Item,
Self::Error> {
33      Err("A generic error goes here")
34    }
35  }
36
37  struct FuturePanic {}
38
39  impl Future for FuturePanic {
40    typc Itom = ();
41    type Error = ();
42
43    fn poll(&mut self, _cx: &mut Context) -> Poll<Self::Item,
      Self::Error> {
44      panic!("It seems like there was a major issue with
      catch_unwind_example")
45    }
46  }
```

4. After that, let's add our generic error handling functions/examples:

```
48  fn using_recover() {
49    let f = MyFuture::new();
50
51    let f_recover = f.recover::<Never, _>(|err| {
52      println!("An error has occurred: {}", err);
53      ()
54    });
55
56    block_on(f_recover).unwrap();
```

```
57  }
58
59  fn map_error() {
60    let map_fn = |err| format!("map_error_example: {}", err);
61
62    if let Err(e) = block_on(map_error_example().map_err(map_fn))
      {
63      println!("block_on error: {}", e)
64    }
65  }
66
67  fn err_into() {
68    if let Err(e) = block_on(err_into_example().err_into::()) {
69      println!("block_on error code: {:?}", e)
70    }
71  }
72
73  fn or_else() {
74    if let Err(e) = block_on(or_else_example()
75      .or_else(|_| Err("changed or_else's error message"))) {
76      println!("block_on error: {}", e)
77    }
78  }
```

5.  And now for our `panic` functions:

```
80  fn catch_unwind() {
81    let f = FuturePanic {};
82
83    if let Err(e) = block_on(f.catch_unwind()) {
84      let err = e.downcast::<&'static str>().unwrap();
85      println!("block_on error: {:?}", err)
86    }
87  }
88
89  fn stream_panics() {
90    let stream_ok = stream::iter_ok::<_, bool>(vec![Some(1),
      Some(7), None, Some(20)]);
91    // We panic on "None" values in order to simulate a stream
      that panics
92    let stream_map = stream_ok.map(|o| o.unwrap());
93
94    // We can use catch_unwind() for catching panics
95    let stream = stream_map.catch_unwind().then(|r| Ok::<_, ()>
      (r));
96    let stream_results: Vec<_> =
       block_on(stream.collect()).unwrap();
97
```

```
 98   // Here we can use the partition() function to separate the Ok
      and Err values
 99   let (oks, errs): (Vec<_>, Vec<_>) =
      stream_results.into_iter().partition(Result::is_ok);
100   let ok_values: Vec<_> =
      oks.into_iter().map(Result::unwrap).collect();
101   let err_values: Vec<_> =
      errs.into_iter().map(Result::unwrap_err).collect();
102
103   println!("Panic's Ok values: {:?}", ok_values);
104   println!("Panic's Err values: {:?}", err_values);
105 }
```

6. And finally, our `main` function:

```
107 fn main() {
108   println!("using_recover():");
109   using_recover();
110
111   println!("\nmap_error():");
112   map_error();
113
114   println!("\nerr_into():");
115   err_into();
116
117   println!("\nor_else():");
118   or_else();
119
120   println!("\ncatch_unwind():");
121   catch_unwind();
122
123   println!("\nstream_panics():");
124   stream_panics();
125 }
```

# How it works...

Let's start with the `using_recover()` function:

- Any errors that have occurred within the future will be transformed into `<Self as Future>::Item`. Any `<Self as Future>::Error` type can be passed through, since we never produce an actual error.

- The `futures::executor::block_on(F: Future)` function will run a future until completion within the invoking thread. Any tasks within futures' `default executor` will also run on the invoking thread, but completion on the tasks may never occur since `F` may finish before the tasks have been completed. If this is the case, then the spawned tasks are dropped. `LocalPool` is often recommended for mitigating this issue, but for our examples `block_on()` will be sufficient.

All of these error handling functions can be found within the `futures::FutureExt` trait.

Now, onto our `map_error()` function:

- The `<Self as Future>::map_err<E, F>(F: FnOnce(Self::Error) -> E)` function will map a future's (`Self`) error into another error while returning a new future. This function is often used in conjunction with combinators, such as select or join, since we can guarantee that the futures will have the same error type to complete the composition.

Next, the `err_into()` function:

- Transforms the `Self::Error` into another `Error` type using the `std::convert::Into` trait
- Like `futures::FutureExt::map_err`, this function is useful for aggregating combinators together

The `or_else()` function:

- If `<Self as Future>` returns an error, `futures::FutureExt::or_else` will execute a closure with the following signature: `FnOnce(Self::Error) -> futures::future::IntoFuture<Item = Self::Item>`
- Useful for chaining failing combinators together
- The closure will not execute if the future has completed successfully, panics, or its future is dropped

Then the `catch_unwind()` function:

- This function is generally not recommended as a way to handle errors, and is only enabled with Rust's `std` option (which is enabled by default)
- Future traits implement the `AssertUnwindSafe` trait as `AssertUnwindSafe<F: Future>` trait

And lastly, the `stream_panics()` function:

- On line 95, this `futures::StreamExt::catch_unwind` function is similar to `futures::FutureExt::catch_unwind`
- If a panic occurs, it will be the last element of the stream for the stream
- This feature is only enabled with Rust's `std` option as well
- The `AssertUnwindSafe` trait is also implemented for streams as `AssertUnwindSafe<S: Stream>`

> The combinators for streams are located in the `futures::StreamExt` trait, which has the same functions as `futures::FutureExt` with some additional stream-specific combinators such as `split()` and `skip_while()` that may prove to be useful for your projects.

# See also

- `Chapter 6`, *Handling Errors*

# Combining futures

Combining, and chaining, our futures allows us to perform multiple operations in sequential order and helps organize our code a bit more. They can be used to transform, splice, filter, and so on `<Self as Future>::Item`s.

# How to do it...

1. Inside the `bin` folder, create a new file called `combinators.rs`.

2. Add the following code and run it with `cargo run --bin combinators`:

```
1   extern crate futures;
2   extern crate futures_util;
3
4   use futures::prelude::*;
5   use futures::channel::{mpsc, oneshot};
6   use futures::executor::block_on;
7   use futures::future::{ok, err, join_all, select_all, poll_fn};
8   use futures::stream::iter_result;
9   use futures_util::stream::select_all as select_all_stream;
10
11  use std::thread;
12
13  const FINISHED: Result<Async<()>, Never> =
    Ok(Async::Ready(()));
```

3. Let's add our `join_all` example function:

```
15  fn join_all_example() {
16    let future1 = Ok::<_, ()>(vec![1, 2, 3]);
17    let future2 = Ok(vec![10, 20, 30]);
18    let future3 = Ok(vec![100, 200, 300]);
19
20    let results = block_on(join_all(vec![future1, future2,
      future3])).unwrap();
21    println!("Results of joining 3 futures: {:?}", results);
22
23    // For parameters with a lifetime
24    fn sum_vecs<'a>(vecs: Vec<&'a [i32]>) -> Box<Future, Error =
      ()> + 'static> {
25      Box::new(join_all(vecs.into_iter().map(|x| Ok::<i32, ()>
        (x.iter().sum()))))
26    }
27
28    let sum_results = block_on(sum_vecs(vec![&[1, 3, 5], &[6, 7,
      8], &[0]])).unwrap();
29    println!("sum_results: {:?}", sum_results);
30  }
31
```

Next, we will write out our `shared` function:

```
32  fn shared() {
33    let thread_number = 2;
34    let (tx, rx) = oneshot::channel::();
35    let f = rx.shared();
36    let threads = (0..thread_number)
```

```
37        .map(|thread_index| {
38          let cloned_f = f.clone();
39          thread::spawn(move || {
40            let value = block_on(cloned_f).unwrap();
41            println!("Thread #{}: {:?}", thread_index, *value);
42          })
43        })
44        .collect::<Vec<_>>();
45      tx.send(42).unwrap();
46
47      let shared_return = block_on(f).unwrap();
48      println!("shared_return: {:?}", shared_return);
49
50      for f in threads {
51        f.join().unwrap();
52      }
53    }
```

And now for our `select_all` example:

```
55  fn select_all_example() {
56    let vec = vec![ok(3), err(24), ok(7), ok(9)];
57
58    let (value, _, vec) = block_on(select_all(vec)).unwrap();
59    println!("Value of vec: = {}", value);
60
61    let (value, _, vec) =
      block_on(select_all(vec)).err().unwrap();
62    println!("Value of vec: = {}", value);
63
64    let (value, _, vec) = block_on(select_all(vec)).unwrap();
65    println!("Value of vec: = {}", value);
66
67    let (value, _, _) = block_on(select_all(vec)).unwrap();
68    println!("Value of vec: = {}", value);
69
70    let (tx_1, rx_1) = mpsc::unbounded::();
71    let (tx_2, rx_2) = mpsc::unbounded::();
72    let (tx_3, rx_3) = mpsc::unbounded::();
73
74    let streams = vec![rx_1, rx_2, rx_3];
75    let stream = select_all_stream(streams);
76
77    tx_1.unbounded_send(3).unwrap();
78    tx_2.unbounded_send(6).unwrap();
79    tx_3.unbounded_send(9).unwrap();
80
81    let (value, details) = block_on(stream.next()).unwrap();
```

```
82
83     println!("value for select_all on streams: {:?}", value);
84     println!("stream details: {:?}", details);
85  }
```

Now we can add our `flatten`, `fuse`, and `inspect` functions:

```
87  fn flatten() {
88     let f = ok::<_, _>(ok::<u32, Never>(100));
89     let f = f.flatten();
90     let results = block_on(f).unwrap();
91     println!("results: {}", results);
92  }
93
94  fn fuse() {
95     let mut f = ok::<u32, Never>(123).fuse();
96
97     block_on(poll_fn(move |mut cx| {
98         let first_result = f.poll(&mut cx);
99         let second_result = f.poll(&mut cx);
100        let third_result = f.poll(&mut cx);
101
102        println!("first result: {:?}", first_result);
103        println!("second result: {:?}", second_result);
104        println!("third result: {:?}", third_result);
105
106        FINISHED
107    }))
108    .unwrap();
109  }
110
111 fn inspect() {
112    let f = ok::<u32, Never>(111);
113    let f = f.inspect(|&val| println!("inspecting: {}", val));
114    let results = block_on(f).unwrap();
115    println!("results: {}", results);
116  }
```

Then we can add our `chaining` example:

```
118 fn chaining() {
119    let (tx, rx) = mpsc::channel(3);
120    let f = tx.send(1)
121       .and_then(|tx| tx.send(2))
122       .and_then(|tx| tx.send(3));
123
124    let t = thread::spawn(move || {
125       block_on(f.into_future()).unwrap();
```

```
126    });
127
128    t.join().unwrap();
129
130    let result: Vec<_> = block_on(rx.collect()).unwrap();
131    println!("Result from chaining and_then: {:?}", result);
132
133    // Chaining streams together
134    let stream1 = iter_result(vec![Ok(10), Err(false)]);
135    let stream2 = iter_result(vec![Err(true), Ok(20)]);
136
137    let stream = stream1.chain(stream2)
138      .then(|result| Ok::<_, ()>(result));
139
140    let result: Vec<_> = block_on(stream.collect()).unwrap();
141    println!("Result from chaining our streams together: {:?}",
         result);
142 }
```

And now for our `main` function:

```
144 fn main() {
145    println!("join_all_example():");
146    join_all_example();
147
148    println!("\nshared():");
149    shared();
150
151    println!("\nselect_all_example():");
152    select_all_example();
153
154    println!("\nflatten():");
155    flatten();
156
157    println!("\nfuse():");
158    fuse();
159
160    println!("\ninspect():");
161    inspect();
162
163    println!("\nchaining():");
164    chaining();
165 }
```

# How it works...

The `join_all()` function:

- Collects results from several futures and returns a new future with the `futures::future::JoinAll<F: Future>` trait
- The new future will perform commands for all of the aggregated futures within the `futures::future::join_all` call, returning a vector of `Vec<T: Future::Item>` in FIFO ordering
- An error will return itself immediately and cancel the other related futures

And the `shared()` function:

- `futures::FutureExt::shared` will create a handle that can be cloned, which resolves to the returning value of `<T as futures::future::SharedItem>` which can be deferred into `T`.
- Useful for polling a future on more than one thread
- This method is enabled only when Rust's `std` option is enabled (which it is by default)
- The underlying result is `futures::future::Shared<Future::Item>`, which implements `Send` and `Sync` traits
- Using `futures::future::Shared::peek(&self)` will return a value without blocking if any single shared handle has been completed

Next, the `select_all_example()` function:

- `futures::FutureExt::select_all` returns a new future that selects from a list of vectors
- The return value is `futures::future::SelectAll`, which allows us to iterate through the results
- The future's item, index of execution, and a list of futures that still need to be processed will be returned by this function as soon as one of the futures completes its execution

Then the `flatten()` function:

- `futures::FutureExt::flatten` will combine futures together with a returning result of their items being flattened

- The resultant item must implement the `futures::future::IntoFuture` trait

Onto the `fuse()` function:

- There is a small chance of `undefined behavior`, such as panicking or blocking forever, when polling a future that has already returned a `futures::Async::Ready` or `Err` value. The `futures::FutureExt::fuse` function allows us to `poll` the future again without worrying about `undefined behavior`, and will always return `futures::Async::Pending`.
- The future that's being fused will be dropped upon completion in order to reclaim resources.

The `inspect()` function:

- `futures::FutureExt::inspect` allows us to peek at an item of a future which is useful for when we are chaining combinators.

And then the `chaining()` function:

- We first create a channel with three values, and `spawn` a thread to send those three values to the channel's receiver using the `futures::FutureExt::and_then` combinator. We collect the results on line 130 from the channel.
- Then we chain two streams together on line 134 and 135 with the collection occurring on line 140. The result of both streams should be chained together on lines 137 and 138.

# See also

- *Using a vector* and *Access collections as iterators* recipes in `Chapter 2`, *Working with Collections*

# Using Streams

A stream is a pipeline for events that returns a value asynchronously to the invoker. Streams are more useful for items that require the Iterator trait, while Futures are more apt for Result values. When an error occurs throughout a stream, the error will not halt the stream, and polling on the stream will still return other results until the None value has been returned.

Streams and Channels can be a bit confusing for some. Streams are used for continuous, buffered data, and Channels are more suited for completed messages between endpoints.

# How to do it...

1. Inside the bin folder, create a new file called streams.rs.
2. Add the following code and run it with cargo run --bin streams:

```
1    extern crate futures;
2
3    use std::thread;
4
5    use futures::prelude::*;
6    use futures::executor::block_on;
7    use futures::future::poll_fn;
8    use futures::stream::{iter_ok, iter_result};
9    use futures::channel::mpsc;
```

3. Now, let's add our constants, implementations, and so on:

```
11   #[derive(Debug)]
12   struct QuickStream {
13     ticks: usize,
14   }
15
16   impl Stream for QuickStream {
17     type Item = usize;
18     type Error = Never;
19
20     fn poll_next(&mut self, _cx: &mut task::Context) ->
         Poll<Option, Self::Error> {
21       match self.ticks {
22         ref mut ticks if *ticks > 0 => {
23           *ticks -= 1;
```

```
24              println!("Ticks left on QuickStream: {}", *ticks);
25              Ok(Async::Ready(Some(*ticks)))
26          }
27          _ => {
28              println!("QuickStream is closing!");
29              Ok(Async::Ready(None))
30          }
31      }
32    }
33  }
34
35  const FINISHED: Result<Async<()>, Never> =
Ok(Async::Ready(()));
```

4. Our `quick_streams` example would be:

```
37  fn quick_streams() {
38    let mut quick_stream = QuickStream { ticks: 10 };
39
40    // Collect the first poll() call
41    block_on(poll_fn(|cx| {
42        let res = quick_stream.poll_next(cx).unwrap();
43        println!("Quick stream's value: {:?}", res);
44        FINISHED
45    }))
46    .unwrap();
47
48    // Collect the second poll() call
49    block_on(poll_fn(|cx| {
50        let res = quick_stream.poll_next(cx).unwrap();
51        println!("Quick stream's next svalue: {:?}", res);
52        FINISHED
53    }))
54    .unwrap();
55
56    // And now we should be starting from 7 when collecting the
        rest of the stream
57    let result: Vec<_> =
        block_on(quick_stream.collect()).unwrap();
58    println!("quick_streams final result: {:?}", result);
59  }
```

5. There are several ways to iterate through streams; let's add them to our code base:

```
61  fn iterate_streams() {
62    use std::borrow::BorrowMut;
63
```

```
64    let stream_response = vec![Ok(5), Ok(7), Err(false), Ok(3)];
65    let stream_response2 = vec![Ok(5), Ok(7), Err(false), Ok(3)];
66
67    // Useful for converting any of the `Iterator` traits into a
      `Stream` trait.
68    let ok_stream = iter_ok::<_, ()>(vec![1, 5, 23, 12]);
69    let ok_stream2 = iter_ok::<_, ()>(vec![7, 2, 14, 19]);
70
71    let mut result_stream = iter_result(stream_response);
72    let result_stream2 = iter_result(stream_response2);
73
74    let ok_stream_response: Vec<_> =
      block_on(ok_stream.collect()).unwrap();
75    println!("ok_stream_response: {:?}", ok_stream_response);
76
77    let mut count = 1;
78    loop {
79      match block_on(result_stream.borrow_mut().next()) {
80        Ok((res, _)) => {
81          match res {
82            Some(r) => println!("iter_result_stream result #{}:
              {}", count, r),
83            None => { break }
84          }
85        },
86        Err((err, _)) => println!("iter_result_stream had an
          error #{}: {:?}", count, err),
87      }
88      count += 1;
89    }
90
91    // Alternative way of iterating through an ok stream
92    let ok_res: Vec<_> = block_on(ok_stream2.collect()).unwrap();
93    for ok_val in ok_res.into_iter() {
94      println!("ok_stream2 value: {}", ok_val);
95    }
96
97    let (_, stream) = block_on(result_stream2.next()).unwrap();
98    let (_, stream) = block_on(stream.next()).unwrap();
99    let (err, _) = block_on(stream.next()).unwrap_err();
100
101   println!("The error for our result_stream2 was: {:?}", err);
102
103   println!("All done.");
104 }
```

6. And now for our channeling example:

```
106 fn channel_threads() {
107   const MAX: usize = 10;
108   let (mut tx, rx) = mpsc::channel(0);
109
110   let t = thread::spawn(move || {
111     for i in 0..MAX {
112       loop {
113         if tx.try_send(i).is_ok() {
114           break;
115         } else {
116           println!("Thread transaction #{} is still pending!",
i);
117         }
118       }
119     }
120   });
121
122   let result: Vec<_> = block_on(rx.collect()).unwrap();
123   for (index, res) in result.into_iter().enumerate() {
124     println!("Channel #{} result: {}", index, res);
125   }
126
127   t.join().unwrap();
128 }
```

7. Dealing with errors and channels can be done as follows:

```
130 fn channel_error() {
131   let (mut tx, rx) = mpsc::channel(0);
132
133   tx.try_send("hola").unwrap();
134
135   // This should fail
136   match tx.try_send("fail") {
137     Ok(_) => println!("This should not have been successful"),
138     Err(err) => println!("Send failed! {:?}", err),
139   }
140
141   let (result, rx) = block_on(rx.next()).ok().unwrap();
142   println!("The result of the channel transaction is: {}",
143         result.unwrap());
144
145   // Now we should be able send to the transaction since we
      poll'ed a result already
146   tx.try_send("hasta la vista").unwrap();
147   drop(tx);
```

```
148
149     let (result, rx) = block_on(rx.next()).ok().unwrap();
150     println!("The next result of the channel transaction is: {}",
151         result.unwrap());
152
153     // Pulling more should result in None
154     let (result, _) = block_on(rx.next()).ok().unwrap();
155     println!("The last result of the channel transaction is:
        {:?}",
156         result);
157 }
```

8. We can even work with buffers and channels together. Let's add our
`channel_buffer` function:

```
159 fn channel_buffer() {
160   let (mut tx, mut rx) = mpsc::channel::(0);
161
162   let f = poll_fn(move |cx| {
163     if !tx.poll_ready(cx).unwrap().is_ready() {
164       panic!("transactions should be ready right away!");
165     }
166
167     tx.start_send(20).unwrap();
168     if tx.poll_ready(cx).unwrap().is_pending() {
169       println!("transaction is pending...");
170     }
171
172     // When we're still in "Pending mode" we should not be able
173     // to send more messages/values to the receiver
174     if tx.start_send(10).unwrap_err().is_full() {
175       println!("transaction could not have been sent to the
         receiver due \
176           to being full...");
177     }
178
179     let result = rx.poll_next(cx).unwrap();
180     println!("the first result is: {:?}", result);
181     println!("is transaction ready? {:?}",
182         tx.poll_ready(cx).unwrap().is_ready());
183
184     // We should now be able to send another message since we've pulled
185     // the first message into a result/value/variable.
186     if !tx.poll_ready(cx).unwrap().is_ready() {
187       panic!("transaction should be ready!");
188     }
189
```

```
190     tx.start_send(22).unwrap();
191     let result = rx.poll_next(cx).unwrap();
192     println!("new result for transaction is: {:?}", result);
193
194     FINISHED
195   });
196
197   block_on(f).unwrap();
198 }
```

9. Just because we're using the futures crate doesn't mean everything has to be concurrent. Add the following example to demonstrate how to block with channels:

```
200 fn channel_threads_blocking() {
201   let (tx, rx) = mpsc::channel::(0);
202   let (tx_2, rx_2) = mpsc::channel::<()>(2);
203
204   let t = thread::spawn(move || {
205     let tx_2 = tx_2.sink_map_err(|_| panic!());
206     let (a, b) =
        block_on(tx.send(10).join(tx_2.send(()))).unwrap();
207
208     block_on(a.send(30).join(b.send(()))).unwrap();
209   });
210
211   let (_, rx_2) = block_on(rx_2.next()).ok().unwrap();
212   let (result, rx) = block_on(rx.next()).ok().unwrap();
213   println!("The first number that we sent was: {}",
        result.unwrap());
214
215   drop(block_on(rx_2.next()).ok().unwrap());
216   let (result, _) = block_on(rx.next()).ok().unwrap();
217   println!("The second number that we sent was: {}",
        result.unwrap());
218
219   t.join().unwrap();
220 }
```

10. Sometimes we'll need concepts such as unbounded channels; let's add our `channel_unbounded` function:

```
222 fn channel_unbounded() {
223   const MAX_SENDS: u32 = 5;
224   const MAX_THREADS: u32 = 4;
225   let (tx, rx) = mpsc::unbounded::();
226
227   let t = thread::spawn(move || {
```

```
228        let result: Vec<_> = block_on(rx.collect()).unwrap();
229        for item in result.iter() {
230          println!("channel_unbounded: results on rx: {:?}", item);
231        }
232    });
233
234    for _ in 0..MAX_THREADS {
235      let tx = tx.clone();
236
237      thread::spawn(move || {
238        for _ in 0..MAX_SENDS {
239          tx.unbounded_send(1).unwrap();
240        }
241      });
242    }
243
244    drop(tx);
245
246    t.join().ok().unwrap();
247 }
```

11. And now we can add our `main` function:

```
249 fn main() {
250    println!("quick_streams():");
251    quick_streams();
252
253    println!("\niterate_streams():");
254    iterate_streams();
255
256    println!("\nchannel_threads():");
257    channel_threads();
258
259    println!("\nchannel_error():");
260    channel_error();
261
262    println!("\nchannel_buffer():");
263    channel_buffer();
264
265    println!("\nchannel_threads_blocking():");
266    channel_threads_blocking();
267
268    println!("\nchannel_unbounded():");
269    channel_unbounded();
270 }
```

# How it works...

First, let's talk about the `QuickStream` structure:

- The `poll_next()` function will continuously be invoked, and with each iteration, `i`'s ticks attribute will be decremented by 1
- Polling will stop when the ticks attribute reaches 0 and returns `futures::Async::Ready<None>`

Within the `quick_streams()` function:

- We build a `futures::task::Context` by using `futures::future::poll_on(f: FnMut(|cx: Context|))`, so that we can explicitly invoke `QuickStream`'s `poll_next()` function on lines 42 and 50
- Since we have declared 10 ticks on line 38, our first two `block_on`'s `poll_next()` calls should yield 9 and 8
- The next `block_on` call, on line 57, will keep polling `QuickStream` until `futures::Async::Ready<None>` is returned from the ticks attribute equaling zero

Within `iterate_streams()`:

- `futures::stream::iter_ok` will convert an `Iterator` into a `Stream`, which will always be ready to return the next value
- `futures::stream::iter_result` does the same thing as `iter_ok`, except we use `Result` values instead of `Ok` values
- On lines 78 through 89, we iterate through the stream's results and print out some information depending on whether the value was `Ok` or an `Error` type. If the `None` type has been returned from our stream, then we will break the loop
- Lines 92 through 95 show an alternative way of iterating through a stream's `Ok` results by using the `into_iter()` calls
- Lines 97 through 99 show an alternative way of iterating through a stream's `Result` return types

Loops, iterated results, and `collect()` calls are synchronous. We used this functions for demonstrative/educational purposes only. Combinators such as `map()`, `filter()`, `and_then()`, etc. would be used in a real application for streams and channels.

The `channel_threads()` function:

- On line 107, we define the maximum number of sends we want to attempt.
- On line 108, we declare a channel to send messages to. Channel capacity is the `buffer size (the argument of futures::channel::mpsc::channel)` + `the number of senders` (each sender is guaranteed a slot within the channel). Channels will return a `futures::channel::mpsc::Receiver<T>`, which implements the `Stream` trait, and a `futures::channel::mpsc::Sender<T>`, which implements the `Sink` trait.
- Lines 110 through 120 is where we `spawn` a thread and attempt to send 10 signals, looping until each send is sent successfully.
- We collect, and display, our results on line 122 through 125, and join our threads on line 127.

The `channel_error()` section:

- On line 131, we declare our channel with a `0 usize` buffer as the argument, which gives us one slot for the initial sender
- We send the first message successfully on line 133
- Lines 136 through 139 should fail, since we are trying to send a message to a channel that is considered full (since we did not receive the value, drop the initial sender, flush the stream, and so on)
- On line 146, we use the sender's `futures::channel::mpsc::Sender::try_send(&mut self, msg: T)` functions, which won't block our thread unless we don't drop/invoke the sender's destroyer method using `drop(T)` on line 147
- Polling the stream any additional times after receiving the last value will always return `None`

Next, the `channel_buffer()` function:

- We set up a future closure with `poll_fn()` on line 162.
- We check to see if our sender is ready to be polled with its `futures::sink::poll_ready(&mut self, cx: &mut futures::task::Context)` method on lines 163 through 165.
- Sinks have a method called `futures::sink::start_send(&mut self, item: <Self as Sink>::SinkItem) -> Result<(), <Self as Sink>::SinkError>`, which prepares the message to be delivered, but won't until we flush or close the sink. `poll_flush()` is often used to guarantee that every message has been sent from the sink.

- Polling the stream for the next value will also alleviate space within the sink/sender using the `futures::stream::poll_next(&mut self, cx: &mut futures::task::Context)` method, as we have done on line 179.
- We can check if our sender is ready, as we have done on line 182 using the `futures::Async::is_ready(&self) -> bool` method.
- Our final value should be `22` and displayed to the console from line 192.

Then the `channel_threads_blocking()` function:

- First, we set up our channels on lines 201 and 202.
- Then we `spawn` a thread that will map all of `tx_2`'s errors into a `panic!` (line 205), and then we send the value of `10` to our first channel while joining a second sender with the `()` value (line 206). On line 208, we send the value of `30` and another empty value `()` to our second channel.
- On line 211 we poll the second channel, which would hold a value of `()`.
- On line 212 we poll the first channel, which would hold a value of `10`.
- We drop the second channel's receiver (line 215), since we need to close or flush for the second `tx_2.send()` call on line 208 (`tx_2` is known as variable `b` on this line).
- After performing the drop, we can finally return our second value from the first channel's sender, which should be `30`.

And the `channel_unbounded()` function:

- On line 225 we declare an `unbounded channel`, which means that sending messages to this channel will always succeed as long as the receiver is not closed. Messages will be buffered on an as-needed basis, and since this channel is unbounded, our application can exhaust our available memory.
- Lines 227 through 232 `spawn` a thread that collects all of the receiver's messages (line 228), and we iterate through them on line 229. The item on line 230 is a tuple of the index in which the message was received and the message's value (in our case, this is always 1).
- Lines 237 through 241 is what will `spawn` the number of threads (using the `MAX_THREADS` constant) as well as the number of times that we want to send per thread using the `MAX_THREADS` constant.
- Lines 244 we will drop (which closes) the channel's sender so that we may collect all of the messages from line 228.

- We join the spawned thread with our current thread on line 246, which will execute the collection and iterations commands (lines 228 through 231).

# Using Sinks

Sinks are the *sending-side* of channels, sockets, pipes, and so on, in which messages can be sent from the sink asynchronously. Sinks communicate by initiating a send signal, and then the rest is polled. One thing to watch out for when using sinks is that they can run out of sending space, which will prevent more messages from being sent.

# How to do it...

1. Inside the `bin` folder, create a new file called `sinks.rs`.
2. Add the following code and run it with `cargo run --bin sinks`:

```
1    extern crate futures;
2
3    use futures::prelude::*;
4    use futures::future::poll_fn;
5    use futures::executor::block_on;
6    use futures::sink::flush;
7    use futures::stream::iter_ok;
8    use futures::task::{Waker, Context};
9
10   use std::mem;
```

3. Let's add our examples with using vectors as `sinks`:

```
12   fn vector_sinks() {
13     let mut vector = Vec::new();
14     let result = vector.start_send(0);
15     let result2 = vector.start_send(7);
16
17     println!("vector_sink: results of sending should both be
         Ok(()): {:?} and {:?}",
18         result,
19         result2);
20     println!("The entire vector is now {:?}", vector);
21
22     // Now we need to flush our vector sink.
23     let flush = flush(vector);
24     println!("Our flush value: {:?}", flush);
```

```
25      println!("Our vector value: {:?}",
        flush.into_inner().unwrap());
26
27      let vector = Vec::new();
28      let mut result = vector.send(2);
29      // safe to unwrap since we know that we have not flushed the
        sink yet
30      let result = result.get_mut().unwrap().send(4);
31
32      println!("Result of send(): {:?}", result);
33      println!("Our vector after send(): {:?}",
        result.get_ref().unwrap());
34
35      let vector = block_on(result).unwrap();
36      println!("Our vector should already have one element: {:?}",
        vector);
37
38      let result = block_on(vector.send(2)).unwrap();
39      println!("We can still send to our stick to ammend values:
        {:?}",
40          result);
41
42      let vector = Vec::new();
43      let send_all = vector.send_all(iter_ok(vec![1, 2, 3]));
44      println!("The value of vector's send_all: {:?}", send_all);
45
46      // Add some more elements to our vector...
47      let (vector, _) = block_on(send_all).unwrap();
48      let (result, _) = block_on(vector.send_all(iter_ok(vec![0, 6,
        7]))).unwrap();
49      println!("send_all's return value: {:?}", result);
50  }
```

We can map/transform our `sinks` values. Let's add our `mapping_sinks` example:

```
52  fn mapping_sinks() {
53      let sink = Vec::new().with(|elem: i32| Ok::<i32, Never>(elem
        * elem));
54
55      let sink = block_on(sink.send(0)).unwrap();
56      let sink = block_on(sink.send(3)).unwrap();
57      let sink = block_on(sink.send(5)).unwrap();
58      println!("sink with() value: {:?}", sink.into_inner());
59
60      let sink = Vec::new().with_flat_map(|elem| iter_ok(vec![elem;
        elem].into_iter().map(|y| y * y)));
61
```

```
62    let sink = block_on(sink.send(0)).unwrap();
63    let sink = block_on(sink.send(3)).unwrap();
64    let sink = block_on(sink.send(5)).unwrap();
65    let sink = block_on(sink.send(7)).unwrap();
66    println!("sink with_flat_map() value: {:?}",
      sink.into_inner());
67  }
```

We can even send messages to multiple `sinks`. Let's add our `fanout` function:

```
69  fn fanout() {
70    let sink1 = vec![];
71    let sink2 = vec![];
72    let sink = sink1.fanout(sink2);
73    let stream = iter_ok(vec![1, 2, 3]);
74    let (sink, _) = block_on(sink.send_all(stream)).unwrap();
75    let (sink1, sink2) = sink.into_inner();
76
77    println!("sink1 values: {:?}", sink1);
78    println!("sink2 values: {:?}", sink2);
79  }
```

Next, we'll want to implement a structure for a customized sink. Sometimes our application will require us to manually flush our `sinks` instead of doing it automatically. Let's add our `ManualSink` structure:

```
81   #[derive(Debug)]
82   struct ManualSink {
83     data: Vec,
84     waiting_tasks: Vec,
85   }
86
87   impl Sink for ManualSink {
88     type SinkItem = Option; // Pass None to flush
89     type SinkError = ();
90
91     fn start_send(&mut self, op: Option) -> Result<(),
       Self::SinkError> {
92       if let Some(item) = op {
93         self.data.push(item);
94       } else {
95         self.force_flush();
96       }
97
98       Ok(())
99     }
100
101    fn poll_ready(&mut self, _cx: &mut Context) -> Poll<(), ()> {
```

```
102        Ok(Async::Ready(()))
103    }
104
105    fn poll_flush(&mut self, cx: &mut Context) -> Poll<(), ()> {
106      if self.data.is_empty() {
107        Ok(Async::Ready(()))
108      } else {
109        self.waiting_tasks.push(cx.waker().clone());
110        Ok(Async::Pending)
111      }
112    }
113
114    fn poll_close(&mut self, _cx: &mut Context) -> Poll<(), ()> {
115      Ok(().into())
116    }
117 }
118
119 impl ManualSink {
120    fn new() -> ManualSink {
121      ManualSink {
122        data: Vec::new(),
123        waiting_tasks: Vec::new(),
124      }
125    }
126
127    fn force_flush(&mut self) -> Vec {
128      for task in self.waiting_tasks.clone() {
129        println!("Executing a task before replacing our values");
130        task.wake();
131      }
132
133      mem::replace(&mut self.data, vec![])
134    }
135 }
```

And now for our manual flush function:

```
137 fn manual_flush() {
138    let mut sink = ManualSink::new().with(|x| Ok::<Option, ()>
       (x));
139    let _ = sink.get_mut().start_send(Some(3));
140    let _ = sink.get_mut().start_send(Some(7));
141
142    let f = poll_fn(move |cx| -> Poll<Option<_>, Never> {
143      // Try to flush our ManualSink
144      let _ = sink.get_mut().poll_flush(cx);
145      let _ = flush(sink.get_mut());
146
```

```
147        println!("Our sink after trying to flush: {:?}",
           sink.get_ref());
148
149        let results = sink.get_mut().force_flush();
150        println!("Sink data after manually flushing: {:?}",
151            sink.get_ref().data);
152        println!("Final results of sink: {:?}", results);
153
154        Ok(Async::Ready(Some(())))
155    });
156
157    block_on(f).unwrap();
158 }
```

And lastly, we can add our main function:

```
160 fn main() {
161    println!("vector_sinks():");
162    vector_sinks();
163
164    println!("\nmapping_sinks():");
165    mapping_sinks();
166
167    println!("\nfanout():");
168    fanout();
169
170    println!("\nmanual_flush():");
171    manual_flush();
172 }
```

# How it works...

First, let's take a look at the futures::Sink trait itself:

```
pub trait Sink {
    type SinkItem;
    type SinkError;

    fn poll_ready(
        &mut self,
        cx: &mut Context
    ) -> Result<Async<()>, Self::SinkError>;
    fn start_send(
        &mut self,
        item: Self::SinkItem
    ) -> Result<(), Self::SinkError>;
    fn poll_flush(
```

```
        &mut self,
        cx: &mut Context
    ) -> Result<Async<()>, Self::SinkError>;
    fn poll_close(
        &mut self,
        cx: &mut Context
    ) -> Result<Async<()>, Self::SinkError>;
}
```

We are already familiar with the `Item` and `Error` concepts from futures and streams, so we will move on to the required functions:

- `poll_ready` must be invoked with the returning value of `Ok(futures::Async::Ready(()))` before each attempt at using `start_send`. If the sink receives an error, the sink will no longer be able to receive items.
- `start_send`, as stated previously, prepares the message to be delivered, but won't until we flush or close the sink. If the sink uses buffers, the `Sink::SinkItem` won't be processed until the buffer has been fully completed.
- `poll_flush` will flush the sink, which will allow us to collect items that are currently being processed. `futures::Async::Ready` will return if the sink does not have any more items within the buffer, otherwise, the sink will return `futures::Async::Pending`.
- `poll_close` will flush and close the sink, following the same return rules as `poll_flush`.

Now, onto our `vector_sinks()` function:

- Sinks are implemented for `Vec<T>` types, so we can declare a mutable vector and use the `start_send()` function, which will immediately poll our values into the vector on lines 13 through 15.
- On line 28 we use the `futures::SinkExt::send(self, item: Self::SinkItem)`, which will complete after the item has been processed and flushed through the sink. `futures::SinkExt::send_all` is recommended for batching multiple items to send through, versus having to manually flush between each send call (as demonstrated on line 43).

Our `mapping_sinks()` function:

- Line 51 demonstrates how you can map/manipulate elements within a sink using the `futures::SinkExt::with` function. This function produces a new sink that iterates through each item and sends the final value *as a future* to the *parent* sink.

- Line 60 illustrates the `futures::SinkExt::flat_with_map` function that has mostly the same functionality as the `futures::SinkExt::with` function except each iterated item is sent as a stream value to the *parent* sink and will return an `Iterator::flat_map` value instead of a `Iterator::map`.

Next, the `fanout()` function:

- The `futures::SinkExt::fanout` function allows us to send messages to multiple sinks at one time, as we have done on line 72.

And then `manual_flush()`:

- We first implement our own `Sink` trait with the `ManualSink<T>` construct (lines 81 through 135). Our `ManualSink`'s `poll_flush` method will only return `Async::Ready()` if our data vector is empty, otherwise, we are going to push the task (`futures::task::Waker`) into a queue line through the `waiting_tasks` attribute. We use the `waiting_tasks` attribute within our `force_flush()` function (line 128) in order to manually *wake up* our tasks (line 130).
- On lines 138 through 140, we build our `ManualSink<Option<i32>>` and start sending some values.
- We use `poll_fn` on line 142 in order to quickly build a `futures::task::Context` so that we may pass this value down to our underlying poll calls.
- On line 144 we manually call our `poll_flush()` function, which will not execute our actual tasks since they are placed within the `waiting_tasks` attribute.
- Until we invoke `force_flush()`, our sink will not return any values (as indicated on lines 150-151). Once this function has been called upon and the underlying `Waker` tasks have finished executing, then we can see the messages (line 152) that we sent earlier (lines 139 and 140).

# Using the oneshot channel

Oneshot channels are useful for when you need to send only one message to a channel. The oneshot channel is applicable for tasks that really only need to be updated/notified once, such as whether or not a recipient has read your message, or as a final destination within a task pipeline to notify the end user that the task has been completed.

# How to do it...

1. Inside the `bin` folder, create a new file called `oneshot.rs`.
2. Add the following code and run it with `cargo run --bin oneshot`:

```
1   extern crate futures;
2
3   use futures::prelude::*;
4   use futures::channel::oneshot::*;
5   use futures::executor::block_on;
6   use futures::future::poll_fn;
7   use futures::stream::futures_ordered;
8
9   const FINISHED: Result<Async<()>, Never> =
    Ok(Async::Ready(()));
10
11  fn send_example() {
12    // First, we'll need to initiate some oneshot channels like
      so:
13    let (tx_1, rx_1) = channel::();
14    let (tx_2, rx_2) = channel::();
15    let (tx_3, rx_3) = channel::();
16
17    // We can decide if we want to sort our futures by FIFO
      (futures_ordered)
18    // or if the order doesn't matter (futures_unordered)
19    // Note: All futured_ordered()'ed futures must be set as a
      Box type
20    let mut ordered_stream = futures_ordered(vec![
21      Box::new(rx_1) as Box<Future>,
22      Box::new(rx_2) as Box<Future>,
23    ]);
24
25    ordered_stream.push(Box::new(rx_3) as Box<Future>);
26
27    // unordered example:
28    // let unordered_stream = futures_unordered(vec![rx_1, rx_2,
      rx_3]);
29
30    // Call an API, database, etc. and return the values (in our
      case we're typecasting to u32)
31    tx_1.send(7).unwrap();
32    tx_2.send(12).unwrap();
33    tx_3.send(3).unwrap();
34
35    let ordered_results: Vec<_> =
      block_on(ordered_stream.collect()).unwrap();
```

```
36      println!("Ordered stream results: {:?}", ordered_results);
37  }
38
39  fn check_if_closed() {
40      let (tx, rx) = channel::();
41
42      println!("Is our channel canceled? {:?}", tx.is_canceled());
43      drop(rx);
44
45      println!("Is our channel canceled now? {:?}",
        tx.is_canceled());
46  }
47
48  fn check_if_ready() {
49      let (mut tx, rx) = channel::();
50      let mut rx = Some(rx);
51
52      block_on(poll_fn(|cx| {
53          println!("Is the transaction pending? {:?}",
54              tx.poll_cancel(cx).unwrap().is_pending());
55          drop(rx.take());
56
57          let is_ready = tx.poll_cancel(cx).unwrap().is_ready();
58          let is_pending =
            tx.poll_cancel(cx).unwrap().is_pending();
59
60          println!("Are we ready? {:?} This means that the pending
            should be false: {:?}",
61              is_ready,
62              is_pending);
63          FINISHED
64      }))
65      .unwrap();
66  }
67
68  fn main() {
69      println!("send_example():");
70      send_example();
71
72      println!("\ncheck_if_closed():");
73      check_if_closed();
74
75      println!("\ncheck_if_ready():");
76      check_if_ready();
77  }
```

# How it works...

Within our `send_example()` function:

- On lines 13 through 15, we set up three `oneshot` channels.
- On lines 20 through 23 we use `futures::stream::futures_ordered`, which will convert a list (any `IntoIterator` value) of futures into a `Stream` yielding results on a first in, first out (FIFO) basis. If any underlying futures do not complete before the next future is invoked, this function will wait until the long-running future has been completed and will then internally re-sort that future into its proper order.
- Line 25 shows us that we can push additional futures into the `futures_ordered` iterator separately.
- Line 28 demonstrates another function that doesn't rely on sorting on a FIFO basis, called `futures::stream::futures_unordered`. This function will have better performance than its counterpart `futures_ordered`, but for our example, we are not sending enough values to make a difference.
- On lines 31 through 33 we send values to our channels, mimicking the process of returning values from an API, a database, and so on. If the send is successful then `Ok(())` will be returned, otherwise, an `Err` type will be returned.
- And on our last two lines (35 and 36), we collect our `futures_ordered` values and display them to the console.

Next, the `check_if_closed()` function:

- Our channel should remain open until we explicitly drop/destroy the receiver (or send a value to the channel). We can check the status of our receiver by invoking the `futures::channel::oneshot::Sender::is_canceled(&self) -> bool` function, which we have done on lines 42 and 45.

Then the `check_if_ready()` function:

- On line 50 we explicitly assign a value to the oneshot's receiver, which would put our receiver in a state of pending (since it already has a value).
- We drop our receiver on line 55 and we can check if our receiver is ready by using our sender's `futures::channel::oneshot::Sender::poll_cancel` function, which we use on lines 57 and 58. `poll_cancel` will return `Ok(Async::Ready)` if the receiver has been dropped or `Ok(Async::Pending)` if the receiver has not been dropped.

# Returning futures

The Future trait relies on three main ingredients: a type, an error, and a poll() function that returns a Result<Async<T>, E> structure. The poll() method will never block the main thread, and Async<T> is an enumerator with two variants: Ready(T) and Pending. Periodically, the poll() method will be invoked by a task's context's waker() trait, located in futures::task::context::waker, until a value is ready to be returned.

## How to do it...

1. In the src/bin folder, create a file called returning.rs.
2. Add the following code and run it with cargo run —bin returning:

```
1    extern crate futures;
2
3    use futures::executor::block_on;
4    use futures::future::{join_all, Future, FutureResult, ok};
5    use futures::prelude::*;
6
7    #[derive(Clone, Copy, Debug, PartialEq)]
8    enum PlayerStatus {
9      Loading,
10     Default,
11     Jumping,
12   }
13
14   #[derive(Clone, Copy, Debug)]
15   struct Player {
16     name: &'static str,
17     status: PlayerStatus,
18     score: u32,
19     ticks: usize,
20   }
```

3. Now comes the implementations for the structs:

```
22   impl Player {
23     fn new(name: &'static str) -> Self {
24       let mut ticks = 1;
25       // Give Bob more ticks explicitly
26       if name == "Bob" {
27         ticks = 5;
28       }
29
```

```
30        Player {
31          name: name,
32          status: PlayerStatus::Loading,
33          score: 0,
34          ticks: ticks,
35        }
36      }
37
38      fn set_status(&mut self, status: PlayerStatus) ->
        FutureResult<&mut Self, Never> {
39        self.status = status;
40        ok(self)
41      }
42
43      fn can_add_points(&mut self) -> bool {
44        if self.status == PlayerStatus::Default {
45          return true;
46        }
47
48        println!("We couldn't add any points for {}!", self.name);
49        return false;
50      }
51
52      fn add_points(&mut self, points: u32) -> Async<&mut Self> {
53        if !self.can_add_points() {
54          Async::Ready(self)
55        } else {
56          let new_score = self.score + points;
57          // Here we would send the new score to a remote server
58          // but for now we will manaully increment the player's
            score.
59
60          self.score = new_score;
61
62          Async::Ready(self)
63        }
64      }
65    }
66
67  impl Future for Player {
68    type Item = Player;
69    type Error = ();
70
71    fn poll(&mut self, cx: &mut task::Context) ->
        Poll<Self::Item, Self::Error> {
72      // Presuming we fetch our player's score from a
73      // server upon initial load.
74      // After we perform the fetch send the Result value.
```

```
75
76        println!("Player {} has been poll'ed!", self.name);
77
78        if self.ticks == 0 {
79          self.status = PlayerStatus::Default;
80          Ok(Async::Ready(*self))
81        } else {
82          self.ticks -= 1;
83          cx.waker().wake();
84          Ok(Async::Pending)
85        }
86      }
87  }
```

4. Next, we'll want to add our `helper` functions and our `Async` function for adding points to our players:

```
89  fn async_add_points(player: &mut Player,
90              points: u32)
91              -> Box<Future + Send> {
92    // Presuming that player.add_points() will send the points to a
93    // database/server over a network and returns an updated
94    // player score from the server/database.
95    let _ = player.add_points(points);
96
97    // Additionally, we may want to add logging mechanisms,
98    // friend notifications, etc. here.
99
100   return Box::new(ok(*player));
101 }
102
103 fn display_scoreboard(players: Vec<&Player>) {
104   for player in players {
105     println!("{}'s Score: {}", player.name, player.score);
106   }
107 }
```

5. And finally, the actual usage:

```
109 fn main() {
110   let mut player1 = Player::new("Bob");
111   let mut player2 = Player::new("Alice");
112
113   let tasks = join_all(vec![player1, player2]);
114
115   let f = join_all(vec![
116     async_add_points(&mut player1, 5),
```

```
117        async_add_points(&mut player2, 2),
118    ])
119      .then(|x| {
120        println!("First batch of adding points is done.");
121        x
122      });
123
124    block_on(f).unwrap();
125
126    let players = block_on(tasks).unwrap();
127    player1 = players[0];
128    player2 = players[1];
129
130    println!("Scores should be zero since no players were
       loaded");
131    display_scoreboard(vec![&player1, &player2]);
132
133    // In our minigame, a player cannot score if they are
       currently
134    // in the air or "jumping."
135    // Let's make one of our players' status set to the jumping
       status.
136
137    let f =
       player2.set_status(PlayerStatus::Jumping).and_then(move |mut
       new_player2| {
138      async_add_points(&mut player1, 10)
139        .and_then(move |_| {
140          println!("Finished trying to give Player 1 points.");
141          async_add_points(&mut new_player2, 2)
142        })
143        .then(move |new_player2| {
144          println!("Finished trying to give Player 2 points.");
145          println!("Player 1 (Bob) should have a score of 10 and
           Player 2 (Alice) should \
146              have a score of 0");
147
148          // unwrap is used here to since
149          display_scoreboard(vec![&player1,
           &new_player2.unwrap()]);
150          new_player2
151        })
152    });
153
154    block_on(f).unwrap();
155
156    println!("All done!");
157 }
```

# How it works...

Let's start by introducing the structures that participate in this example:

- `PlayerStatus` is an enumerator for maintaining a *global* state on the player's instance. The variants are:
    - `Loading`, which is the initial state
    - `Default`, which is applied after we are done loading the player's stats
    - `Jumping` is a special state that won't allow us to add points to the player's scoreboard due to the rules of the game
- `Player` holds our player's main attributes, along with a special attribute called ticks that stores the amount of cycles that we want to run through with `poll()` before assigning the player's status from `Loading` to `Default`.

Now, onto our implementations:

- Jumping down to the `fn set_status(&mut self, status: PlayerStatus) -> FutureResult<&mut Self, Never>` function on our `Player` structure, we will notice a return value of `FutureResult`, which tells futures that this function will immediately return a computed value from the `result()`, `ok()`, or `err()` functions from `futures::futures`. This is useful for quickly prototyping our application while being able to utilize our `executors` and futures combinators.
- At the `fn add_points(&mut self, points: u32) -> Async<&mut Self>` function we return our `Async` value immediately, since we currently do not have a server to use, but we would implement the `Async<T>` value over `FutureResult` for functions that require computations asynchronously.
- We mimic the time it takes for a network request using our player's `ticks` attribute. `Poll<I, E>` will keep executing as long as we are returning `Async::Pending` (line [x]). The executor needs to know whether or not a task needs to be polled again. The task's `Waker` trait is what handles these notifications, and we can manually invoke it using `cx.waker().wake()` on line 83 . Once our player's `ticks` attribute reaches zero we send an `Async::Ready(self)` signal, which tells the executor to no longer poll this function.

For our `async_add_points()` helper method:

- We return `Box<Future<Item = Player, Error = Never> + Send`, which tells futures that this function will eventually return a value of `Player` (since we `Never` return an error).
- The `+ Send` part of the return is not necessary for our current code base, but in the future, we may want to offload some of these tasks onto other threads which executors require. Spawning across threads requires us to return the `futures::prelude::Never` type as an error and a `'static` variable as well.
- When calling future functions with combinators (such as `then` and `and_then`), we will need to return a `Never` error type or the same error type as every other future function that is being called within the same combinator flow.

Finally, onto our main block:

- We use the `futures::future::join_all` function, which accepts any `IntoIterator` that contains all `InfoFuture` trait elements (which should be all future functions). This either collects and returns `Vec<T>` sorted FIFO, or cancels executing as soon as the first error returns from any of the future functions within the collection, which becomes the returning value for the `join_all()` call.
- `then()` and `and_then()` are combinators that internally use `future::Chain` and return a `Future` trait value, which allows us to add more combinators if we wanted. See the *Using combinators and utilities* section for more information on combinators.
- `block_on()` is an executor method that handles any future function or value as its input and returns a `Result<Future::Item, Future::Error>`. When running this method, the function containing the method will block until the future(s) have been completed. Spawned tasks will execute on the default executor, but they may not be completed before `block_on` finishes its task(s). If `block_on()` finishes before the spawned tasks, then those spawned tasks will be dropped.
- We can also use `block_on()` as a quick way to run our cycles/ticks and execute task(s), which invokes our `poll()` functions. We used this method on line 124 for *initially loading players* onto the game.

# There's more...

The box() method for returning futures does cause an additional allocation to the heap. Another method of returning futures relies on using a nightly version of Rust or for this issue https://github.com/rust-lang/rust/issues/34511 to be resolved. The new async_add_points() method would return an implied Future trait and would look as follows:

```
fn async_add_points<F>(f: F, player: &mut Player, points: u32) -> impl
Future<Item = Player, Error = F::Error>
where F: Future<Item = Player>,
{
    // Presuming that player.add_points() will send the points to a
    // database/server over a network and returns
    // an updated player score from the server/database.
    let _ = player.add_points(points).flatten();

    // Additionally, we may want to add logging mechanisms, friend
    notifications, etc. here.

    return f.map(player.clone());
}
```

Rust may cause undefined behavior if we were to call poll() more than once for a future. This problem can be mitigated by converting the future into a stream by using the into_stream() method or using the fuse() adapter, which adds a tiny bit of runtime overhead.

Tasks are usually executed/polled from using an executor such as the block_on() helper function. You can manually execute tasks by creating a task::Context and calling poll() directly from the task. As a general rule, it is recommended to not invoke poll() manually and to have an executor manage polling automatically.

# See also

- *Boxing data* recipe in Chapter 5, *Advanced Data Structures*
- Chapter 7, *Parallelism and Rayon*

# Locking resources with BiLocks

BiLocks are used when we need to store a value across multiple threads with up to two owners associated with that value. Applicable uses for a BiLock type would be splitting TCP/UDP data for reading and writing, or adding a layer between a sink and a stream (for logging, monitoring, and so on), or it can be a sink and a stream at the same time.

When using futures with an additional crate (such as tokio or hyper), knowing BiLocks can help us wrap data around the other crate's common methods. This would allow us to build futures and concurrency on top of existing crates without having to wait until the crate's maintainers support concurrency explicitly. BiLocks are a very low-level utility, but understanding how they work can help us further down the road with our (web) applications.

In the next chapter, we will mostly focus on networking with Rust, but we will also get to practice integrating futures with other crates. BiLocks can be used throughout these next examples, if you wanted to split a TCP/UDP stream in a mutex state, although it is not necessary to do so with the crates that we will be using.

# How to do it...

1. In the `src/bin` folder, create a file called `bilocks.rs`.
2. Add the following code and run it with `cargo run —bin bilocks`:

```
1   extern crate futures;
2   extern crate futures_util;
3
4   use futures::prelude::*;
5   use futures::executor::LocalPool;
6   use futures::task::{Context, LocalMap, Wake, Waker};
7   use futures_util::lock::BiLock;
8
9   use std::sync::Arc;
10
11  struct FakeWaker;
12  impl Wake for FakeWaker {
13    fn wake(_: &Arc) {}
14  }
15
16  struct Reader {
17    lock: BiLock,
18  }
19
```

```
20  struct Writer {
21    lock: BiLock,
22  }
23
24  fn split() -> (Reader, Writer) {
25    let (a, b) = BiLock::new(0);
26    (Reader { lock: a }, Writer { lock: b })
27  }
29  fn main() {
30    let pool = LocalPool::new();
31    let mut exec = pool.executor();
32    let waker = Waker::from(Arc::new(FakeWaker));
33    let mut map = LocalMap::new();
34    let mut cx = Context::new(&mut map, &waker, &mut exec);
35
36    let (reader, writer) = split();
37    println!("Lock should be ready for writer: {}",
38        writer.lock.poll_lock(&mut cx).is_ready());
39    println!("Lock should be ready for reader: {}",
40        reader.lock.poll_lock(&mut cx).is_ready());
41
42    let mut writer_lock = match writer.lock.lock().poll(&mut cx).unwrap() {
43      Async::Ready(t) => t,
44      _ => panic!("We should be able to lock with writer"),
45    };
46
47    println!("Lock should now be pending for reader: {}",
48        reader.lock.poll_lock(&mut cx).is_pending());
49    *writer_lock = 123;
50
51    let mut lock = reader.lock.lock();
52    match lock.poll(&mut cx).unwrap() {
53      Async::Ready(_) => {
54        panic!("The lock should not be lockable since writer has
      already locked it!")
55      }
56      _ => println!("Couldn't lock with reader since writer has
      already initiated the lock"),
57    };
58
59    let writer = writer_lock.unlock();
60
61    let reader_lock = match lock.poll(&mut cx).unwrap() {
62      Async::Ready(t) => t,
63      _ => panic!("We should be able to lock with reader"),
64    };
65
```

```
66    println!("The new value for the lock is: {}", *reader_lock);
67
68    let reader = reader_lock.unlock();
69    let reunited_value = reader.reunite(writer).unwrap();
70
71    println!("After reuniting our locks, the final value is
      still: {}",
72        reunited_value);
73 }
```

# How it works...

- First, we need to implement a fake `futures::task::Waker` for when we create a new context (this is what our `FakeWaker` structure is for on lines 11 through 14)
- Since BiLocks require two owners, we will divide the ownership into two different structures, called `Reader<T>` (on lines 16 through 18) and `Writer<T>` (on lines 20 through 22)
- Our `split() -> (Reader<u32>, Writer<u32>)` function is just to structure/organize our code a bit better, and when calling `BiLock::new(t: T)` the return type is a tuple of two `futures_util::lock::BiLock` elements

Now that the preliminary code has been explained, let's dive into our `main()` function:

- On lines 30 through 34 we set up a new `LocalPool`, `LocalExecutor`, `Waker` (`FakeWaker`), and a `LocalMap` (map storage of local data within tasks) for creating a new `Context`, since we will be polling our locks manually for demonstration purposes.
- Lines 38 and 40 use the `futures_util::lock::BiLock::poll_lock` function, which returns an `Async<futures_util::lock::BiLockGuard<T>>` value if the lock is available. If the lock is not available then the function will return `Async::Pending`. The lock (the `BiLockGuard<T>`) will unlock when the reference is dropped.
- On line 42 we execute `writer.lock.lock()`, which will block the lock and a `BiLockAcquire<T>` will be returned, which is a future that can be polled. When `BiLockAcquire` is polled, a `Poll<BiLockAcquired<T>, ()>` value is returned and that value can be dereferenced mutably.
- On line 48, we can now see that the lock is currently in an `Async::Pending` state, which would not allow us to lock the BiLock again, as shown on lines 51 through 57.

- After modifying our lock's value (line 49), we should now unlock it (line 59) so that the other owner can reference it (lines 61 through 64).
- When we call `BiLockAcquired::unlock()` (line 68), the original `BiLock<T>` is returned and the lock is officially unlocked.
- On line 69 we perform `futures_util::lock::BiLock::reunite(other: T)`, which recovers the value of the lock and destroys the *two halves* of the BiLock references (presuming that `T` is the other half of the BiLock from the `BiLock::new()` call).

# 9
# Networking

In this chapter, we will cover the following recipes:

- Setting up a basic HTTP server
- Configuring an HTTP server to perform echoing and routing
- Configuring an HTTP server to perform file serving
- Making requests to APIs
- Setting up a basic UDP Socket
- Configuring a UDP socket to perform echoing
- Setting up a secure connection via TLS

# Introduction

Through the internet, the world is getting smaller every day. The web connects people in amazing ways. Countless services are available at your fingertips for free. Millions of people can use your apps without even installing it.

As a developer wanting to take advantage of this, porting your app to the internet can be quite easy if you have set your architecture up in a clean way. The only thing you need to change is the layer that interacts with the outside world.

This chapter is going to show you how to create this layer by allowing your application to accept requests, respond to them, and show you how to create requests to other web services on your own.

# Setting up a basic HTTP server

Let's start our chapter by bringing the famous Hello World program into the 21$^{st}$ century by hosting it on a server. We are going to use the `hyper` crate for this, which is a strongly typed wrapper around all things HTTP. In addition to being one of the fastest HTTP implementations in the world (`https://www.techempower.com/benchmarks/#section=data-r15hw=phtest=plaintext`), it is used by nearly *all* major high-level frameworks (`https://github.com/flosse/rust-web-framework-comparison#high-level-frameworks`), the only exception being the ones that reimplemented it all on the extremely basic *stringly-typed* TCP library that Rust provides under `std::net::TcpStream`.

## Getting ready

All `hyper` recipes work with `futures`, so you should read all of Chapter 8, *Working with Futures*, before continuing.

At the time of writing, `hyper` has not yet upgraded to `futures v0.2` (tracking issue: `https://github.com/hyperium/hyper/issues/1448`), so we going to use `futures v0.1`. This should be no problem in the future (no pun intended), as all relevant code is written in a way that should be compatible with `0.2` when it's released.

If some unexpected API change breaks the recipes, you will be able to find a fixed version of them at the book's GitHub repository (`https://github.com/jnferner/rust-standard-library-cookbook/tree/master/chapter-nine/src/bin`), which will always be updated in order to work with the newest versions of all libraries.

## How to do it...

1. Create a Rust project to work on during this chapter with `cargo new chapter-nine`
2. Navigate into the newly created `chapter-nine` folder. For the rest of this chapter, we will assume that your command line is currently in this directory
3. Open the `Cargo.toml` file that has been generated for you
4. Under `[dependencies]`, add the following lines:

```
futures = "0.1.18"
hyper = "0.11.21"
```

5. If you want, you can go to futures' (`https://crates.io/crates/futures`) and hyper's (`https://crates.io/crates/hyper`) *crates.io* pages to check for the newest version and use that one instead

6. Inside the folder `src`, create a new folder called `bin`

7. Delete the generated `lib.rs` file, as we are not creating a library

8. In the folder `src/bin`, create a file called `hello_world_server.rs`

9. Add the following code and run it with `cargo run --bin hello_world_server`:

```
1    extern crate futures;
2    extern crate hyper;
3
4    use futures::future::Future;
5    use hyper::header::{ContentLength, ContentType};
6    use hyper::server::{const_service, service_fn, Http, Request,
Response, Service};
7    use std::net::SocketAddr;
8
9    const MESSAGE: &str = "Hello World!";
10
11   fn main() {
12     // [::1] is the loopback address for IPv6, 3000 is a port
13     let addr = "[::1]:3000".parse().expect("Failed to parse
address");
14     run_with_service_function(&addr).expect("Failed to run web
server");
15   }
```

Run a server by creating a service with `service_fn`:

```
17   fn run_with_service_function(addr: &SocketAddr) -> Result<(),
     hyper::Error> {
18     // Hyper is based on Services, which are construct that
19     // handle how to respond to requests.
20     // const_service and service_fn are convenience functions
21     // that build a service out of a closure
22     let hello_world = const_service(service_fn(|_| {
23       println!("Got a connection!");
24       // Return a Response with a body of type hyper::Body
25       Ok(Response::::new()
26         // Add header specifying content type as plain text
27         .with_header(ContentType::plaintext())
28         // Add header specifying the length of the message in
           bytes
29         .with_header(ContentLength(MESSAGE.len() as u64))
30         // Add body with our message
```

```
31          .with_body(MESSAGE))
32    }));
33
34    let server = Http::new().bind(addr, hello_world)?;
35    server.run()
36  }
```

Run a server by manually creating a `struct` that implements `Service`:

```
38  // The following function does the same, but uses an explicitly
    created
39  // struct HelloWorld that implements the Service trait
40  fn run_with_service_struct(addr: &SocketAddr) -> Result<(),
    hyper::Error> {
41    let server = Http::new().bind(addr, || Ok(HelloWorld))?;
42    server.run()
43  }
44
45  struct HelloWorld;
46  impl Service for HelloWorld {
47    // Implementing a server requires specifying all involved
      types
48    type Request = Request;
49    type Response = Response;
50    type Error = hyper::Error;
51    // The future that wraps your eventual Response
52    type Future = Box<Future>;
53
54    fn call(&self, _: Request) -> Self::Future {
55      // In contrast to service_fn, we need to explicitly return
        a future
56      Box::new(futures::future::ok(
57        Response::new()
58          .with_header(ContentType::plaintext())
59          .with_header(ContentLength(MESSAGE.len() as u64))
60          .with_body(MESSAGE),
61      ))
62    }
63  }
```

# How it works...

In `main`, we first parse a string representing our IPv6 loopback address (think `localhost`) as an `std::net::SocketAddr`, which is a type holding an IP address and a port [13]. Granted, we could have used a constant for our address, but we are showing how to parse it from a string, because in a real application you will probably fetch the address from an environment variable, as shown in `Chapter 1`, *Learning the Basics; Interacting with environment variables*.

We then run our `hyper` server, which we create in `run_with_service_function` [17]. Let's take a look at that function by learning a bit about `hyper`.

The most fundamental trait in `hyper` is the `Service`. It is defined as follows:

```
pub trait Service where
    <Self::Future as Future>::Item == Self::Response,
    <Self::Future as Future>::Error == Self::Error, {
    type Request;
    type Response;
    type Error;
    type Future: Future;
    fn call(&self, req: Self::Request) -> Self::Future;
}
```

It should be easy to read the signature of `call`: It takes a `Request` and returns a `Future` of a `Response`. `hyper` uses this trait to answer to an incoming request. We generally have two ways to define a `Service`:

- Manually create a `struct` that implements `Service`, explicitly setting its associated types to whatever `call` returns
- Let a `Service` be built for you by passing a closure that returns a `Result` to `service_fn`, which you wrap in a `const_service`

Both variants result in the exact same thing, so this example contains both versions to give you a taste of them.

`run_with_service_function` uses the second style [22]. It returns a `Result` of a `Response`, which `service_fn` converts to a `Future` of `Response` because `Result` implements `Future`. `service_fn` then does some type deduction for us and creates a kind of `Service`. But we aren't done yet. You see, when `hyper` receives a new connection, it will not call our `Service` directly with the `Request`, but first makes a copy of it in order to handle every connection with its very own `Service`. This means that our `Service` must have the ability to create new instances of itself, which is indicated by the `NewService` trait. Luckily, we don't need to implement it ourselves either. The closure at the heart of our `Service` doesn't manage any state, so we can call it a constant function. Constants are very easy to copy, as all copies are guaranteed to be identical. We can mark our `Service` as constant by calling `const_service` on it, which basically just wraps the `Service` in an `Arc` and then implements `NewService` by simply returning a copy of it. But what exactly is our `Service` returning anyways?

`Response<hyper::Body>` creates a new HTTP response [25] and manages its body as a `hyper::Body`, which is a future `Stream<Chunk>`. A `Chunk` is just a piece of an HTTP message. This `Response` is a builder, so we can change the contents of it by calling various methods. In our code, we set its `Content-Type` header to `plaintext`, which is a `hyper` shortcut for the MIME type `text/plain` [27].

 A MIME type is a label for data served over HTTP. It tells the client how to treat the data it receives. For example, most browsers will not render the message `<p>Hello World!</p>` as HTML unless it comes with the header `Content-Type: text/html`.

We also set its `Content-Length` header to the length (in bytes) of our message so the client knows how much data they should expect [29]. Finally, we set the message's body to the message, which then gets sent to the client as `"Hello World!"` [31].

Our service can now be bound to a new instance of `hyper::server::Http`, which we then run [34 and 35]. You can now open your browser of choice and point it to `http://localhost:3000`. If everything went right, you should be greeted by a `Hello World!` message.

The same thing would happen if we called `run_with_service_struct` instead, which uses a manually created `Service` instead [40]. A quick inspection of its implementation shows us the key differences to the last approach [45 to 63]:

```
struct HelloWorld;
impl Service for HelloWorld {
    type Request = Request;
    type Response = Response;
```

```
    type Error = hyper::Error;
    type Future = Box<Future<Item = Self::Response, Error =
    Self::Error>>;

    fn call(&self, _: Request) -> Self::Future {
        Box::new(futures::future::ok(
            Response::new()
                .with_header(ContentType::plaintext())
                .with_header(ContentLength(MESSAGE.len() as u64))
                .with_body(MESSAGE),
        ))
    }
}
```

As you can see, we need to explicitly specify the concrete type of basically everything [48 to 52]. We also can't simply return a `Result` in our `call` method and need to return the actual `Future`, wrapped in a `Box` [56], so we don't need to think about which exact flavor of `Future` we are using.

On the other hand, this approach has one big advantage over the other: It can manage state in the form of members. Because all `hyper` recipes in this chapter work with constant Services, that is Services that will return the same `Response` to equal Requests, we will use the first variant to create Services. This is simply a stylistic decision based on simplicity, as they are all small enough that it wouldn't be worth it to extract them into an own `struct`. In your projects, use whichever form suits the current use case best.

## See also

- *Using the builder pattern* and *Interacting with environment variables* recipe in Chapter 1, *Learning the Basics*

# Configuring an HTTP server to perform echoing and routing

We learned how to serve the same response forever, but that would get pretty dull after a while. In this recipe, you are going to learn how to read requests and respond to them individually. For this, we will use routing to differentiate between requests to different endpoints.

# Getting ready

To test this recipe, you will need a way to easily send HTTP requests. An excellent free tool for this is Postman (https://www.getpostman.com/), which features a nice and self-explanatory UI. If you'd rather not download anything, you can use your terminal for this. If you're on Windows, you can open PowerShell and enter the following to do an HTTP request:

```
Invoke-WebRequest -UseBasicParsing <Your URL> -Method <Your method in
CAPSLOCK> -Body <Your message as a string>
```

So, if you wanted to POST the message hello there, my echoing friend to http://localhost:3000/echo, as you will be asked to later in the recipe, you'd need to enter the following command:

```
Invoke-WebRequest -UseBasicParsing http://localhost:3000/echo -Method POST
-Body "Hello there, my echoing friend"
```

On Unix systems, you can use cURL for that (https://curl.haxx.se/). The analog command is the following:

```
curl -X <Your method> --data <Your message> -g <Your URL>
```

cURL will resolve localhost to its entry in /etc/hosts. In some configurations, this will only be the IPv4 loopback address (127.0.0.1). In some others, you will have to use ip6-localhost. Check your /etc/hosts to find out what to use. In any case, an explicit [::1] will always work. As an example, the following command will again POST the message hello there, my echoing friend to http://localhost:3000/echo:

```
curl -X POST --data "Hello there my echoing friend" -g
"http://[::1]:3000/echo"
```

# How to do it...

1. Open the Cargo.toml file that has been generated for you
2. Under [dependencies], if you didn't do so in the last recipe, add the following lines:

```
futures = "0.1.18"
hyper = "0.11.21"
```

3. If you want, you can go to futures' (`https://crates.io/crates/futures`) and hyper's (`https://crates.io/crates/hyper`) *crates.io* pages to check for the newest version and use that one instead

4. In the folder `src/bin`, create a file called `echo_server_with_routing.rs`

5. Add the following code and run it with `cargo run --bin echo_server_with_routing`:

```
1    extern crate hyper;
2
3    use hyper::{Method, StatusCode};
4    use hyper::server::{const_service, service_fn, Http, Request,
     Response};
5    use hyper::header::{ContentLength, ContentType};
6    use std::net::SocketAddr;
7
8    fn main() {
9      let addr = "[::1]:3000".parse().expect("Failed to parse
        address");
10     run_echo_server(&addr).expect("Failed to run web server");
11   }
12
13   fn run_echo_server(addr: &SocketAddr) -> Result<(),
     hyper::Error> {
14     let echo_service = const_service(service_fn(|req: Request| {
15       // An easy way to implement routing is
16       // to simply match the request's path
17       match (req.method(), req.path()) {
18         (&Method::Get, "/") => handle_root(),
19         (&Method::Post, "/echo") => handle_echo(req),
20         _ => handle_not_found(),
21       }
22     }));
23
24     let server = Http::new().bind(addr, echo_service)?;
25     server.run()
26   }
```

The functions are handling the routes:

```
28   type ResponseResult = Result<Response, hyper::Error>;
29   fn handle_root() -> ResponseResult {
30     const MSG: &str = "Try doing a POST at /echo";
31     Ok(Response::new()
32       .with_header(ContentType::plaintext())
33       .with_header(ContentLength(MSG.len() as u64))
34       .with_body(MSG))
35   }
```

```
36
37  fn handle_echo(req: Request) -> ResponseResult {
38    // The echoing is implemented by setting the response's
39    // body to the request's body
40    Ok(Response::new().with_body(req.body()))
41  }
42
43  fn handle_not_found() -> ResponseResult {
44    // Return a 404 for every unsupported route
45    Ok(Response::new().with_status(StatusCode::NotFound))
46  }
```

## How it works...

This recipe begins like the last one, so let's skip straight into the definition of our
Service[14 to 22]:

```
|req: Request| {
    match (req.method(), req.path()) {
        (&Method::Get, "/") => handle_root(),
        (&Method::Post, "/echo") => handle_echo(req),
        _ => handle_not_found(),
    }
}
```

We are now using the Request parameter that the last recipe simply ignored.

Because Rust allows us to pattern match on tuples, we can directly differentiate between
HTTP methods and path combinations. We then pass on the control flow of our program to
dedicated route handlers, which in turn are responsible for returning the response.

 In bigger programs with tons of routes, we would not specify them all in
one function, but spread them across namespaces and split them into
subrouters.

The code for handle_root [29] looks nearly identical to the hello world Service from the
last chapter, but instructs the caller to POST at the /post route.

Our match for said POST leads to handle_echo [37], which simply returns the request's
body as the response's body [40]. You can try this for yourself by POSTing a message to
http://localhost:3000/echo, as described in the *Getting ready* section. If everything
goes right, your message will come right back at you.

Last, but not least, `handle_not_found` [43] is called when no routes matched. This time, we don't send a message back, but instead, return the possible most famous status code of the world: `404 Not Found` [45].

# Configuring an HTTP server to perform file serving

The last recipes were really useful for building web services, but let's take a look at how to do the thing HTTP was originally created for: serving HTML files to the web.

# How to do it...

1. Open the `Cargo.toml` file that has been generated for you.
2. Under `[dependencies]`, if you didn't do so in the last recipe, add the following lines:

```
futures = "0.1.18"
hyper = "0.11.21"
```

3. If you want, you can go to futures' (`https://crates.io/crates/futures`) and hyper's (`https://crates.io/crates/hyper`) *crates.io* pages to check for the newest version and use that one instead.
4. In the folder `chapter-nine`, create a folder called `files`.
5. In the folder `files`, create a file called `index.html` and add the following code to it:

```
<!doctype html>
<html>

<head>
    <link rel="stylesheet" type="text/css" href="/style.css">
    <title>Home</title>
</head>

<body>
    <h1>Home</h1>
    <p>Welcome. You can access other files on this web server
    aswell! Available links:</p>
    <ul>
        <li>
```

```
                <a href="/foo.html">Foo!</a>
        </li>
        <li>
                <a href="/bar.html">Bar!</a>
        </li>
    </ul>
</body>

</html>
```

6. In the folder `files`, create a file called `foo.html` and add the following code to it:

```
<!doctype html>
<html>

<head>
    <link rel="stylesheet" type="text/css" href="/style.css">
    <title>Foo</title>
</head>

<body>
    <p>Foo!</p>
</body>

</html>
```

7. In the folder `files`, create a file called `bar.html` and add the following code to it:

```
<!doctype html>
<html>

<head>
    <link rel="stylesheet" type="text/css" href="/style.css">
    <title>Bar</title>
</head>

<body>
    <p>Bar!</p>
</body>

</html>
```

8. In the folder `files`, create a file called `not_found.html` and add the following code to it:

```
<!doctype html>
<html>

<head>
    <link rel="stylesheet" type="text/css" href="/style.css">
    <title>Page Not Found</title>
</head>

<body>
    <h1>Page Not Found</h1>
    <p>We're sorry, we couldn't find the page you requested.</p>
    <p>Maybe it was renamed or moved?</p>
    <p>Try searching at the
        <a href="/index.html">start page</a>
    </p>
</body>

</html>
```

9. In the folder `files`, create a file called `invalid_method.html` and add the following code to it:

```
<!doctype html>
<html>

<head>
    <link rel="stylesheet" type="text/css" href="/style.css">
    <title>Error 405 (Method Not Allowed)</title>
</head>

<body>
    <h1>Error 405</h1>
    <p>The method used is not allowed for this URL</p>
</body>

</html>
```

10. In the folder `src/bin`, create a file called `file_server.rs`.

11. Add the following code and run it with `cargo run --bin echo_server_with_routing`:

```
1    extern crate futures;
2    extern crate hyper;
3
```

```
4   use hyper::{Method, StatusCode};
5   use hyper::server::{const_service, service_fn, Http, Request,
    Response};
6   use hyper::header::{ContentLength, ContentType};
7   use hyper::mime;
8   use futures::Future;
9   use futures::sync::oneshot;
10  use std::net::SocketAddr;
11  use std::thread;
12  use std::fs::File;
13  use std::io::{self, copy};
14
15  fn main() {
16    let addr = "[::1]:3000".parse().expect("Failed to parse
      address");
17    run_file_server(&addr).expect("Failed to run web server");
18  }
19
20  fn run_file_server(addr: &SocketAddr) -> Result<(),
    hyper::Error> {
21    let file_service = const_service(service_fn(|req: Request| {
22      // Setting up our routes
23      match (req.method(), req.path()) {
24        (&Method::Get, "/") => handle_root(),
25        (&Method::Get, path) => handle_get_file(path),
26        _ => handle_invalid_method(),
27      }
28    }));
29
30    let server = Http::new().bind(addr, file_service)?;
31    server.run()
32  }
```

The following are the route handlers:

```
34  // Because we don't want the entire server to block when
    serving
      a file,
35  // we are going to return a response wrapped in a future
36  type ResponseFuture = Box<Future>;
37  fn handle_root() -> ResponseFuture {
38    // Send the landing page
39    send_file_or_404("index.html")
40  }
41
42  fn handle_get_file(file: &str) -> ResponseFuture {
43    // Send whatever page was requested or fall back to a 404
    page
```

```
44     send_file_or_404(file)
45   }
46
47   fn handle_invalid_method() -> ResponseFuture {
48     // Send a page telling the user that the method he used is
not
       supported
49     let response_future = send_file_or_404("invalid_method.html")
50       // Set the correct status code
51       .and_then(|response|
         Ok(response.with_status(StatusCode::MethodNotAllowed)));
52     Box::new(response_future)
53   }
```

The following is the code for the functions returning the futures with our files:

```
55   // Send a future containing a response with the requested file
     or a 404 page
56   fn send_file_or_404(path: &str) -> ResponseFuture {
57     // Sanitize the input to prevent unwanted data access
58     let path = sanitize_path(path);
59
60     let response_future = try_to_send_file(&path)
61       // try_to_send_file returns a future of Result<Response,
         io::Error>
62       // turn it into a future of a future of Response with an
         error of hyper::Error
63       .and_then(|response_result| response_result.map_err(|error|
         error.into()))
64       // If something went wrong, send the 404 page instead
65       .or_else(|_| send_404());
66     Box::new(response_future)
67   }
68
69   // Return a requested file in a future of Result<Response,
     io::Error>
70   // to indicate whether it exists or not
71   type ResponseResultFuture = Box<Future, Error = hyper::Error>>;
72   fn try_to_send_file(file: &str) -> ResponseResultFuture {
73     // Prepend "files/" to the file
74     let path = path_on_disk(file);
75     // Load the file in a separate thread into memory.
76     // As soon as it's done, send it back through a channel
77     let (tx, rx) = oneshot::channel();
78     thread::spawn(move || {
79       let mut file = match File::open(&path) {
80         Ok(file) => file,
81         Err(err) => {
```

```
82          println!("Failed to find file: {}", path);
83          // Send error through channel
84          tx.send(Err(err)).expect("Send error on file not
            found");
85          return;
86        }
87      };
88
89      // buf is our in-memory representation of the file
90      let mut buf: Vec = Vec::new();
91      match copy(&mut file, &mut buf) {
92        Ok(_) => {
93          println!("Sending file: {}", path);
94          // Detect the content type by checking the file
            extension
95          // or fall back to plaintext
96          let content_type =
            get_content_type(&path).unwrap_or_else
            (ContentType::plaintext);
97          let res = Response::new()
98            .with_header(ContentLength(buf.len() as u64))
99            .with_header(content_type)
100           .with_body(buf);
101         // Send file through channel
102         tx.send(Ok(res))
103           .expect("Send error on successful file read");
104       }
105       Err(err) => {
106         // Send error through channel
107         tx.send(Err(err)).expect("Send error on error reading
            file");
108       }
109     };
110   });
111   // Convert all encountered errors to hyper::Error
112   Box::new(rx.map_err(|error|
      io::Error::new(io::ErrorKind::Other,
      error).into()))
113 }
114
115 fn send_404() -> ResponseFuture {
116   // Try to send our 404 page
117   let response_future =
      try_to_send_file("not_found.html").and_then(|response_result|
      {
118     Ok(response_result.unwrap_or_else(|_| {
119       // If the 404 page doesn't exist, sent fallback text
            instead
```

```
120        const ERROR_MSG: &str = "Failed to find \"File not
found\"
           page. How ironic\n";
121        Response::new()
122          .with_status(StatusCode::NotFound)
123          .with_header(ContentLength(ERROR_MSG.len() as u64))
124          .with_body(ERROR_MSG)
125      }))
126    });
127    Box::new(response_future)
128 }
```

The following are some helper functions:

```
130  fn sanitize_path(path: &str) -> String {
131    // Normalize the separators for the next steps
132    path.replace("\\", "/")
133      // Prevent the user from going up the filesystem
134      .replace("../", "")
135      // If the path comes straigh from the router,
136      // it will begin with a slash
137      .trim_left_matches(|c| c == '/')
138      // Remove slashes at the end as we only serve files
139      .trim_right_matches(|c| c == '/')
140      .to_string()
141  }
142
143  fn path_on_disk(path_to_file: &str) -> String {
144    "files/".to_string() + path_to_file
145  }
146
147  fn get_content_type(file: &str) -> Option {
148    // Check the file extension and return the respective MIME
type
149    let pos = file.rfind('.')? + 1;
150    let mime_type = match &file[pos..] {
151      "txt" => mime::TEXT_PLAIN_UTF_8,
152      "html" => mime::TEXT_HTML_UTF_8,
153      "css" => mime::TEXT_CSS,
154      // This list can be extended for all types your server
      should support
155      _ => return None,
156    };
157    Some(ContentType(mime_type))
158  }
```

# How it works...

Wow! That was a lot of files. Of course, the exact content of the HTML and CSS doesn't matter for this recipe, as we're going to be focused on Rust. We've put them all in the `files` folder because we are going to make its contents publicly accessible by name for any client.

The basics of the server setup are the same as with the echoing recipe: create a `Service` with `const_service` and `service_fn` [21], match the request's method and path, and then handle the routes in different functions. When looking at our return type, however, we can notice a difference [36]:

```
type ResponseFuture = Box<Future<Item = Response, Error =
hyper::Error>>;
```

We are no longer returning a `Response` directly, but instead, wrapping it in a `Future`. This allows us to not block the server when loading a file into memory; we can continue handling requests in the main thread while the file serving `Future` is run in the background.

When looking at our route handlers, you can see that they all use the `send_file_or_404` function. Let's take a look at it [56]:

```
fn send_file_or_404(path: &str) -> ResponseFuture {
    let path = sanitize_path(path);

    let response_future = try_to_send_file(&path)
        .and_then(|response_result| response_result.map_err(|error|
        error.into()))
        .or_else(|_| send_404());
    Box::new(response_future)
}
```

First, the function sanitizes our input. The implementation of `sanitize_path` [130 to 141] should be pretty straightforward. It filters out potential troublemakers so that a malicious client cannot do any shenanigans, such as requesting the file `localhost:3000/../../../../home/admin/.ssh/id_rsa`.

We then call `try_to_send_file` on the sanitized path [72]. We are going to look at that function in a minute, but for now, it's enough to look at its signature. It tells us that it returns a `Future` of a `Result` that can be a `Response` or an `io::Error`, as that's the error encountered on invalid filesystem access. We cannot return this `Future` directly, since we already told `hyper` that we are going to return a `Future` of `Response`, so we need to convert the types. If the file retrieving `Future` generated from `try_to_send_file` succeeded, we act on its item, which is a `Result<Response, io::Error>`.

Because `hyper::Error` implements `From<io::Error>`, we can convert them easily by calling `.into()` [63] (see `Chapter 5`, *Advanced Data Structures*; *Converting types*, for an introduction to the `From` trait). This will return a `Result<Response, hyper::Error>`. Because a `Future` is constructable from a `Result`, it will be implicitly converted to a `Future<Response, hyper::Error>` for us, which is exactly what we want. A little cherry on top is our handling of `try_to_send_file` returning an error, in which case we can safely assume that the file doesn't exist, so we return a `Future` with a custom `404 Not Found` page by calling `send_404()` [65]. Before looking at its implementation, let's check out `try_to_send_file` first [72].

First, we convert the requested path into a local filesystem path with `path_on_disk` [74], which is simply implemented as follows [144]:

```
"files/".to_string() + path_to_file
```

We created an own function for this so it will be easy for you to extend the filesystem logic. For example, for Unix systems, it is usual to put all static HTML in `/var/www/`, while Windows web servers usually put all of their data in their own installation folder. Or you may want to read a configuration file provided by the user and store its value in a `lazy_static`, as shown in `Chapter 5`, *Advanced Data Structures*; *Using lazy static variable*, and use that path instead. You can implement all of those rules in this function.

Back in `try_to_send_file`, we create a `oneshot::channel` to send data as a `Future` [77]. This concept is explained in detail in `Chapter 8`, *Working with Futures*; *Using the oneshot channel*. The rest of the function now creates a new thread to load the file into memory in the background [78]. We first open the file [79] and return an error through the channel if it doesn't exist. We then copy the entire file into a local vector of bytes [91] and again propagate any error that might occur [107]. If the process of copying into RAM succeeded, we return a `Response` with the content of the file as its body [100]. Along the way, we have to figure out the file's appropriate MIME type [96], as promised in the recipe *Setting up a basic HTTP server*. For that, we simply match the extension of the file [147 to 158]:

```rust
fn get_content_type(file: &str) -> Option<ContentType> {
    let pos = file.rfind('.')? + 1;
    let mime_type = match &file[pos..] {
        "txt" => mime::TEXT_PLAIN_UTF_8,
        "html" => mime::TEXT_HTML_UTF_8,
        "css" => mime::TEXT_CSS,
        _ => return None,
    };
    Some(ContentType(mime_type))
}
```

You may think this implementation is pretty lazy and that there should be a better way, but, trust me, this is exactly how all big web servers do it. Case in point, you can find nginx (`https://nginx.org/en/`) mime detection algorithm here: `https://github.com/nginx/nginx/blob/master/conf/mime.types`. If you plan on serving new file types, you can extend the `match` for their extensions. The `nginx` source is a good resource for this.

`get_content_type` returns `None` if there was no match [155] instead of a default content type, so that every caller can decide on a default for themselves. In `try_to_send_file`, we use `.unwrap_or_else(ContentType::plaintext);` [96] to set the fallback MIME type to `text/plain`.

The last unexplained function left in our example is `send_404`, which we use a lot as a fallback. You can see that all it really does is call `try_to_send_file` on the 404 page [117] and on error send a static message instead [124].

The fallback in `send_404` really shows us the beauty in Rust's error handling concept. Because strongly typed errors are part of a function's signature, as opposed to languages such as C++, where you never know who might throw an exception, you are forced to consciously handle the error cases. Try to remove `and_then` and its associated closure and you'll see that the compiler doesn't let you compile your program because you didn't handle the `Result` of `try_to_send_file` in any way.

Go ahead now and see the results of our file server with your own eyes by pointing your browser to `http://localhost:3000/`.

## There's more...

Despite being relatively easy to understand, our implementation of `try_to_send_file` is not endlessly scalable. Imagine serving and loading huge files into memory for millions of clients at the same time. That would bring your RAM to its limits pretty quickly. A more scalable solution is to send the file in chunks, that is part by part, so that you only need to hold a small part of it in memory at any given time. To implement this, you'll need to copy the contents of your file to a limited `[u8]` buffer with a fixed size and send that through an additional channel as an instance of `hyper::Chunk`, which implements `From<Vec<T>>`.

# See also

- *Converting types into each other* and *Creating lazy static variables* recipe in `Chapter 5`, *Advanced Data Structures*
- *Using the oneshot channel* recipe in `Chapter 8`, *Working with Futures*

# Making requests to APIs

Our last destination in this chapter brings us away from the server in favor of the other party participating in internet communication: the client. We will use `reqwest`, which is built around `hyper`, to create HTTPS requests to web services and parse their data into nicely usable Rust structures. You can also use the content of this recipe to write integration tests for your own web services.

# How to do it...

1. Open the `Cargo.toml` file that has been generated for you
2. Under `[dependencies]`, if you didn't do so in the last recipe, add the following lines:

   ```
   reqwest = "0.8.5"
   serde = "1.0.30"
   serde_derive = "1.0.30"
   ```

3. If you want, you can go to `request`'s (https://crates.io/crates/reqwest), `serde`'s (https://crates.io/crates/serde), and `serde_derive`'s (https://crates.io/crates/serde_derive) *crates.io* pages to check for the newest versions and use those ones instead
4. In the folder `src/bin`, create a file called `making_requests.rs`
5. Add the following code and run it with `cargo run --bin making_requests`:

   ```
   1   extern crate reqwest;
   2   #[macro_use]
   3   extern crate serde_derive;
   4
   5   use std::fmt;
   6
   7   #[derive(Serialize, Deserialize, Debug)]
   8   // The JSON returned by the web service that hands posts out
   ```

```
 9   // it written in camelCase, so we need to tell serde about that
10   #[serde(rename_all = "camelCase")]
11   struct Post {
12     user_id: u32,
13     id: u32,
14     title: String,
15     body: String,
16   }
17
18   #[derive(Serialize, Deserialize, Debug)]
19   #[serde(rename_all = "camelCase")]
20   struct NewPost {
21     user_id: u32,
22     title: String,
23     body: String,
24   }
25
26   #[derive(Serialize, Deserialize, Debug)]
27   #[serde(rename_all = "camelCase")]
28   // The following struct could be rewritten with a builder
29   struct UpdatedPost {
30     #[serde(skip_serializing_if = "Option::is_none")]
31     user_id: Option,
32     #[serde(skip_serializing_if = "Option::is_none")]
33     title: Option,
34     #[serde(skip_serializing_if = "Option::is_none")]
35     body: Option,
36   }
37
38   struct PostCrud {
39     client: reqwest::Client,
40     endpoint: String,
41   }
42
43   impl fmt::Display for Post {
44     fn fmt(&self, f: &mut fmt::Formatter) -> fmt::Result {
45       write!(
46         f,
47         "User ID: {}\nID: {}\nTitle: {}\nBody: {}\n",
48         self.user_id, self.id, self.title, self.body
49       )
50     }
51   }
```

The following code shows the requests being implemented:

```
53   impl PostCrud {
54     fn new() -> Self {
```

```
55        PostCrud {
56          // Build an HTTP client. It's reusable!
57          client: reqwest::Client::new(),
58          // This is a link to a fake REST API service
59          endpoint:
            "https://jsonplaceholder.typicode.com/posts".to_string(),
60        }
61      }
62
63      fn create(&self, post: &NewPost) -> Result<Post,
        reqwest::Error> {
64        let response =
self.client.post(&self.endpoint).json(post).send()?.json()?;
65        Ok(response)
66      }
67
68      fn read(&self, id: u32) -> Result<Post, reqwest::Error> {
69        let url = format!("{}/{}", self.endpoint, id);
70        let response = self.client.get(&url).send()?.json()?;
71        Ok(response)
72      }
73
74      fn update(&self, id: u32, post: &UpdatedPost) -> Result<Post,
        reqwest::Error> {
75        let url = format!("{}/{}", self.endpoint, id);
76        let response =
            self.client.patch(&url).json(post).send()?.json()?;
77        Ok(response)
78      }
79
80      fn delete(&self, id: u32) -> Result<(), reqwest::Error> {
81        let url = format!("{}/{}", self.endpoint, id);
82        self.client.delete(&url).send()?;
83        Ok(())
84      }
85    }
```

The following code shows us using our CRUD client:

```
87   fn main() {
88     let post_crud = PostCrud::new();
89     let post = post_crud.read(1).expect("Failed to read post");
90     println!("Read a post:\n{}", post);
91
92     let new_post = NewPost {
93       user_id: 2,
94       title: "Hello World!".to_string(),
95       body: "This is a new post, sent to a fake JSON API
```

```
               server.\n".to_string(),
96      };
97      let post = post_crud.create(&new_post).expect("Failed to
        create post");
98      println!("Created a post:\n{}", post);
99
100     let updated_post = UpdatedPost {
101        user_id: None,
102        title: Some("New title".to_string()),
103        body: None,
104     };
105     let post = post_crud
106        .update(4, &updated_post)
107        .expect("Failed to update post");
108     println!("Updated a post:\n{}", post);
109
110     post_crud.delete(51).expect("Failed to delete post");
111 }
```

# How it works...

At the top, we define our structures. Post[11], NewPost [20], and UpdatedPost [29] all just represent convenient ways to handle the different requirements of the API. The particular JSON API we are interacting with uses camelCase variables, so we need to specify this on every struct, otherwise serde won't be able to parse them correctly [10, 19 and 27].

Because the PATCH method we're communicating with doesn't accept null values on unchanged variables, we mark them all in UpdatedPost as not serialized when equal to None [30, 32 and 34]:

```
#[serde(skip_serializing_if = "Option::is_none")]
```

Additionally, we implement the fmt::Display trait on Post, so we can print it nicely [43 to 51].

But enough about our models; let's take a look at PostCrud [53]. Its purpose is to abstract a CRUD (Create, Read, Update, Delete) service. For this, it is equipped with a reusable HTTP client via reqwest::Client [57] and a mock JSON API endpoint from https://jsonplaceholder.typicode.com/

Its methods show you how easy `reqwest` is to use: you simply use the required HTTP method directly as a function on the client, pass optional data to it, which it will automatically deserialize for you with `.json()`, `.send()` the request, and then parse the response again as JSON with a second call to `.json()` [64].

## There's more...

Of course, `reqwest` is able to work with non-JSON-based web services as well. It has various methods for this such as `query`, which adds an array of key-value queries to the URL, or `form`, which will add `url-encoded` form bodies to the request. While using all these methods, `reqwest` will manage the headers for you, but you can manage them however explicitly you want using the `headers` method.

## See also

- *Using the builder pattern* recipe in `Chapter 1`, *Learning the Basics*
- *Serialization basics with Serde* recipe in `Chapter 4`, *Serialization*

# 10
# Using Experimental Nightly Features

In this chapter, we will cover the following recipes:

- Iterating over an inclusive range
- Returning abstract types
- Composing functions
- Filtering strings efficiently
- Stepping through an iterator in regular intervals
- Benchmarking your code
- Using generators

## Introduction

This final chapter leads us to the most important experimental features in Rust, provided on the newest `nightly` toolchain. As of the time of writing, this is `rustc 1.25.0-nightly`. If you are using `rustup` (`https://rustup.rs/`), you can set it as your default toolchain like this:

```
rustup default nightly
```

These recipes will ensure that you stay ahead in your knowledge of Rust, and are ready to use them effectively once they are stabilized, or right now in your own unstable apps.

All of the recipes in this chapter have varying stability guarantees. Many will undergo drastic changes before they land in the `stable` toolchain, and others are nearly done. This means that some of the example code provided is expected not to work on your newest `nightly`. When this happens, you can find help in two places:

- If the feature is still experimental, it will have an entry in *The Unstable Book* (`https://doc.rust-lang.org/unstable-book/`), and a link to the relevant GitHub issue and its surrounding discussion
- If the feature has been stabilized, there is a good chance you will find it listed in the appendix of *The Rust Programming Language, Second Edition* (`https://doc.rust-lang.org/stable/book/second-edition/appendix-06-newest-features.html`)

# Iterating over an inclusive range

We begin the chapter with a small feature that can make your code a bit more readable. The inclusive range syntax (`..=`) will create a range up to a value *including* it. This helps you eliminate ugly instances of things like `n .. m+1` by rewriting them as `n ..= m`.

# How to do it...

1. Create a Rust project to work on during this chapter with `cargo new chapter-ten`.
2. Navigate into the newly-created `chapter-ten` folder. For the rest of this chapter, we will assume that your command line is currently in this directory.
3. Delete the generated `lib.rs` file, as we are not creating a library.
4. Inside the `src` folder, create a new folder called `bin`.
5. In the `src/bin` folder, create a file called `inclusive_range.rs`.
6. Add the following code, and run it with `cargo run --bin inclusive_range`:

```
1    #![feature(inclusive_range_syntax)]
2
3    fn main() {
4      // Retrieve the entire alphabet in lower and uppercase:
5      let alphabet: Vec<_> = (b'A' .. b'z' + 1) // Start as u8
6        .map(|c| c as char)        // Convert all to chars
7        .filter(|c| c.is_alphabetic()) // Filter only alphabetic
         chars
8        .collect(); // Collect as Vec
```

```
9      println!("alphabet: {:?}", alphabet);
10
11     // Do the same, but using the inclusive range syntax:
12     let alphabet: Vec<_> = (b'A' ..= b'z') // Start as u8
13       .map(|c| c as char)      // Convert all to chars
14       .filter(|c| c.is_alphabetic()) // Filter only alphabetic
          chars
15       .collect(); // Collect as Vec
16     println!("alphabet: {:?}", alphabet);
17   }
```

# How it works...

In this example, the code is the promised rewrite of a snippet in `Chapter 2`, *Working with Collections*; *Accessing collections as iterators*.

The traditional range syntax (n .. m) is exclusive, meaning that 0 .. 5 will only include the numbers 0, 1, 2, 3, and 4. This is good for uses cases where you count up to a length of something, but in our case, we want to iterate over the alphabet, including Z [5]. The inclusive range syntax (n ..= m) helps us by including the last element, so that 0 ..= 5 will yield 0, 1, 2, 3, 4, and 5.

# See also

- *Accessing collections as iterators* recipe in `Chapter 2`, *Working with Collections*

# Returning abstract types

Remember when we used `Box` to create trait objects in order to hide the exact implementation returned, and instead only give guarantees about implemented traits? That required us to accept some overhead, as a `Box` allocates its resources on the heap; however, on the current `nightly`, things are different. You can use the `impl trait` syntax introduced in this recipe to return objects as their trait directly on the stack, all without boxes. At the moment, this only works for returned types, but the syntax is planned to be extended to most places where you could write a concrete type.

# How to do it...

1. Open the `Cargo.toml` file that has been generated earlier for you.

2. In the `bin` folder, create a file called `return_abstract.rs`.

3. Add the following code, and run it with `cargo run --bin return_abstract`:

```
1   #![feature(conservative_impl_trait)]
2
3   trait Animal {
4     fn do_sound(&self);
5   }
6
7   struct Dog;
8   impl Animal for Dog {
9     fn do_sound(&self) {
10       println!("Woof");
11     }
12  }
13
14  fn main() {
15    // The caller doesn't know which exact object he gets
16    // He knows only that it implements the Animal trait
17    let animal = create_animal();
18    animal.do_sound();
19
20    for word in caps_words_iter("do you feel lucky, punk?") {
21      println!("{}", word);
22    }
23
24    let multiplier = create_multiplier(23);
25    let result = multiplier(3);
26    println!("23 * 3 = {}", result);
27  }
28
29  // The impl trait syntax allows us to use abstract return types
30  // This means that we don't specify which exact struct we return
31  // but which trait(s) it implements
32  fn create_animal() -> impl Animal {
33    Dog {}
34  }
35
36  // Any iterator can be returned as an abstract return type
37  fn caps_words_iter<'a>(text: &'a str) -> impl Iterator + 'a {
```

```
38      // Return an iterator over every word converted into ALL_CAPS
39      text.trim().split(' ').map(|word| word.to_uppercase())
40   }
41
42   // Same goes for closures
43   fn create_multiplier(a: i32) -> impl Fn(i32) -> i32 {
44      move |b| a * b
45   }
```

# How it works...

If you've read `Chapter 5`, *Advanced Data Structures; Boxing data*, this recipe doesn't need much explanation. By returning an `impl trait`, we tell the caller of a function to not care about the specific struct that is returned, and that its only guarantee about it is that it implements some trait. In this sense, abstract return types work like the trait objects discussed in the said recipe, with the added bonus of being way faster, as they don't have any overhead. This is useful for returning iterators [37] and closures [43], which we adapted from the recipe about boxes, but also to hide implementation details. Consider our function `create_animal`[32]. A caller will only care that it returns a struct that implements `Animal`, but not which exact animal. If a `Dog` [7] doesn't prove to be the right thing because of changing requirements, you can create a `Cat`, and return that one without touching the rest of the code, as it all just depends on `Animal`. This is a form of *dependency inversion* (`https:/ /en.wikipedia.org/wiki/Dependency_inversion_principle`).

The `conservative` in `conservative_impl_trait` [1] tells us that this is just a part of a bigger feature. At the moment, you can only use it in return types of functions. In the future, you'll be able to use it in traits, constraints, and bindings as well.

# There's more...

Of all the recipes in this chapter, this one is probably the most stable, as it is being considered for immediate stabilization. The discussion can be found at `https://github.com/rust-lang/rust/issues/34511`.

While you can use abstract return types for some forms of dependency inversion, you cannot use them for traditional Java-style factories that return different objects depending on a parameter. This is because abstract return types only hide the specific struct returned on the outside of the function, but still internally rely on a specific return value. Because of this, the following code will not compile:

```rust
trait Animal {
    fn do_sound(&self);
}

struct Dog;
impl Animal for Dog {
    fn do_sound(&self) {
        println!("Woof");
    }
}
struct Cat;
impl Animal for Cat {
    fn do_sound(&self) {
        println!("Meow");
    }
}

enum AnimalType {
    Dog,
    Cat,
}

fn create_animal(animal_type: AnimalType) -> impl Animal {
    match animal_type {
        AnimalType::Cat => Cat {},
        AnimalType::Dog => Dog {},
    }
}
```

While the outside world doesn't know which animal is going to be returned by `create_animal`, the function itself needs a specific return type internally. Because the first possible return from our match is an instance of `Cat`, `create_animal` assumes that we are going to return no other type. We break that expectation in the next line by returning a `Dog`, so the compiler fails:

```
error[E0308]: match arms have incompatible types
  --> src/main.rs:26:5
   |
26 | /       match animal_type {
27 | |           AnimalType::Cat => Cat {},
28 | |           AnimalType::Dog => Dog {},
   | |                               ------ match arm with an incompatible type
29 | |       }
   | |_____^ expected struct `Cat`, found struct `Dog`
   |
   = note: expected type `Cat`
              found type `Dog`
```

If we want this factory to compile, we need to resort back to `Box` again:

```
fn create_animal(animal_type: AnimalType) -> Box<Animal> {
    match animal_type {
        AnimalType::Cat => Box::new(Cat {}),
        AnimalType::Dog => Box::new(Dog {}),
    }
}
```

 By the way, this is also exactly what Java does under the hood.

For most purposes, you won't need a factory such as the one presented here. It is considered more idiomatic to use generics with trait bounds.

# See also

- *Boxing data* recipe in `Chapter 5`, *Advanced Data Structures*

# Composing functions

Because we have now learned how to return arbitrary closures with no overhead, we can combine that with macros that accept any number of parameters (`Chapter 1`, *Learning the Basics*; *Accepting a variable number of arguments*) to create an easy way to chain actions as you would be used to in functional languages such as *Haskell*.

# How to do it...

1. Open the `Cargo.toml` file that has been generated earlier for you.

2. In the `bin` folder, create a file called `compose_functions.rs`.

3. Add the following code, and run it with `cargo run --bin compose_functions`:

```
1    #![feature(conservative_impl_trait)]
2
3    // The compose! macro takes a variadic amount of closures and
     returns
4    // a closure that applies them all one after another
5    macro_rules! compose {
6      ( $last:expr ) => { $last };
7      ( $head:expr, $ ($tail:expr), +) => {
8        compose_two($head, compose!($ ($tail), +))
9      };
10   }
11
12   // compose_two is a helper function used to
13   // compose only two closures into one
14   fn compose_two<FunOne, FunTwo, Input, Intermediate, Output>(
15     fun_one: FunOne,
16     fun_two: FunTwo,
17   ) -> impl Fn(Input) -> Output
18   where
19     FunOne: Fn(Input) -> Intermediate,
20     FunTwo: Fn(Intermediate) -> Output,
21   {
22     move |x| fun_two(fun_one(x))
23   }
24
25   fn main() {
26     let add = |x| x + 2.0;
27     let multiply = |x| x * 3.0;
28     let divide = |x| x / 4.0;
29     // itermediate(x) returns ((x + 2) * 3) / 4
30     let intermediate = compose!(add, multiply, divide);
31
32     let subtract = |x| x - 5.0;
33     // finally(x) returns (((x + 2) * 3) / 4) - 5
34     let finally = compose!(intermediate, subtract);
35
36     println!("(((10 + 2) * 3) / 4) - 5 is: {}", finally(10.0));
```

```
37   }
```

# How it works...

By the usage of `compose!` in main [30 and 34], you should see clearly what it does: it takes as many closures as you want, and combines them into a new closure that runs them one by one. This is really useful for runtime user-driven functionality composition.

The macro is implemented similarly to the standard macro for variable arguments from `Chapter 1`, *Learning the Basics*; *Accepting a variable number of arguments*, with its edge case being a single closure [6]. When encountering more, it will recursively go through them and combine them in pairs by calling the helper function `compose_two` [14]. Usually, type parameters are written as a single character, but we are using full words for them in this recipe for readability reasons, as there are quite a number of types involved. The type constraints used should illustrate how the types are used pretty well [18 to 20]:

```
where
    FunOne: Fn(Input) -> Intermediate,
    FunTwo: Fn(Intermediate) -> Output,
```

`FunOne` is a closure that takes an `Input`, turns it into an `Intermediate`, and passes it to `FunTwo`, which returns an `Output`. As you can see from the implementation, the only thing we do is call `fun_one` on a value, and then call `fun_two` on its returned value [22]:

```
move |x| fun_two(fun_one(x))
```

# See also

- *Accepting a variable number of arguments* recipe in `Chapter 1`, *Learning the Basics*

# Filtering strings efficiently

While you can filter characters out of a `String` on the stable channel already, this requires creating a new `String` with the filtered characters. On `nightly`, you can do this in place of the same `String`, helping you a lot with performance if you need to perform this kind of action many, many times, or on very large strings.

# How to do it...

1. Open the `Cargo.toml` file that has been generated earlier for you.

2. In the `bin` folder, create a file called `retain_string.rs`.

3. Add the following code, and run it with `cargo run --bin retain_string`:

```
1   #![feature(string_retain)]
2
3   fn main() {
4       let mut some_text = "H_el_l__o_ ___Wo_r__l_d_".to_string();
5       println!("Original text: {}", some_text);
6       // retain() removes all chars that don't fulfill a
7       // predicate in place, making it very efficient
8       some_text.retain(|c| c != '_');
9       println!("Text without underscores: {}", some_text);
10      some_text.retain(char::is_lowercase);
11      println!("Text with only lowercase letters: {}", some_text);
12
13      // Before retain, you had to filter the string as an iterator
         over chars
14      // This will however create a new String, generating overhead
15      let filtered: String = "H_el_l__o_ ___Wo_r__l_d_"
16          .chars()
17          .filter(|c| *c != '_')
18          .collect();
19      println!("Text filtered by an iterator: {}", filtered);
20  }
```

# How it works...

In `Chapter 2`, *Working with Collections; Using a Vector*, we learned about `Vec::retain`, which filters a vector in place. On the `nightly` toolchain, this functionality has arrived in `String` and works the same way, as if a `String` was a `Vec<char>`—which, if you think about it, it really is.

The functionality of filtering a `String` was always there, but it required going over the string as an `Iterator` and creating a new `String` with the filtered characters; or worse yet, converting a `String` to a newly-created `Vec<char>`, using `retain` on it, and then converting the chars back into another newly-created `String`.

# See also

- *Using a vector* recipe in Chapter 2, *Working with Collections*

# Stepping through an iterator in regular intervals

Have you ever wanted to step through data by only looking at every nth item? On stable Rust, the best solution to this problem is using the third-party crate itertools (https://crates.io/crates/itertools), which brings you a whole lot of iterator goodies, or allows you to code the functionality yourself; however, you have a built-in step_by method doing exactly this.

# How to do it...

1. Open the Cargo.toml file that has been generated earlier for you.

2. In the bin folder, create a file called iterator_step_by.rs.

3. Add the following code, and run it with cargo run --bin iterator_step_by:

```
1   #![feature(iterator_step_by)]
2
3   fn main() {
4       // step_by() will start on the first element of an iterator,
5       // but then skips a certain number of elements on every
         iteration
6       let even_numbers: Vec<_> = (0..100).step_by(2).collect();
7       println!("The first one hundred even numbers: {:?}",
         even_numbers);
8
9       // step_by() will always start at the beginning.
10      // If you need to skip the first few elements as well, use
         skip()
11      let some_data = ["Andrei", "Romania", "Giuseppe", "Italy",
         "Susan", "Britain"];
12      let countries: Vec<_> =
         some_data.iter().skip(1).step_by(2).collect();
```

```
13      println!("Countries in the data: {:?}", countries);
14
15      let grouped_stream = "Aaron 182cm 70kg Alice 160cm 90kg Bob
        197cm 83kg";
16      let weights: Vec<_> = grouped_stream
17        .split_whitespace()
18        .skip(2)
19        .step_by(3)
20        .collect();
21      println!("The weights of the people are: {:?}", weights);
22   }
```

# How it works...

This recipe shines when you are being handed an unstructured data stream that follows a certain pattern. For example, sometimes some old APIs that don't use JSON, or other programs you might want to interact with, hand you streams of data that are grouped by position, like the data we stored in `grouped_stream`[15], which follows the following pattern:

```
person0 height0 weight0 person1 height1 weight1 person2 height2 weight2
```

`step_by` lets us parse this structure very easily. It works by handing you current element, and then skipping a certain amount of elements on every iteration. In our example, we parse `grouped_stream` by first creating an iterator over every substring that is not whitespace with `split_whitespace` [17], then, because we are only interested in the weights, `skip` the first two elements (`"Aaron"` and `"182cm"`), which places our iterator at `"70kg"`. We then tell the iterator to only look at every third element from now on with `step_by(3)` [19], resulting in us iterating over `"70kg"`, `"90kg"`, and `"83kg"`. Finally, we `collect` the elements into a vector [20].

# See also

- *Using a string* and *Accessing collections as iterators* recipes in `Chapter 2`, *Working with Collections*

# Benchmarking your code

The Rust project has developed a testing crate for the compiler itself. Because it includes some quite useful features, most importantly a benchmarker, it is accessible on nightly builds as the built-in `test` crate. Because it gets shipped with every nightly build, you don't need to add it to your `Cargo.toml` to use it.

The `test` crate is marked unstable because of its tight coupling to the compiler.

# How to do it...

1. Open the `Cargo.toml` file that has been generated earlier for you.

2. In the `bin` folder, create a file called `benchmarking.rs`.

3. Add the following code, and run it with `cargo bench`:

```rust
#![feature(test)]
// The test crate was primarily designed for
// the Rust compiler itself, so it has no stability guaranteed
extern crate test;

pub fn slow_fibonacci_recursive(n: u32) -> u32 {
  match n {
    0 => 0,
    1 => 1,
    _ => slow_fibonacci_recursive(n - 1) +
    slow_fibonacci_recursive(n - 2),
  }
}

pub fn fibonacci_imperative(n: u32) -> u32 {
  match n {
    0 => 0,
    1 => 1,
    _ => {
      let mut penultimate;
      let mut last = 1;
      let mut fib = 0;
      for _ in 0..n {
        penultimate = last;
        last = fib;
        fib = penultimate + last;
```

```
26          }
27          fib
28        }
29      }
30    }
31
32    pub fn memoized_fibonacci_recursive(n: u32) -> u32 {
33      fn inner(n: u32, penultimate: u32, last: u32) -> u32 {
34        match n {
35          0 => penultimate,
36          1 => last,
37          _ => inner(n - 1, last, penultimate + last),
38        }
39      }
40      inner(n, 0, 1)
41    }
42
43    pub fn fast_fibonacci_recursive(n: u32) -> u32 {
44      fn inner(n: u32, penultimate: u32, last: u32) -> u32 {
45        match n {
46          0 => last,
47          _ => inner(n - 1, last, penultimate + last),
48        }
49      }
50      match n {
51        0 => 0,
52        _ => inner(n - 1, 0, 1),
53      }
54    }
```

4. Running benchmarks:

```
56    #[cfg(test)]
57    mod tests {
58      use super::*;
59      use test::Bencher;
60
61      // Functions annotated with the bench attribute will
62      // undergo a performance evaluation when running "cargo
bench"
63      #[bench]
64      fn bench_slow_fibonacci_recursive(b: &mut Bencher) {
65        b.iter(|| {
66          // test::block_box is "black box" for the compiler and
          LLVM
67          // Telling them to not optimize a variable away
68          let n = test::black_box(20);
69          slow_fibonacci_recursive(n)
```

```
70       });
71     }
72
73     #[bench]
74     fn bench_fibonacci_imperative(b: &mut Bencher) {
75       b.iter(|| {
76         let n = test::black_box(20);
77         fibonacci_imperative(n)
78       });
79     }
80
81     #[bench]
82     fn bench_memoized_fibonacci_recursive(b: &mut Bencher) {
83       b.iter(|| {
84         let n = test::black_box(20);
85         memoized_fibonacci_recursive(n)
86       });
87     }
88
89     #[bench]
90     fn bench_fast_fibonacci_recursive(b: &mut Bencher) {
91       b.iter(|| {
92         let n = test::black_box(20);
93         fast_fibonacci_recursive(n)
94       });
95     }
96   }
```

# How it works...

The bread and butter of the test crate is the Bencher struct [59]. An instance of it is passed automatically to every function annotated with the #[bench] attribute [63] when running cargo bench. Its iter method takes a closure [65], and runs it multiple times to determine how long one iteration of it takes. While doing this, it also discards time measurements that are far off the others to eliminate one-off extremes.

Another useful part of the test crate is its black_box struct [68], which wraps any value and tells the compiler and LLVM to not optimize it away, no matter what. If we didn't use it in our benchmarks, they might get optimized away and result in a rather optimistic and unhelpful measurement of 0 ns/iter, or zero nanoseconds per execution of the closure.

We can use the tools at our disposal to test out some theories. Remember the recursive **Fibonacci** implementation discussed in Chapter 7, *Parallelism and Rayon; Running two operations together*? Well, it is repeated here as slow_fibonacci_recursive[6].

This implementation is slow because both calls to `slow_fibonacci_recursive(n - 1)` and `slow_fibonacci_recursive(n - 2)` need to recalculate *all* values individually. Worse yet, every call also splits up into a call to `slow_fibonacci_recursive(n - 1)` and `slow_fibonacci_recursive(n - 2)` once more, recalculating everything again and again! In terms of *Big O*, this is an efficiency of $O(1.6^n)$ (proof at https://stackoverflow.com/a/360773/5903309). In comparison, the imperative algorithm, `fibonacci_imperative` [14] is a simple loop, so it's at $O(n)$. By this theory, it should be *a lot* faster than the slow, recursive one. Running `cargo bench` lets us verify these assertions easily:

```
running 4 tests
test tests::bench_fast_fibonacci_recursive     ... bench:            3 ns/iter (+/- 2)
test tests::bench_fibonacci_imperative         ... bench:            4 ns/iter (+/- 3)
test tests::bench_memoized_fibonacci_recursive ... bench:           11 ns/iter (+/- 1)
test tests::bench_slow_fibonacci_recursive     ... bench:       28,663 ns/iter (+/- 7,639)
```

What a difference! On my computer, the slow, recursive implementation is more than 7,000 times slower than the imperative one! Surely, we can do better.

**StackOverflow** user **Boiethios** helpfully provided us with `memoized_fibonacci_recursive` at https://stackoverflow.com/a/49052806/5903309. As the name suggests, this implementation uses a concept known as *memoization*. This means that the algorithm has some way of passing around already-calculated values. An easy way of doing this would be to pass around a `HashMap` with all calculated values, but that would again bring its own overhead, as it operates on the heap. Instead, we go for the route of *accumulators*. This means that we just pass the relevant values directly as parameters, which in our case are `penultimate`, which represents the Fibonacci of n-2, and `last`, which represents the Fibonacci of n-1. If you want to read more about these functional concepts, check out http://www.idryman.org/blog/2012/04/14/recursion-best-practices/.

Checking the benchmarks, we can see that we managed to improve the algorithm quite a bit with `memoized_fibonacci_recursive`. But it's still a bit slower than `fibonacci_imperative`. One of many possible ways to further improve the algorithm is by extracting the n == 1 match that would be checked in every recursive call outside, as demonstrated in `fast_fibonacci_recursive` [43], which clocks in at a great three nanoseconds per iteration!

# There's more...

Our implementation also employs another optimization: *tail call optimization*, or *TCO* for short. In oversimplified terms, TCO happens when the compiler is able to rewrite a recursive algorithm into an imperative one. More generally, TCO is when the compiler can compile a recursive call into a form that doesn't add a new stack frame per call, and as a consequence, can't cause a stack overflow (not the website, but the error). For a good discussion on the topic, see `https://stackoverflow.com/questions/310974/what-is-tail-call-optimization`.

Although Rust doesn't support TCO per se (see the RFC at `https://github.com/rust-lang/rfcs/issues/271`), the lower-level LLVM does. It requires the last call of a function to be a call to itself. The last line of `inner` [40] is a call to `inner`, so it's eligible for TCO.

This is somewhat hard to guarantee in bigger Rust algorithms, though, as objects implementing the `Drop` trait will inject a call to `drop()` at the end of a function, removing any possibility of TCO.

# See also

- *Running two operations together* recipe in `Chapter 7`, *Parallelism and Rayon*

# Using generators

The biggest concept that is still not quite usable yet in Rust is *easy async*. One reason for that is a lack of compiler support for certain things, which is being worked on right now. One important part of the road to async is *generators*, which are implemented similarly to how they're used in C# or Python.

# How to do it...

1. Open the `Cargo.toml` file that has been generated earlier for you.
2. In the `bin` folder, create a file called `generator.rs`.
3. Add the following code, and run it with `cargo run --bin generator`:

```
1    #![feature(generators, generator_trait,
     conservative_impl_trait)]
2
```

```
3    fn main() {
4      // A closure that uses the keyword "yield" is called a
       generator
5      // Yielding a value "remembers" where you left off
6      // when calling .resume() on the generator
7      let mut generator = || {
8        yield 1;
9        yield 2;
10     };
11     if let GeneratorState::Yielded(value) = generator.resume() {
12       println!("The generator yielded: {}", value);
13     }
14     if let GeneratorState::Yielded(value) = generator.resume() {
15       println!("The generator yielded: {}", value);
16     }
17     // When there is nothing left to yield,
18     // a generator will automatically return an empty tuple
19     if let GeneratorState::Complete(value) = generator.resume() {
20       println!("The generator completed with: {:?}", value);
21     }
22
23     // At the moment, you can return a different type
24     // than you yield, although this feature is considered for
       removal
25     let mut generator = || {
26       yield 100;
27       yield 200;
28       yield 300;
29       "I'm a string"
30     };
31     loop {
32       match generator.resume() {
33         GeneratorState::Yielded(value) => println!("The generator
           yielded: {}", value),
34         GeneratorState::Complete(value) => {
35           println!("The generator completed with: {}", value);
36           break;
37         }
38       }
39     }
40
41     // Generators are great for implementing iterators.
42     // Eventually, all Rust iterators are going to be rewritten
       with generators
43     let fib: Vec<_> = fibonacci().take(10).collect();
44     println!("First 10 numbers of the fibonacci sequence: {:?}",
       fib);
45   }
```

```
46
47   // As of the time of writing, a generator does not have a
48   // direct conversion to an iterator yet, so we need a wrapper:
49   use std::ops::{Generator, GeneratorState};
50   struct GeneratorIterator(T);
51   impl Iterator for GeneratorIterator
52   where
53     T: Generator,
54   {
55     type Item = T::Yield;
56     fn next(&mut self) -> Option {
57       match self.0.resume() {
58         GeneratorState::Yielded(value) => Some(value),
59         GeneratorState::Complete(_) => None,
60       }
61     }
62   }
63
64   fn fibonacci() -> impl Iterator {
65     // Using our wrapper
66     GeneratorIterator(move || {
67       let mut curr = 0;
68       let mut next = 1;
69       loop {
70         yield curr;
71         let old = curr;
72         curr = next;
73         next += old;
74       }
75     })
76   }
```

# How it works...

A `Generator` is currently defined as any closure that uses the new `yield` keyword. When it is executed with `.resume()` [11], it will run until it hits a `yield`. If run again, the generator will continue where it left off until it reaches another `yield` or encounters a `return`. If there are no more yields left in the generator, it will simply return an empty tuple, behaving as if encountering `return ();`.

Because there are two scenarios of what a generator does (`yield` vs `return`), you have to check the result of `.resume()` every time you use it, as it could be `GeneratorState::Yielded` or `GeneratorState::Complete`.

At the time of writing, you can `return` a different type than you `yield`. The situation around this is somewhat unclear, as the reason for this quirk is the aforementioned convention to `return ();` when running out of yields. Maybe the final version of generators in Rust will not rely on this behavior, and only allow returning the same type as yielding. You can find the discussion about this and more at `https://github.com/rust-lang/rust/issues/43122`.

Besides async, another big use case for generators is iterators. So much so that the Rust standard library iterators are planned to eventually be rewritten with generators. At the moment, the exact way of how this transition should happen has not been figured out, so there is no generic implementation of `Iterator for Generator`. To work around this, you can create a little wrapper type like we did with `GeneratorIterator`[50], which implements `Iterator` for its wrapped `Generator`.

We illustrate how to use it by rewriting the Fibonacci iterator from Chapter 2, *Working with Collections*; *Creating an own iterator*, with a generator in the `fibonacci` function [64]. The implementation looks pretty clean, doesn't it? As a reminder, here is how we wrote the original implementation using the `Iterator` trait directly, which not only needed a function, but also a `struct` and a trait implementation:

```
fn fibonacci() -> Fibonacci {
    Fibonacci { curr: 0, next: 1 }
}
struct Fibonacci {
    curr: u32,
    next: u32,
}
impl Iterator for Fibonacci {
    type Item = u32;
    fn next(&mut self) -> Option<u32> {
        let old = self.curr;
        self.curr = self.next;
        self.next += old;
        Some(old)
    }
}
```

# See also

- *Creating an own iterator* recipe in Chapter 2, *Working with Collections*

# Other Books You May Enjoy

If you enjoyed this book, you may be interested in these other books by Packt:

**Rust Cookbook**

Vigneshwer Dhinakaran

ISBN: 978-1-78588-025-4

- Understand system programming language problems and see how Rust provides unique solutions
- Get to know the core concepts of Rust to develop fast and safe applications
- Explore the possibility of integrating Rust units into existing applications to make them more efficient
- Achieve better parallelism, security, and performance
- Explore ways to package your Rust application and ship it for deployment in a production environment
- Discover how to build web applications and services using Rust to provide high-performance to the end user

## Network Programming with Rust
Abhishek Chanda

ISBN: 978-1-78862-489-3

- Appreciate why networking is important in implementing distributed systems
- Write a non-asynchronous echo server over TCP that talks to a client over a network
- Parse JSON and binary data using parser combinators such as nom
- Write an HTTP client that talks to the server using request
- Modify an existing Rust HTTP server and add SSL to it
- Master asynchronous programming support in Rust
- Use external packages in a Rust project

# Leave a review - let other readers know what you think

Please share your thoughts on this book with others by leaving a review on the site that you bought it from. If you purchased the book from Amazon, please leave us an honest review on this book's Amazon page. This is vital so that other potential readers can see and use your unbiased opinion to make purchasing decisions, we can understand what our customers think about our products, and our authors can see your feedback on the title that they have worked with Packt to create. It will only take a few minutes of your time, but is valuable to other potential customers, our authors, and Packt. Thank you!

# Index

www.ingramcontent.com/pod-product-compliance
Lightning Source LLC
Chambersburg PA
CBHW080616060326
40690CB00021B/4713